Taylor's Guides to Gardening

Frances Tenenbaum, Editor

HOUGHTON MIFFLIN COMPANY
Boston • New York   1996

Taylor's Guide to Seashore Gardening

Copyright © 1996 by Houghton Mifflin Company
Drawings copyright © 1996 by Steve Buchanan

All rights reserved

For information about permission to reproduce selections from
this book, write to Permissions, Houghton Mifflin Company,
215 Park Avenue South, New York, New York 10003.

For information about this and other Houghton Mifflin trade
and reference books and multimedia products, visit The
Bookstore at Houghton Mifflin on the World Wide Web at
http://www.hmco.com/trade/.

Taylor's Guide is a registered trademark
of Houghton Mifflin Company.

Library of Congress Cataloging-in-Publication Data

Taylor's guide to seashore gardening / Frances Tenenbaum, editor.
    p. cm. — (Taylor's guides to gardening)
  Includes index.
  ISBN 0-395-73532-7
  1. Seashore gardening. I. Tenenbaum, Frances. II. Series.
SB460.T39 1996
635.9'0973'09146 — dc20   95-48906
                                     CIP

Printed in Hong Kong

DNP 10 9 8 7 6 5 4 3 2 1

Cover photograph © by George Taloumis

Contents

Contributors

Rita Buchanan, who developed the plant list and wrote the encyclopedia for this book, has worked as a botanist and horticulturist in Texas, Colorado, Virginia, Connecticut, England, and Costa Rica. She was coeditor of *Taylor's Master Guide to Gardening* and editor of several other guides, including *Taylor's Guide to Herbs* and *Taylor's Guide to Gardening in the South*. A former editor of *Fine Gardening* magazine, she writes and edits gardening books from her home in Winsted, Connecticut.

Patrick Chasse, who wrote about gardening on the Northeast coast, is a landscape architect. His company, Landscape Design Associates on Mt. Desert Island, Maine, specializes in restoration and preservation of historic landscapes and reconstruction of natural plant communities from Maine to the Bahamas. He lectures at Radcliffe College and the New York Botanical Garden and at botanical gardens and symposia across the country and abroad.

William Flemer III wrote two essays in this guide, "How to Garden by the Sea" and "Trees for the Seashore." A third-generation nurseryman, he is vice president of Princeton Nurseries in Allentown, New Jersey. His specialty is the breeding of shade trees, flowering trees, and shrubs; many of his introductions are among the most popular shade and flowering trees in the horticultural world. He has served three terms as chairman of the U.S. National Arboretum and is the author of four books, including *Nature's Guide to Successful Gardening and Landscaping*.

Daniel J. Foley has spent a lifetime working with plants. A landscape architect and horticulturist, he was editor of *Horticulture* magazine in the 1950s. He is the author of many books, most notably the classic *Gardening by the Sea*. The introductory essay in this Taylor's Guide was adapted from that book. He lives in Salem, Massachusetts.

Judith Kehs, who wrote the essay on herbs, has owned and operated Cricket Hill Herb Farm in the coastal town of Rowley, Massachusetts, since 1976. She has lectured and taught extensively about all aspects of growing and using herbs and has consulted on the design and preparation of restoration gardens at historic sites. In her greenhouses and gardens she grows more than 300 varieties of common and uncommon herbs.

Des Kennedy, author of the essay on the Pacific Northwest, lives and gardens on Denman Island in British Columbia's Georgia Strait. He writes regularly for Canadian and U.S. gardening magazines and contributes a gardening column to the *Globe and Mail* newspaper. He is the author of *Crazy About Gardening* and *Nature's Outcasts.*

Judith Larner Lowry, author of the essay on the California coast, has been the proprietor of Larner Seeds, a mail-order company specializing in California native plants and seeds. She also designs and installs native-plant gardens in San Francisco's Bay Area. She has written a series of educational pamphlets and is working on a book on gardening with California native plants.

Glenn Morris, who wrote about the south Atlantic seashore, is a landscape consultant and writer who lives in Greensboro, North Carolina. Trained as a landscape architect, he served as the first landscape design editor of *Southern Living* magazine and has contributed to *Taylor's Guide to Gardening in the South* as well as *Taylor's Master Guide to Gardening.* He is the author of *North Carolina Beaches.*

Peter Schneider wrote the essay on roses. He publishes his own newsletter, the *American Rose Rambler,* and is the author of *Peter Schneider on Roses.* With Beverly R. Dobson, he is coeditor of the *Combined Rose List,* the annual directory of all roses known to be in commerce worldwide. He edited the revision of *Taylor's Guide to Roses.* He lives and gardens in Freedom Township, Ohio.

Carol Stocker wrote the essay on vacation-home gardening. A former New England newspaper Woman of the Year, she is a longtime journalist, gardener, and environmental writer. She has been a reporter for the *Providence Journal* and the *Detroit Free Press.* Since becoming the staff garden columnist for the *Boston Globe* in 1993, she has twice won the top newspaper writing award from the Garden Writers Association of America.

Introduction: The Lure of Seaside Gardens

DANIEL J. FOLEY

If I had my choice, it would be a garden by the sea. A place where untempered winds and ocean spray challenge the most competent of gardeners. A place where sunlit dew makes even the tiniest plants appear like jewels in the early morning sun. A place where the mingled fragrances of flowers, mixed with the salt of sea breezes, give the air a bracing freshness.

What is it that gives coastal gardens their rare enchantment? Is it the sun on overcast days filtering through the recurring mist and fog, or is it the vast backdrop of sea and sky that encompasses them? Or, in a different mood, is it the gleaming brilliance of that same sun on cloudless days that lights and warms the world so comfortably, all the while enhancing the landscape with a strange kind of glow that relaxes the spirit and makes everything about us pleasant and vibrant? For those who have lived near the ocean, on the East Coast or the West, the lure of the sea is an unforgettable experience, and all the more so when your house is in or near a garden.

In the seashore garden, the colors of blossoms and foliage appear to glow brighter, the tints and shades more distinct. The blues are bluer and the pinks are pinker and dew-drenched flowers in the morning light have a freshness that is not found in gardens inland. The subtle softness of silvery dusty miller, blue-green sea hollies, and gray lavender is all the more apparent in oceanside plantings. The diaphanous quality of the light near the sea gives flowers and foliage their true color value.

Within reach of the sea, plants frequently assume curious and picturesque forms, contorted by the prevailing winds. Nature with all the force of its power holds dominant sway, often using wind pruning and salt spray to sculpt trees and shrubs in the most elemental of art forms, stripping ruthlessly leaf and flower, branch and twig.

The possibilities, limitations, and success of any seaside garden are to a large extent determined by wind, sand, salt spray, and tide. When the garden site is perched high above the shoreline, tides have little or no immediate effect — and sand may not be a factor on a high, rocky coast. But for centuries, despite hurricanes and tornadoes, vegetation of a special kind, both woody and herbaceous, has endured the buffeting of wind and salt spray. Not even the shifting dunes of Cape Cod or those of the Jersey shore, or the seemingly endless stretches of Florida's coastline and the pounding of the surf on the Pacific shores have eliminated the beach grass, the bayberry, the beach plum, the dusty miller, the beach pea, the seaside goldenrod, and other denizens of these ever-changing strands that line our coastlines east and west.

Clearly, there is more to gardening by the sea than the sheer enjoyment of color. It is not just one delightful day after another spent weeding and cultivating, tying up plants and removing dead flowers. There are times when storms come suddenly, full of wind and rain, taking their toll of beds and borders. Seaside gardening has its hazards; the relentless wind often leaves its imprint in various ways. Yet there are always plants that survive the roughest weather, and gardeners, too, begin each spring with new courage and enthusiasm. For gardeners, the greater the challenge, the richer the rewards.

Adapted from *Gardening by the Sea,* by Daniel J. Foley, copyright 1965 by Daniel J. Foley.

Seashore Gardening in the Pacific Northwest

DES KENNEDY

The Pacific Northwest coast — the coastlines of Oregon, Washington, and southern British Columbia — is renowned both for its extravagant natural beauty and for its luxuriant gardens. This is a region of panoramas that defy hyperbole, of landscapes forged through massive tectonic heaving and glacial scraping, of seascapes made doubly dramatic by towering mountains, sinuous fjords, and windswept islands. The shoreline includes rocky headlands and sweeping beaches, sand dunes, mud flats, and estuaries. The greatest coastal temperate rain forests on Earth grow here — massive spruce, red cedar, fir, and hemlock trees, their canopies festooned with mosses and lichens, their huge roots fluted and splayed across rotting logs. Two of the North American continent's great rivers — the Columbia and the Fraser — as well as many others meet the Pacific along this coast.

The challenge that this environment poses to a gardener is how to best fit into nature's grand designs. With an abundance of excellent native plants and a benign climate that readily accommodates exotics from other places, the Pacific Northwest is one of the continent's most fervent horticultural hotspots. A tremendous diversity of gardening opportunities and styles occurs along the coast, in large part driven by topography and the various climatic regimes it helps create.

Topography and Soils

The coast embraces a wide array of geographic forms and soil types, with a fundamental division found between the outer and inner coast. The outer coast — "the wild west side" — faces the open Pacific, with its gales and drenching rains and somber fogs. Along the southern coast of Oregon, rugged mountains press hard against the shore, creating spectacular sea cliffs and bluffs. Farther north, the mountains drop away and the coastline alternates between rocky headlands and vast sandy beaches. Extensive sand dunes dominate the central coast and reach into southern Washington. North of the Columbia River, the mountains build again, culminating in the icy crags of the Olympic Mountains.

Then the nature of the coast alters dramatically. The glacial trough of Juan de Fuca Strait slices inland, funneling salt water and a maritime climate into the myriad channels and islands of Puget Sound and Georgia Strait. This inner coast is shielded by the Olympic Mountains and the mountains of Vancouver Island. Its surrounding lowlands are formed from glacial deposits, uplifted marine sediments such as sandstones and shales, and the alluvial deposits of rivers, notably the broad Fraser estuary. Most of the region's people reside along the inner coast, and it's here where gardening activity achieves its apex. North of the Fraser, the inner coast becomes a jigsaw puzzle of rocky islands, channels, and fjords, with more cobble beaches and rocky coves than sandy shores or mud flats.

The tortured topography of the coast offers gardeners priceless habitat variations — hillocks and gullies, slopes, rocky outcrops, and trickling streams — that can be exploited to good advantage. With the exception of the inner coast estuaries, especially the Fraser and the Skagit, and alluvial soils found along some coastal valleys, the region's soils tend to be sparse and infertile. Dunes and other sandy areas are severely nutrient-deprived and require substantial additions of organic matter to build up any tilth and fertility. Some have exceptionally high salt content from ocean spray. Elsewhere soils tend to be rather thin and quite acidic, often with a pH level of 5.0 or less. These need extensive and repeated sweetening with lime to make them amenable to any plants other than the acid lovers. Peaty soils occurring in upland bogs or meadows can be especially acidic and sterile.

Weather

The benign climate of the coast is legendary, for although its latitudes parallel those of Maine and Minnesota, this region is spared their frigid winters by the warm and moist influences of the Pacific. Average winter temperatures throughout the region hover above the freezing point — the January mean in Vancouver, British Columbia is 36°F; in Seattle, 38°F; and in Brookings on the southern Oregon coast, a balmy 46°F. Some spots in the Brookings area seldom ever experience a frost and are mild enough for growing subtropicals. The San Juan and Gulf islands bask in a Mediterranean climate. Still, coastal gardeners have their share of weather perils to face — gale-force winds and torrential rains, sudden killing frosts, and summer drought.

The overall weather pattern is described as winter wet/summer dry, which is a relatively rare combination. Winter storms track across the Pacific and pound against the coastal mountains. Strong winds gust from the southwest or come funneling up the straits from the southeast. Rising against the coast mountains, the warm and mild Pacific air cools and its moisture condenses out as rain, with rainfall amounts varying substantially along the coast. Some spots on the outer coast of Vancouver Island, where the worst of the storms strike land, can be inundated with 260 inches of rain a year. Astoria, Oregon, at the mouth of the Columbia, receives 77 inches. But in the rain shadows cast by the Olympics and the mountains of Vancouver Island, precipitation levels plummet sharply. Seattle receives about 39 inches a year; Victoria, British Columbia, a scant 23 inches. The little town of Sequim, huddled on the shore of Juan de Fuca Strait in the Olympics' rain shadow, gets a paltry 15 inches a year, about the same as the coast of southern California. Although rainfall amounts vary among these microclimates, humidity levels tend to remain generally high through much of the year.

Most of the rainfall, along with an occasional snowstorm, occurs in winter. In some places, more than 80 percent of annual precipitation falls between October and April. Thereafter, rain may be sporadic and scarce. In spring, maritime breezes begin to blow from the west or northwest. These are dry offshore breezes, and they may alternate with even drier winds blowing from the northeast, off the continental mass. The combination of thin topsoil underlain with rock or sand, scant rainfall, and drying winds can quickly cause drought conditions and plant desiccation. This can occur quite early in the growing season, often in May when many plants are in their most vigorous growth period, and can have a serious impact on new growth and flowering. Late summer generally is a time of extreme dryness. Successful planting schemes in this climatic regime require plants that will tolerate excessive moisture in winter and severe dryness in the summer months.

Additionally, many areas of the outer coast lie in the summer fog belt, which is caused by a combination of ocean currents and prevailing breezes that creates thick bands of low-lying fog. These drift ashore overnight, clinging to the coastline and settling in pockets, and may or may not eventually burn off during the day. Where it commonly occurs, summer fog greatly limits the growing of sun- and warmth-loving fruits, vegetables, and flowers. Throughout the region, summers, particularly summer nights, are relatively cool — average July temperatures range between the high 50s and low 60s — limiting the success of many heat-loving plants.

Perhaps most damaging of all, especially for certain areas along the inner coast, is the occasional outpouring of frigid air down valleys and inlets from the northeast interior. This results in brief but bitter cold snaps that can occur as early as November, before plants have hardened off, causing severe damage to marginally hardy plants and in extreme cases even to hardy natives. Because the cold air mass is also very dry, it seldom produces snowfall to protect plants from its chilling effects. Thus some coastal gardeners are required to buffer both the prevailing southwest gales and the rarer, but more lethal, northeast outflow winds.

Again, these weather effects can vary greatly within short distances. Bellingham, Washington, at the northern end of Puget Sound, averages 186 growing-season days, with an average first fall frost in the first week of October and a final spring frost around May 10. Less than 100 miles to the south, Seattle enjoys 255 growing days, with killing frosts starting, on average, in early November and finishing by the first week of March. Many of the more tender rhododendrons for which Seattle gardens are renowned will not flourish in Bellingham or Vancouver. Topographical features within a local area, particularly the pooling of cold air in hollows, can impose similar limitations. Generally, however, the region is favored with mild winters, and most areas along the coast enjoy a growing season of more than 200 days.

Native Vegetation

Nowhere is the advisability of anchoring a garden to its landscape more pressing than along the shore. Nature is so demanding and so wildly extravagant at this interface of land, sea, and open sky that successful gardens incorporate as many native elements as possible. Pacific Northwest gardeners are endowed with a rich palette of native plants to work with.

The coastal forests are dominated by magnificent conifers — Sitka spruce *(Picea sitchensis)*, western hemlock *(Tsuga heterophylla)*, western red cedar *(Thuja plicata)*, Douglas fir *(Pseudotsuga menziesii)*, and giant fir *(Abies grandis)*. These are generally too large and fast-growing, particularly giant fir and Sitka spruce, for use in smaller gardens. Shade-loving western hemlock can make an attractive garden specimen, especially when young, and can be sheared as a hedge, as can red cedar, but neither tree takes wind well. Douglas fir is both stout and wind-firm. Its beautiful, thick, reddish bark and twisted limbs in exposed situations make it a valuable overstory tree, and young Douglas fir can be sheared to a dense hedge.

One of the most valuable smaller native conifers in the shorefront garden is the shore pine, *Pinus contorta*. Widespread along the inner and outer coast, it is tolerant of salt spray, fierce winds, and impoverished sandy soil. It grows as a bushy, thickly branched small tree, bearing dark green needles along its twig tips. Ideal for an evergreen windscreen, it's often seen in the wild with its windward sides sculpted dramatically.

Equally useful, and better adapted to a range of garden applications, is the Port Orford cedar, or Lawson cypress, *Chamaecyparis lawsoniana*. A native of the southern Oregon and northern California coast, this lacy-foliaged conifer has been extensively cultivated, and there are now more than 200 named cultivars in a wide range of shapes and sizes. Tolerant of poor soils and coastal weather, it is happiest in the sun. A number of its cultivars are effective as screens or hedges.

An even smaller native conifer, found in the wild as either a shrub or a small tree, is the Rocky Mountain juniper, *Juniperus scopulorum*. It occurs frequently on dry, rocky bluffs on the San Juan and Gulf islands and is a good choice for areas of poor soil and drought.

Native deciduous trees are less widespread than conifers, with the exception of red alder *(Alnus rubra)* and bigleaf maple *(Acer macrophyllum)*, which have limited use in smaller gardens owing to their rapid growth, invasive seeding, and branch shedding. Growing in cool, moist, and shady sites, the vine maple *(Acer circinatum)* is a crooked little tree that resembles Japanese maples. Like its bigleaf cousin, it produces clusters of beautiful early-spring flowers, thereafter leafing out in attractive horizontal layers, and has brilliant autumn colors. The Garry oak, *Quercus garryana,* occurs sporadically along the inner coast, most spectacularly in now-rare open meadows with spring-flowering bulbs. Its elegantly contorted limbs and rough bark are very attractive, particularly in silhouette against sky or water. It thrives in poor, well-drained soil and enjoys southern exposures. Two native elderberries, *Sambucus caerulea* with blue berries and *S. racemosa* with red, enjoy moist and sunny locations and are excellent for attracting birds, which feed on the berries. The native Pacific dogwood, *Cornus nuttallii,* is an admirable tree, but it is so susceptible to anthracnose that it should not be planted.

The coast is blessed with two outstanding broad-leaved evergreen trees. The California bay laurel, *Umbellularia californica,* also called Oregon myrtle, is both beautiful and adaptable, equally at home in a shady understory and in full sun. Tolerant of wind and salt, it can develop as either a tree or a bushy shrub and readily accepts shearing. Its elegant limbs and lustrous green foliage provide a handsome foil for flowering shrubs or perennials. As a multipurpose windscreen for the southern coast, it has no peer. An equally lovely evergreen, the Pacific madrone, *Arbutus menziesii,* grows throughout the lowlands and islands of the inner coast. With sinuous limbs sheathed in smooth, reddish brown bark and an open canopy of glossy green leaves, the madrone etches exquisite outlines against the glare of the sea. It is impervious to drought and will not tolerate wet soils, favoring rocky southern exposures along shorelines or ridges. Drawbacks include its habit of withdrawing moisture and nutrients from soil, so underplanting is difficult; its perpetual shedding of bark fragments and leaves; and its seasonal shedding of flowers and fruit.

Native relatives of the madrone, all members of the heath family, *Ericacea,* and well adapted to coastal gardens, include two huckleberries, a rhododendron and an azalea, manzanitas, and salal. The most widespread is salal, *Gaultheria shallon,* an evergreen shrub with thick, glossy leaves, much used in floral arrangements. Growing in impenetrable thickets in either exposed or understory situations, salal makes a rugged windscreen up to 10 feet high. Its dark berries and habitat are highly attractive to birds. Aggressive underground runners make it ideal for anchoring loose, sandy soils, but its invasiveness needs to be checked in the garden.

The native huckleberries are happy in either sun or shade. The evergreen species, *Vaccinium ovatum,* is a splendid foliage plant that can be treated like boxwood. Sheared into dense mounds or hedges beneath the slender stems of madrone or California bay laurel, it makes an outstanding shoreline display. Its deciduous relative, *V. parvifolium,* is airy and graceful in a woodland setting but gets bushier in the open or when sheared. Its delicate tracery of twigs is attractive in all seasons, and its salmon-pink berries are a favorite of birds.

The evergreen West Coast rhododendron, *Rhododendron macrophyllum,* which has pale purple flowers, and the deciduous western azalea, *R. occidentale,* which has white to pale rose flowers, are admirable natives, though neither is as showy as introduced rhodos. Several manzanitas (species of *Arctostaphylos*) also make good seashore plants.

Two native members of the rose family, *Rosaceae,* are important for seaside gardeners. The Nootka rose, *Rosa nutkana,* is a tough, thicket-forming shrub with single flowers and large, shiny hips. Ocean-spray, *Holodiscus discolor,* spills cascades of small frothy white flowers on weeping branches and is most at home in sunny glades amid groves of Douglas fir.

Other native shrubs of use to seaside gardeners include the glossy-leaved Oregon grapes, *Mahonia aquifolium* and the smaller *Mahonia nervosa,* both of which are outstanding. With lilac-blue flowers and lustrous evergreen leaves, blue-blossom, *Ceanothus thyrsiflorus,* is a splendid oceanside performer. The list is rounded out with the deciduous red-flowering currant *(Ribes sanguineum),* the graceful serviceberry *(Amelanchier alnifolia),* and the dune-loving Hooker's willow *(Salix hookeriana).*

A number of handsome native ferns adapt themselves to seaside gardens, but most require sheltered sites. The deer fern *(Blechnum spicant),* the lady fern *(Athyrium filix femina),* and the maidenhair fern *(Adiantum pedatum)* are all choice if given cool, moist conditions. The robust sword fern, *Polystichum munitum,* will survive in sunnier and drier spots, while the licorice fern, *Polypodium scouleri,* lives close to the surf, impervious to salt spray.

Several native wildflowers lend themselves to seacoast gardens and as transition plantings between the garden and the wild. The California poppy, *Eschscholzia californica,* thrives along the sea cliffs of Oregon and California. With blue-gray foliage and brilliant custard-gold flowers, it naturalizes well on dry and stony banks. From the same region, the Pacific Coast iris, *Iris douglasiana* (also known as Douglas iris), grows in evergreen clumps and produces flowers in a variety of colors. On exposed rocky outcrops, spreading stonecrop, *Sedum divergens,* roots along horizontal stems, offering succulent small leaves and bright yellow flowers. On beaches, the sweetly scented yellow sand verbena, *Abronia latifolia,* sprawls up to 6 feet in diameter, its succulent stems and leaves catching sand to help anchor it. The shore lupine, *Lupinus littoralis,* also thrives on dunes or beaches, as does the beach silver-top, *Glehnia leiocarpa.* Sea pink, *Armeria maritima,* produces lovely little papery pink flowers in niches along rocky sea cliffs. In similar crannies the hairy cinquefoil, *Potentilla villosa,* shows clusters of striking golden flowers. Further down the rock face, within the reach of sea spray, glossy-leaved mist maidens, *Romanzoffia tracyi,* produce springtime blooms of delicate white flowers.

Among the native grasses recommended for shorefront gardens are beach grass *(Ammophila arenaria)* and rye grass *(Elymus mollis).*

Exotics

Plants complementary to these natives come from other regions with similar climatic and cultural conditions, and the Pacific Northwest, especially the inner coast, can accommodate a vast array of exotics. Southern Japan, with a moist and mild climate (although wetter in the summer than the Pacific Northwest), has provided the region with a wealth of plant material, particularly broad-leaved evergreens and deciduous flowering trees. Among these are excellent hollies such as *Ilex crenata* and *I. pedunculosa,* as well as *Osmanthus* and the many plants with *japonica* in their botanical names, including camellia, pieris, fatsia, skimmia, aucuba, euonymus, lonicera, and cryptomeria, along with many splendid rhododendrons and Japanese maples. Two sedums from Japan, *Sedum sieboldii* and *S. spectabile,* are valuable seaside perennials. The Japanese black pine, *Pinus thunbergiana,* is especially recommended for sandy soil and exposed conditions, and it revels in ocean spray.

Other rhododendrons and azaleas, which adapt well to the mild, moist, and acidic conditions on the coast (but may require irrigation during summer droughts), originate from Korea, western China, the Himalayas, and Britain. Flowering heathers, largely from Britain, fit in equally well, and the British strawberry tree, *Arbutus unedo,* makes a good companion to the native madrone. The English holly, *Ilex aquifolium,* performs well in coastal locations.

Certain mountainous areas bordering the Mediterranean have a winter-wet/summer-dry regime almost identical to the inner coast's and provide many of the shrubs, annuals, and perennials best suited to surviving the region's extended summer dry spell. These include the lavenders (*Lavendula* spp.) and rosemary *(Rosmarinus officinalis),* along with aubretias, bellflowers, evergreen candytuft *(Iberis sempervirens),* hellebores, thymes, mulleins, alyssums, lavender cotton *(Santolina chamaecyparrissus),* dusty miller *(Centaurea cineraria)* and drought-tolerant cornflowers *(C. cyanus)*, sea holly *(Eryngium maritimum)*, the rock roses, *(Cistus* spp.), and a wide range of rock-garden plants and bulbs. The mugo pine *(Pinus var. mugo mugo)*, the holly oak *(Quercus ilex)*, and the Russian olive *(Elaeagnus angustifolia)* are three reliable seashore trees from this area. Also from the Mediterranean region is laurustinus *(Viburnum tinus)*, a glossy-leaved evergreen that can be clipped to a hedge.

Selected plants from the temperate regions of the Southern Hemisphere — particularly New Zealand, Australia, South Africa, and southern South America — are appropriate for Pacific Northwest coastal gardens. Hebes, berberis, alstroemeria, and escallonias are excellent, but many others are not sufficiently hardy for the occasional cold weather that assails the coast.

Perennials from other parts of Europe and Asia that have proved useful for seacoast plantings include the pincushion flower *(Scabiosa caucasica)*; lamb's ears *(Stachys byzantina)*; speedwell, especially *Veronica longifolia* (also listed as *V. maritima)*; the globe thistles, *(Echinops* spp.); *Bergenia* spp.; the thrifts, especially *Armeria maritima;* and the pinks *(Dianthus* spp.).

A number of trees native to other parts of the United States are well suited here, including the red oak *(Quercus rubra)*, the red maple *(Acer rubrum)*, and the American holly *(Ilex opaca)*, as well as sweet gums *(Liquidambar* spp.), which have fine foliage and brilliant autumn colors. Other European trees recommended for coastal plantings are the sycamore maple *(Acer pseudoplantanus);* the mountain ash *(Sorbus aucuparia)*, whose bright red or orange berries are very popular with birds; and the hawthorn *(Crataegus monogyna)*. The latter is the classic hawthorn of English hedgerows, a tough little tree well adapted to coastal conditions and amenable to being clipped into dense hedges; several varieties are available. Another European, the common sea buckthorn, *Hippophae rhamnoides*, is a marvelous seaside performer. Content in sandy soil and dry conditions, it can be trained as a small tree or left as a shrub for screening. Its small silvery leaves catch the marine light beautifully in a breeze.

Many roses do well near the sea, none better than the rugosas, *Rosa rugosa*. Equally tolerant of wind, frost, drought, and salt spray, the rugosas form dense and prickly hedges of glossy green foliage. They are largely pest-resistant, their flowers are wonderfully fragrant, and their hips are bold. Among the most popular rugosas are 'Hansa' (double reddish purple flowers), 'Blanc Double de Coubert' (double white), and 'Frau Dagmar Hastrup' (single pink).

Other drought- and wind-tolerant plants recommended for

Pacific Northwest seacoast plantings include the <u>cotoneasters,</u> especially rockspray *(Cotoneaster horizontalis);* the photinias and hardy fuchsias, especially *Fuchsia magellanica;* the Mexican orange *(Choisya ternata);* the tamarisks; and two fine junipers: the shrub form of *Juniperus chinensis,* and the ground-cover shore juniper, *J. conferta littoralis,* especially the selected form 'Blue Pacific'.

Design Principles

Pacific Northwest gardens show influences of various gardening traditions, most notably those of Britain and Japan. Similarities of climate, topography, and vegetation types accommodate the massed plantings of the traditional English mixed border as readily as the meticulous Japanese interplanting of evergreens clipped to reveal subtle shadings of texture and form. Outstanding examples and blendings of these traditions are to be seen throughout the region. Their adaptability to seashore conditions and native vegetation is evidenced at a restored estate garden in Shore Acres State Park Botanical Garden near Coos Bay, Oregon. Protected by a windscreen of conifers, but within earshot of surf pounding against sea cliffs, is a formal garden with geometrical parterres bordered with clipped boxwood alongside a tranquil Japanese pond garden.

As these gardens illustrate, the fundamental design choice confronting the seashore gardener, particularly on the outer coast, concerns enclosure and openness. The more enclosed and sheltered the garden, the more protected it is from the elements and the greater the diversity of garden plants and the formality of garden schemes it will accommodate. A perennial border with herbaceous peonies and delphiniums is a realistic possibility only if marine winds are largely excluded. Naturally sheltered from the brunt of ocean storms, many sites along the inner coast are appropriate for gardening schemes not markedly different from those of inland gardens.

Formal gardens in an oceanfront setting generally require a definitive separation from the surrounding natural landscape. This is best achieved through unambiguous lines created by hedges, fences, or walls. Perimeter plantings should serve both as a backdrop to the formal garden within and as a transition zone between the garden and the natural shorefront landscape.

An open view of sea and sky is often best enhanced by a natural or informal gardening scheme. Informal plantings are designed to segue into the landscape, and they do so both by including native species and by mirroring wild plant associations. Plants are grouped in irregular drifts or masses and reflect the natural configuration of overstory, understory, and herbaceous layers. The ambience of the natural, the wild, the carefree precludes fussy-looking or overly manicured elements. Structures and features are best fashioned from indigenous, or at least harmonious, materials — in a beachfront setting, perhaps red cedar planking weathered to silver-gray by wind and rain; in a rocky cove, perhaps retaining walls formed of native sandstone. Here nature itself is the defining element, and the garden's success is measured by its harmonious convergence with the land- and seascape.

As an ocean view is often the dominant feature of the site, thoughtful consideration must be given to the impact the view creates within the garden. In some cases, the garden will function as a small, three-sided enclosure that opens out onto a far larger vista. On a practical level, plantings help provide privacy and shelter; but they also work aesthetically to frame the view, to give it a foreground, and to incorporate it into an aesthetic whole. A single gnarled Japanese black pine or a grove of slender-stemmed madrone can serve to break an unrelieved expanse of sea and sky, furnishing a vertical line to intersect the horizontal and thereby give it scale and a comfortingly human dimension. Mounds of shore junipers or sheared evergreen huckleberry might afford a foreground that establishes a frame of reference between the garden and the immense sea beyond. In certain circumstances, as Japanese design principles particularly illustrate, a glimpse of the distant sea, bracketed by artful plantings, can be more vivid and profound than an open and overwhelming exposure.

In brilliant seaside sunshine, and within the pearly gray light of summer fogs, flower colors can be especially vibrant. Blues, which are invaluable in any garden, are particularly useful here in reflecting and connecting with the distant hues of water and sky and in playing against evergreen foliage. Bold splashes of color — perhaps imitating the radiant gold of California poppies blooming by the thousands in sea-cliff meadows — are best achieved with mass plantings. Subtle pastels, such as those of the rugosa roses, complement the soft pinks and yellows of native wildflowers. The silver-gray foliage of sea buckthorn or Russian olive picks up the bleached colors of the shore and, trembling in the sea breeze, reflects the dappled light of sunshine on waves.

The California Coast

JUDITH LARNER LOWRY

The crashing surf, quiet inlets, dramatic bluffs, and sheltered forests of California's varied and glorious 1,200-mile coastline provide opportunities to create uniquely beautiful seashore gardens. Fog drip in the otherwise dry summers coupled with temperatures moderated by the ocean give coastal gardeners advantages that inland gardeners can only envy. With the right plants, gardening on the coast is one of the easiest kinds of gardening California has to offer.

Though many plants that grow inland will also thrive on the coast, by choosing an appropriate palette of native coastal plants, coastal gardeners can take advantage of the resistance to wind, salt air, and drought that marks this group of plants. Plants from the dunes and bluff edges; from the marine terraces, canyons, and riparian areas; and from the mixed-evergreen and redwood forests will serve the gardener well.

General Guidelines

You can learn a lot from the experiences of other coastal gardeners by examining their successes and profiting from their mistakes.

1. Look at the **vegetation architecture** of the area in which you are gardening, and don't plant species that will result in what ecologists call a "type conversion." In other words, don't change your coastal prairie to a pine forest, your coastal bluff to a lawn, or your oak grove to a redwood forest.

If you live in the coastal scrub, where few plants are over 10 feet high, don't try to make a woodland garden; it may have been just that soothing, gray-blue coastal scrub foliage that drew you to this area in the first place. Furthermore, trying to create an entirely different kind of landscape can lead to a host of problems. For example, planting large trees, such as blue gum eucalyptus *(Eucalyptus globulus)* or Monterey pine *(Pinus radiata),* both of which reseed vigorously, on seaside cliffs can increase erosion. The cliffs can't sustain the weight of a massive trunk and branching structure. The ubiquitous *E. globulus,* planted as windbreak and lumber crops, has many disadvantages for the homeowner, including constant litter and limb drop, the difficulty of growing other plants underneath it, and its shallow root system, which often cannot support the top growth. Since it sprouts from the crown when cut, it is difficult to remove or to contain.

2. Choose a **keynote** species or combination of species to be repeated throughout the garden. Since so many plants do well on the California coast, there is a tendency to plant one of this and one of that, so that the garden becomes a miscellaneous, disorganized hodgepodge. The number of specimen plants should be limited so that each one is set off by a background of repeated species.

3. Winds along the shore can be severe, and the gardener beginning a garden usually wants to create **shelter from coastal winds.** Screen and hedge plants should be chosen with care. The Monterey pine, recommended for that purpose for years, has proved unsuitable in many situations. In its native environs, which include shallow soil and extreme winds, it is contained and relatively long-lived. In other coastal areas, where the soil is deeper or where a high water table stimulates growth, the Monterey pine grows quickly, beyond what its root system can support. As it grows, it shades out its own lower limbs, creating dangerous fire ladders, and destroying its effectiveness as a windscreen and hedge — wind is interrupted only at the top of the tree and not down below, where the garden needs protection.

The Monterey cypress, *Cupressus macrocarpa,* has also been widely planted as a hedge and windbreak. Though it takes well to pruning and forms a satisfactorily dense, formal hedge when scrupulously maintained, all too often that rigorous routine is not kept up. Without those twice-yearly ministrations, Monterey cypresses will shoot up into unsightly and unmanageable trees, particularly where a high water table and rich clay soil stimulate their growth.

Once let go, the Monterey cypress cannot be brought back to hedge form. A useful slower-growing conifer species is the shore pine, *Pinus contorta*. Dense above and below, and moderate in growth rate, water use, and tree-surgeon bills, it makes an excellent hedge component or specimen plant. For quicker protection, add a shrub such as ceanothus to the planting. The faster the growth, the shorter the life, so mixing quick-growing, short-lived species with slow-growing, long-lived ones is a good idea.

Research has shown that shrubs 10 feet high cast a "wind shadow" 100 feet long. A hedge made of shrubs or small trees 20 feet high will offer protection to a person 6 feet tall standing 50 feet away. Wind protection can therefore be obtained from such relatively low-growing coastal shrubs as Pacific wax myrtle *(Myrica californica)*, coffeeberry *(Rhamnus californicus)*, toyon *(Heteromeles arbutifolia)*, Catalina cherry *(Prunus lyonii)*, and the fast-growing, adaptable, semi-woody tree mallow *(Lavatera assurgentiflora)*.

The most effective wind and noise barriers are multilayered, dense plants in the large-shrub/small-tree category, with fore and aft plantings of lower-growing shrubs. It is pleasant to include deciduous shrubs as well, such as the California hazel *(Corylus cornuta)* or the flowering currant *(Ribes sanguineum)*, with evergreen species. From the northern coastal scrub comes the shrub coyote bush *(Baccharis pilularis* var. *consanguinea)*, with its associates, the silvery and fragrant California sagebrush *(Artemisia californica)*, the orange-flowering sticky monkey flower *(Diplacus aurantiacus)*, and lizardtail *(Eriophyllum stoechadifolium)*. From the south-central coast come the beautiful salvias, such as *Salvia brandegei, S. leucophylla,* and *S. mellifera*. In their native habitat, they are "drought-deciduous," that is, they lose many of their leaves in the summer, but planted in more-northern gardens, they add a beautiful silvery or gray-green note to the garden all year long.

4. **Erosion control** is a concept that has caught on with gardeners, but sometimes the plants chosen can exacerbate the problem. German ivy *(Senecio mikanioides)*, English ivy *(Hedera helix)*, ice plant *(Mesembryanthemum chilense)*, and capeweed *(Arctotheca calendula)* are low-growing plants that root at all nodes and have been widely planted for bank con-

trol in riparian areas and on coastal bluffs for erosion control. Ice plant, with its heavy, succulent leaves, quickly covers a sandy cliff, but the weight of its foliage on unstable
sandstone can work to pull chunks of cliff down. Also, the
concentrated salt in its succulent tissues changes the soil
chemistry of the bluff, and thus other, more benign species
can't replace it.

Algerian ivy, *Hedera canariensis,* is widely planted along
the coast to cover fences and banks. The erosion control it
provides is superficial, since its shallow roots don't serve to
tie the soil layers together. Look to the native sea-bluff plants
on relatively intact cliffs for planting ideas; they allow the
rain to filter through to the soil, and their roots hold the soil
layers together in the best way for our coastal environment.

5. Accept, work with, and learn to enjoy **seasonality**. The
annual wildflowers will bloom, set seed, and die. The coastal
scrub plants will go into semidormancy at the end of the summer and into the fall. The deciduous shrubs, such as the
graceful California hazel, *Corylus cornuta* var. *californica,*
and the early-blooming *Ribes sanguineum,* will drop their
leaves by summer's end. The beauty of their buds and new
growth can then be enjoyed.

The temptation to create eternal spring in the garden always exists in California, as our subtle seasons can give the
impression that eternal spring is possible. Accepting seasonal
change adds a deeper dimension to the coastal garden. Those
plants that do remain always verdant are often dangerously
invasive. Which leads to the last, and probably most important, guideline for coastal gardeners.

6. Look around at vacant lots and notice what garden
plants have escaped beyond the garden fence. Learn the **invasive problem plants**, of which the coast has many, and
avoid them. In most of the coastal gardens we work with, the
largest proportion of time and money goes to controlling or
removing those plants, either purposely planted by gardeners
or spreading from other gardens, that in the relatively hos-
pitable coastal climate know no bounds. Yet at the same time,
we see innocent new coastal gardeners leaving nurseries with
flats and containers of exactly the same plants.

The California Exotic Pest Plant Council particularly rec-
ommends avoiding and removing whenever possible the following species that thrive only too well along the California
coast: English ivy, German ivy, Algerian ivy, ice plant, French
broom *(Genista monspessulana),* Scotch broom *(Cytisus scoparius),* pampas grass *(Cortaderia jubata),* blue gum eucalyptus, passionflower vine *(Passiflora jamesonii)* and capeweed.

California Regions

Since coastal gardening encompasses so many different situations in California, it makes sense to discuss these areas separately. Though other ecosystems exist along the coast, it is in the following six plant communities that most gardening takes place. The concept of plant communities is, of course, a human one, and in California exceptions abound. Still, general distinctions will be useful.

Redwood forest

Fortunate is the coastal gardener who lives in the shade of these glorious trees. Fog drip that can add 10 inches to the annual rainfall, deep humus that muffles sound, fine-textured leaves through which shafts of sunlight pour, and wordless association with a relict species over 10 million years old are priceless values to be treasured. Invasive species tend to be less of a problem for redwood gardeners also.

In old-growth or relatively intact redwood forests, a layer of low-growing plants brightens the forest floor. In areas regrown after numerous loggings, that plant layer can be conspicuously absent. Once a sufficient humus layer is built up from needle drop, plants can be introduced easily. Try low-growing species such as redwood sorrel, *Oxalis oregana,* which has sour, edible leaves and pink and purple flowers; redwood violet, *Viola sempervirens,* for its bright yellow blossoms; wild ginger, *Asarum caudatum,* which has handsome, heart-shaped leaves; redwood ivy, *Vancouveria parviflora;* and two beautiful native ferns often seen in the redwoods, the sturdy and adaptable sword fern, *Polystichum munitum,* and the elegant, black-stemmed five-finger fern, *Adiantum pedatum.*

In clearings or openings in the redwoods, two worthy grasses may be found, both easy to grow. *Hierochloe occidentale,* California sweetgrass, lives up to its name. Its bright green leaves, when dried, emanate an intoxicating vanilla fragrance, long-lasting in sachets. The tall and striking California bottlebrush grass, *Elymus californica,* also found in clearings in the redwoods and mixed-evergreen forests, has a graceful droop to its striking, 5-foot-tall flower stalks.

Gardeners often ask for annual wildflowers for redwood shade, but it is with the above-mentioned perennials rather than annuals that the most successful wildflower plantings will be made. Redwood shade is too dense for most annual wildflowers. (Two exceptions are *Claytonia sibirica,* peppermint candy flower, and the edible miner's lettuce, *Claytonia perfoliata.*) The above-mentioned species are all rhizomatous or stoloniferous, spreading perennials that ask only for the shade and soil and fog that the redwoods can provide.

Some choice shrubs can thrive in the redwoods, providing

flowers, foliage, and even berries, as in the case of *Vaccinium ovatum*, the evergreen huckleberry. This shrub has striking bronze-colored new growth, pale pink bell-shaped blossoms, and highly edible, deep blue-black berries in late summer. It is difficult to grow in any but its chosen environs of redwoods or mixed-evergreen forest. *Rhododendron macrophyllum*, the West Coast rhododendron, bears fragrant blossoms in several shades of pink and is similarly picky. It is a superior shrub for the lucky redwood gardener, its large, whorled, dark green leaves attractive all year.

Trees such as *Umbellularia californica*, the California bay laurel, and *Lithocarpus densiflorus*, or tan oak, are success ful in the redwoods where shade is not too severe.

Though planting choices may be more limited in the redwoods than in other coastal areas, the redwood gardener is still to be envied. You can grow what others can not.

Mixed-evergreen forest

This pleasant, complex, and interesting plant community, on a more human scale than the redwood forest, makes up in livability what it lacks in grandeur. The gardener in this kind of terrain will find a woodland rich with diversity of plants, birds, and mammals. Carving a garden out of these woods might begin with a careful evaluation of existing trees. Fire and safety considerations dictate that trees should be at least 30 feet from the house. Overhanging branches, though picturesque, are probably not a good idea.

Still, trees are an invaluable garden asset. A venerable coast live oak, *Quercus agrifolia*, with its massive and striking branching structure, can set the tone for a woodland garden. Its sculptural qualities can be emphasized by careful pruning and the clearing out of invasive understory plants such as *Hedera helix* and *Vinca major*, often found in these situations. Oaks should be underplanted only with those species that do not require summer water, such as *Satureja douglasii* (yerba buena), *Phacelia bolanderii* (Bolander's phacelia), *Ribes viburnifolium* (Catalina currant), and *Polystichum munitum* (sword fern). Oak leaf litter alone makes an attractive and beneficial cover under oak trees.

Small clearings can be made for the enjoyment of shady meadows, where such grasses as the native *Festuca rubra*, with its lax, rich green foliage, and the stately *Festuca californica* (California fescue) can be interspersed with *Iris macrosiphon*, *Silene californica* (Indian pink), *Aquilegia formosa* (western columbine), and other wildflowers that enjoy filtered light. One of the largest native grasses, the dramatic *Calamagrostis nutkaensis*, or Pacific reed grass, thrives with either full sun or part shade where soils are moist.

Coastal scrub

Perhaps more gardens are being made in this plant community than in any other. Particularly in southern California, the southern coastal sage scrub is being disrupted by development to the point where its associated bird and mammal life is becoming endangered. Gardening so as to maintain and enhance the original vegetation type has many benefits.

Plants from these groups make wonderful garden subjects; the wind only makes them sturdier and more shapely and sea air is just what they require. Reminiscent of the moors and fens of Ireland and Scotland, coastal scrub coats the hills and flats of the coast with an array of shrubs and subshrubs in silvers, gray-greens, blue-greens, and olives. A mounding growth habit enables them to withstand wind onslaughts.

Northern coastal scrub has a rich herb layer of bunchgrasses and perennial and annual wildflowers. The southern coastal scrub does not have this herb layer, but some of its components, such as *Salvia leucophylla* (purple-flowered sage) and *Salvia mellifera* are extremely showy in flower, with long spikes of purple flowers. These shrubs are drought-deciduous, losing most of their leaves during the dry summer and fall. When planted in wetter north coast gardens, however, they lose that characteristic, keeping their leaves throughout the year. Planted as they grow, in large masses, these species form the background of a coastal rug of many colors and textures.

In northern coastal scrub gardens, use of the basic plant combination found in central and north-central scrub can provide a beautiful backdrop for other plants. *Baccharis pilularis* var. *consanguinea* (coyote bush), *Artemisia californica* (California sagebrush), *Eriophyllum stoechadifolium* (lizard-tail), and *Diplacus aurantiacus* (sticky monkey flower) create a medley of foliage texture and color that is "just right" for the coast.

Once established, these plants need little or no supplemental irrigation. Late-summer prunings to keep them at their best may be in order. The gardener's pruning shears can accomplish what was once the task of both natural and human-set fires.

Coastal scrub intergrades with all the other plant communities mentioned here, so openings of coastal prairie and borders of dune and bluff plants are appropriate in these gardens. Trees from the mixed-evergreen forests can delineate the edge of the property. Like many parts of the coast, marine terraces and coastal hills typically have a great variety of soils and moisture, so one often sees willow thickets emerging in the midst of otherwise dry scrubland. Showy shrubs such as the silk-tassel bush, *Garrya elliptica,* striking for its pale green catkins that hang on for months, make good specimen plants.

The islands off southern California's coast provide many horticulturally valuable plants for the coastal scrub garden. *Dendromecon harfordii,* island bush poppy, is an evergreen, ever-blooming, handsome shrub with gray-blue leaves and masses of bright yellow flowers throughout the year. Suited for the larger garden, it spreads to almost 15 feet, growing 12 feet in height, and thrives with an occasional pruning to just above the ground.

Coastal prairie

Here we find homes and gardens where cows once grazed. In many cases these grasslands, once a rich mix of perennial bunchgrasses and wildflowers, have, through a complex series of events, undergone a "type conversion" to mostly annual grasslands. This permutation has taken place all over California, but on the coast the perennial bunchgrasses are still to be found in abundance. Extra moisture created by fog gives the perennials an edge over the aggressive European annual weedy grasses.

The gardener in the coastal prairie, often gardening on an uplifted marine terrace, may discover remnants of the original grassland community to work with. Look for grasses growing in discrete, tufted bunches with massive, perennial root systems. If you find them, you are lucky enough to be gardening in one of the rarest plant communities in California. To enhance the health and spread of these survivors, biannual mowings, once in the early spring and once in the fall, will help to curb the growth of weedy annual grasses and to remove dead stalks from the bunches. Seed of your own native grasses may be collected in May and June and broadcast or grown in flats for later transplanting into other areas.

Perennial and annual wildflowers were a part of the original grasslands, and they can easily be added to the grassland. Such species as Douglas iris *(Iris douglasiana),* mule's ears *(Wyethia angustifolia),* pussy ears *(Calochortus tolmiei),* and the coastal form of blue-eyed grass *(Sisyrinchium bellum)* will add color. Some of our coastal hills turn pink with the spring-blooming checkerbloom, *Sidalcea malviflora,* a valuable larval food plant for the butterfly called West Coast Lady.

Use enough of each species to have an impact, 20 to 30 plants of each species. Smaller grasses, such as foothill stipa *(Nasella lepida),* the blue fescue *(Festuca idahoensis),* and California oatgrass *(Danthonia californica),* should be planted 8 inches apart so that they may quickly knit together. California fescue, *Festuca californica,* will usually be happiest with a bit of shade, though some strains of this grass adapt to coastal scrub blasted by winds, to clearings in mixed-evergreen forests, and to prairie settings.

Avoid planting rhizomatous lawn grasses nearby that may invade your prairie. Cut nearby areas of weedy grasses before they go to seed. Leave openings for fall and winter sowings of annual wildflowers. Coastal areas have a broad planting window for annual wildflowers, which may begin as early as October and continue through early March. Sequential sowings will provide bloom beginning in February and continuing through December of some years. Such coastal species as tidy tips *(Layia platyglossa),* baby blue eyes *(Nemophila menziesii),* goldfields *(Lasthenia glabrata),* farewell-to-spring *(Clarkia amoena* and *C. rubicunda),* bird's-eye gilia *(Gilia tricolor),* Chinese houses *(Collinsia heterophylla),* and globe gilia *(Gilia capitata)* make spring a Californian's delight.

Bluff edge and dune

The precipitous, unstable coastal bluffs of California offer spectacular views and not always deep sleep at night for the homeowners perched on them. Surface erosion, slumps, and landslides are a part of life. Irrigated lawns or plantings that require regular water are to be avoided anywhere near coastal cliffs, as water saturating and moving through the cliffs can contribute to their instability. A group of tough, tenacious, drought-tolerant, deep-rooted, floriferous, and easy-to-grow perennials and subshrubs help hold the California sea bluffs, and the bluff-edge gardener would do well to explore this plant palette.

Low-growing forms of coyote bush and California sagebrush mingle with beach aster *(Erigeron glaucus),* sea pink *(Armeria maritima),* and the coastal form of the California poppy *(Eschscholzia californica* var. *maritima).* Perennial, low-growing Bolinas lupine, *Lupinus variicolor,* surges over rocks and sandy outcroppings, its silvery leaves blending with the fuzzy foliage of sandhill sage, *Artemisia pycnocephala.* Another silvery shrub, purple shrub lupine *(Lupinus propinquus),* will be found on northern bluffs, with San Francisco lupine *(L. chamissonis)* farther south. Both are short-lived shrubs that reseed vigorously and have long bloom periods on the coast.

A companion often found growing with sea pink is chalk buckwheat, *Eriogonum latifolium.* A crucial larval food plant and nectar source for many butterflies, it has attractive pale pink flowers on short stems and silvery green foliage that can be kept neat by fall prunings. A closely related species from the Channel Islands, rosy buckwheat, *E. l.* ssp. *grande* var. *rubescens,* is similar in its ground-hugging habit but has flowers of a deep rosy red.

A number of succulent species hug California's coastal cliffs from north to south, including sea lettuce, *Dudleya farinosa*, in the north and central coasts, and chalk lettuce, *D. pulverulentea*, in the south. *Sedum spathulifolium* is a small, flat succulent that can be found on wind-blasted bluffs or shaded, more protected rock formations, thriving as long as it has good drainage.

Riparian

A small and fortunate percentage of coastal gardeners find themselves planting gardens along coastal creeks and rivers. Watering won't be a problem for most of them, and rich soils and high humidity make gardening easy if they choose species that like some shade and wet feet but won't overstep their bounds. In that regard, particularly avoid the ivies *Hedera canariensis* and *Senecio mikanioides*, and periwinkle, *Vinca major*.

For bank covers, consider the alumroots *(Heuchera micrantha* and *H. maxima)*; the giant chain fern *(Woodwardia fimbriata)*; the tall, graceful lady fern *(Athyrium filix-femina)*; California woodland strawberry *(Fragaria californica)*; and yerba buena *(Satureja douglasii)*. Appropriate grasses include California melic grass, *Melica californica*, and small-flowered melic grass, *M. imperfecta*.

Appropriate shrubs abound in this habitat beloved by birds and mammals. Redberry elderberry *(Sambucus callicarpa)*, numerous willows (Salix spp.), and redwood alder *(Alnus oregona)* up north, as well as black cottonwood *(Populus trichocarpa)*, are typical of northern and central coastal regions. Fremont cottonwood, *Populus fremontii*, and western sycamore, *Platanus racemosa*, are common riparian trees in central and southern coastal regions. All lend grace to the riverine scene.

Predominantly deciduous trees make seasonal changes particularly noticeable along creeks and rivers. Different species of willows show from a distance a fine blur of reddish to pumpkin orange to yellow new growth in the fall and winter, which, when examined closely, reveals buds of a tender salmon color. Bigleaf maple, *Acer macrophyllum*, turns bright gold before dropping its leaves. Twinberry, *Lonicera hispidula*, and canyon gooseberry, *Ribes menziesii*, have subtle flowers that reward a close examination.

With the right plants, the California coastal gardener can become at home with what earthquakes and ocean, spring winds and summer fog, salt spray and seasonal drought are continually creating on the shifting, changing coast of California.

The Southeast Coast

GLENN MORRIS

Along the humid Southeast coast, nothing is more symbolic of the romance of this region than the magnificent live oak *(Quercus virginiana)* and the gossamer epiphyte, Spanish moss *(Tillandsia usneoides)*. This environmentally symbiotic pair is indelibly poetic, and few pairs of plants from any region are as evocative. If you scatter beneath this canopy some large-blossomed indica azaleas and a leggy dogwood or two, you can almost see the fireflies winking in the warm night.

A lovely picture, but alas, for the seashore gardener, not a realistic one. These plants do not thrive where beach blankets are spread, but prefer conditions inland, on the elevated sites of permanent settlements — Wilmington, Charleston, Savannah. The edges of the land can be a harsh place for any plant, and even live oaks cower before salt-laden wind. So let's part the frail veil of Spanish moss to see beyond the moonlight and magnolias to catch a glimpse of the vigor of the seashore, a place of sun, salt spray, and the sculpting of the wind.

Changes in Latitude

Cape Henry, Virginia, is the logical northern starting point for the southeastern seashore. In this essay, we'll span a geography that ranges from the mid-Atlantic eastern maritime hardwood forest to the semitropical verdancy of Florida and all blends in between, a generally well-populated coast nearly 1,000 miles in length.

Such a range in latitude creates a plant palette of extremes with a great blending of north and south in the midranges of the geography, essentially South Carolina to northern Florida. Gardeners who are nimble successfully exploit the idiosyncrasy of local conditions to push the limits of hardiness for some surprising, sometimes exotic effects.

Horticultural conditions shift around substantially at the seashore. Besides the gradual, north-south shift in hardiness, there's typically a much more acute seaward-to-landward change. Since creating a garden is a "local" challenge, this latter shift has the most profound effect on plant selection. This text will begin at the swash line — the last mark of the high tide and wander inland to point out the lovely unsameness of the broader "edge of the sea."

"Where's the Beach?"

It is the presence of barrier islands that distinguishes the southeastern coast from other stretches of North American coastline. With a few exceptions, barrier islands continuously line the coast from Virginia to Miami, part of Florida's west coast and panhandle. These islands are fundamentally alike, great piles of sand shaped by the forces of wind and wave. Nature strings these barriers along the edge of the mainland as so many pearls, varying them in length from less than a mile to more than twenty.

The shape varies too, depending on a complicated web of forces that includes the source of sand, prevailing winds, and the shape of the ocean bottom. Some, such as Bogue Banks in North Carolina, Hilton Head Island in South Carolina, and Cumberland Island, Georgia, do have substantial high ground that is heavily forested and, within a lifetime, quite "stable." Others are spartan and geologically nomadic, figuratively as still as a gull before the wind.

The oceanfront is the least stable yet frequently most sought after location on an island. Oceanfront property owners live with the reality that there is a natural tendency for a lot to disappear, sometimes dramatically. Keeping real estate real kindles an interest in seaside horticulture.

Not Every Beach Is an Island

While sandy islands are the prevailing landform at the edge of the sea, there are some mainland coastal locations: Virginia Beach, Virginia; Fort Fisher, North Carolina, the Grand Strand of South Carolina; and some of the Florida coast (near Jacksonville and Flagler). In these areas, the mainland comes to the edge of the sea, or barrier islands have migrated landward to merge into the mainland. These locations have higher ground, standing fresh water, and richer soil with more organic matter.

The Briny Wind Will Blow

Typically, there are three vegetative "zones" on barrier islands: the pioneer or grass zone closest to the water; a middle zone of environmentally stressed shrubs; and, lastly, a zone of forest. In some locations, it is possible to cross from beach to mainland within as little as a mile as the tern flies.

Plant species on the islands have evolved in response to the following primary factors: the prevailing winds, the effects of salt spray borne by those winds, temperature, and soil conditions. Almost every other factor influencing plant selection and growth — water, shade, and nutrients — can be modified or enhanced as needed. But the first conditions are givens and immutable. Gardeners, much as the very islands, must adapt to them.

Prevailing winds actually help determine the physical shape of the oceanfront. On coasts such as the Grand Strand of South Carolina (Myrtle Beach) where the prevailing winds blow parallel to the alignment of the beach, the dune line is typically low, and the wind does not deposit salt spray far inland. Accordingly, gardeners do not need to be as wary of salt tolerance in their plant selection. On Bogue Banks, North Carolina, the wind pushes salt spray on-island, piling loose sand into a dune line or dune field and sculpting vegetation behind it — an "in your face" environment for planting.

The "coastal zone" (USDA Plant Hardiness Zone 9, with average minimum temperatures of 20° to 30°F) is the most uniform horticultural hardiness zone in the Southeast, with remarkable consistency from southern North Carolina to Biloxi, Mississippi.

True, there's some species "creep" both north and south in the coastal expanse, but the natural shift in plant communities is not evident as an abrupt change. An observant yachtsman would note vegetation blending, a smearing of shapes and greens as new species are dabbed into the passing landscape and others, confronted with natural limits, fade from the canvas.

The Pioneer or Grass Zone

On most barrier islands, the first two rows of property back from the mean (sometimes snarling) high-tide line harbor vicious conditions for plants. Beach sand not only retains little moisture, is low or absent in organic matter, and has a slightly alkaline pH, but, in summer, it's hot as hell. Air temperatures of 95° to 97°F yield dune-sand temperatures of easily 140° to 147°F. If you didn't know the ocean was just on the other side of the dunes, would you choose this as a place to visit, let alone put down roots?

The pioneer zone is typically subject to blowing sand and salt-spray-laden winds. Salt spray deforms magnificently but kills absolutely. At this proximity to the ocean, few plants can withstand the exposure to such a combination of temperature, drought ,and windblown salt water. Fortunately, this slice of an island, the pioneer zone, is sometimes more descriptively referenced as the grass zone. Among the native plants that thrive in these xeric conditions are American beach grass, sea oats, and pressure-treated wooden posts.

Of those three, American beach grass and sea oats perform such a critical role in maintaining the stability of the dune line that states prohibit any destruction or removal of them. Efforts to introduce more easily cultivated substitutes for these native plants are limited; however, these alternative plants are available in nurseries.

The "Scrub" Zone

Blending landward from the grass-anchored dunes is an area with a mixture of forbs and shrubs. These plants are able to press close to the beach, sheltered from salt spray and sand movement by the height of the dunes but still having to contend with high temperatures and poor soil. This zone's descriptive title comes from the scruffy character these plants may take on due to the stressed conditions. This modulated setting includes such plants as seaside goldenrod *(Solidago sempervirens)*, dollar weed *(Hydrocotyle bonariensis)*, and the ubiquitous blanket flower *(Gaillardia aristata)*. Shrubbier species such as northern bayberry *(Myrica pensylvanica)* and southern wax myrtle *(M. cerifera)*, and eastern baccharis *(Baccharis halimifolia)* appear, as do some native trees, eastern red cedar *(Juniperus virginiana)* and yaupon holly *(Ilex vomitoria)*.

This can be one of the most enchanting places on an island, for here the salt-laden winds work magic shearing woody vegetation in great sculpted topiaries, scrubby close to the dunes but growing tall enough to create shelter as distance increases from the water's edge. Beneath the sheared tops, shade appears, leaf litter decays and collects, and the process of creating topsoil begins.

Buffered from the salt and wind by such sheared protection, gardeners can start to establish more-domesticated gardens by careful soil preparation and attention to watering and fertilization. The key to gardening here is a natural one: "shelter from the storm." In other words, as one moves off of the beach and out of the wind, the environment lightens up on plants considerably. From here, it is possible to walk right into the forest.

The Maritime Forest

Few of the barrier islands of the Southeast do not have some high forested ground, the safest and most desirable location for a permanent home. Historically, the first permanent settlements were in the maritime forests, which offered shade, good soil, and to some extent sources of fresh water. This is rich gardening ground; the native undisturbed soil is typically an excellent sandy loam with such superb drainage that water retention can be a problem. The canopy of the natural tree cover provides a varying density of shade that permits extraordinary freedom in plant selection (Georgia's Cumberland Island National Seashore features a nearly magical forest of live oaks that yield a stunning dappled shade). If there is a difficulty here it is the fact that there can be insufficient sunlight to grow the warm-season grasses that do best in the coastal hardiness zone.

Here is where nature performs its most magical mixing. In Virginia's Seashore State Park in Virginia Beach, there are natural freshwater cypress ponds. The undergrowth includes thickets of devilwood (*Osmanthus americanus*), and the perfume of sweet bay (*Magnolia virginiana*) and native azaleas luxuriates the late spring air. Spanish moss, at the northern limits of its range, streams from the cypress and black gum trees, genteel drapery by the waters of Broad Bay.

By the time a southward traveler reaches Amelia Island, Florida, the reigning tree of the coastal environs (if it has not been harvested) is the live oak, a partner with the sharp-leaved exclamation points of the cabbage palmetto *(Sabal palmetto)* and the bayonet-leaved saw palmetto *(Serenoa repens)*. As the landscape edges into the semitropical climate, the gardener's art builds on the near-perpetual verdancy, where the cue for winter is not fall color in the foliage of trees and shrubs but a browning of the salt marsh and lawn grasses — except for the golf greens, of course.

South of Orlando, especially on the balmy west coast at St. Petersburg, where approximate average annual minimum temperatures rarely fall below 30°F, familiar houseplants (*Ficus* spp., *Strelitzia* spp.) become hardy out-of-doors and the tropical palms become important landscape plants.

A Plan of Attack

The struggle to establish a seashore garden begins behind the dune line with an effort to make blowing sand stable, deflect prevailing winds slightly, and ameliorate the killing effect of salt spray. This is true regardless of whether wind makes a frontal assault on the beach or slides along parallel to the water's edge. Once this is accomplished, the garden of choice, whether shady or sunny, naturalistic or meticulously organized and grouped around a lawn, is possible.

The quickest way to ensure the sanctity of the planting zone is to build a windbreak, either with masonry or with plants. The plants that are best suited to do this will survive throughout the entire range of this geography. A mix of these trees and shrubs will create a benign enclosure for less-tolerant plants.

Plants native to the garden area are among the best — live oak, eastern red cedar, and yaupon holly have proved their durability at the cutting edge of seaside abuse. The wind is sure to prune them into slanted leaning shapes, reminiscent of cirrus clouds being pushed across the sky. While cabbage palmetto can withstand the salt spray, its naturally poodled form does not make it useful as a barrier.

Japanese black pine (*Pinus thunbergiana*) can be pushed right to the edge of the frontal dunes, and the very aggressive import, French tamarisk (*Tamarix gallica*), can itself create a living sand fence with its vigorous root system, which, incidentally, is capable of seeking out the field lines of a septic system.

Several shrubs are indispensable to this line of defense (or definition). Northern bayberry and its local relative, southern wax myrtle, are practically mandatory. The wax myrtle may easily reach 15 to 20 feet tall. Devilwood (Osmanthus), which may reach 15 feet, is hardy in Virginia and thrives behind the dunes.

Exotics that do well include elaeagnus (*Elaeagnus pungens* 'Fruitlandii'), oleander (*Nerium oleander*); pittosporum (*Pittosporum tobira*); Yeddo hawthorn (*Rhaphiolepis umbellata*) and its smaller relative, Indian hawthorn (*R. indica*); and pampas grass (*Cortaderia selloana*).

Elaeagnus is rangy and willowy, having a character as ragged as the wild edge of the sea. Importantly, it is tough, manageable, and wonderfully fragrant in fall. Pittosporum is simply handsome, and oleander, offering August flowers in multiple colors, reaches a seaside zenith from Charleston south. Give both of these room, since they will grow 10 feet in every direction. Smaller Yeddo hawthorn (8 feet) is dressy

PALMS

Few forms are as bold in the coastal landscape as the palms, which become an immediate focal point in the garden. Although associated with warmer, tropical locations, several species of palms are adaptable to open locations in North Carolina. Cabbage palmetto, for example, meets the northern limits of its natural hardiness on Bald Head Island at the mouth of the Cape Fear River in North Carolina.

In Zone 10, gardeners may establish groves of the larger palms, but farther north, designers employ palms as punctuation points in the garden, typically in protected locations. Landscape designers group palms by their size—some are tree form, others are shrubbier in habit. The smaller palms serve as understory accents (vis à vis Cumberland Island National Seashore). The larger tree-sized palms can actually cast a light, if wispy, shade.

Horticulturists, on the other hand, group palms into two major groups according to foliage: the feather-leaved palms and the fan-leaved palms. Feather-leaved, or pinnate, palms have foliage that is divided into leaflets that originate from a central midrib. The pindo and the date palms are pinnate. Fan-leaved types are named for their resemblance to an open fan. The sturdy cabbage palmetto straddles the two in form.

It is possible to stretch the recommended hardiness limits of palms, especially in protected locations, but temperatures below 20°F will hurt even the most cold-tolerant palms.

The Large Palms

Cabbage palmetto *(Sabal palmetto)*, Canary Island date palm *(Phoenix canariensis)*, and windmill palm *(Trachycarpus fortunei)* are the tallest-growing palms maturing at over 35 feet. The cabbage palmetto (to 90 feet) is most dependable; extremely tolerant of salt, drought, heat, and cold; and easily transplanted. Its natural range extends to North Carolina.

The Canary Island date palm is massive but slow-growing and has an umbrella-shaped crown 15 to 20 feet wide and a mature height of 50 feet. It is also salt-tolerant and useful in seafront landscapes, but it thrives best in rich,

and salt-tolerant and sparkles with white flowers in midsummer. Indian hawthorn boasts the same characteristics, though it is slightly dressier, has more flower color, and is lower in

moist soil. It is not reliably hardy where temperatures frequently drop below 20°F.

A close relative, the Senegal date palm *(Phoenix reclinata)*, forms clumps with many slender, leaning trunks. It is both less massive (to 35 feet, spread 10 to 15 feet) and less hardy and will work best from Orlando south.

Windmill palm is a slow-growing, slender palm between 6 and 20 feet high (or higher in south Florida). The foliage is very dark green and the plant is very hardy; its range could be extended with some protection. Tolerant of both salt spray and sandy soil, it's a good beach palm, durable in Myrtle Beach. For best growth, plant it in fertile soil.

The Small Palms

The smaller palms (under 35 feet) include the European fan palm *(Chamaerops humilis)*, the lady palm *(Rhapis excelsa)*, the needle palm *(Rhapidophyllum hystrix)*, the pindo palm *(Butia capitata)*, and the saw palmetto *(Serenoa repens)*.

European fan palm grows slowly to form a clump (to 20 feet high, 6 feet wide), but it is not as salt-tolerant as other species. It can be hardy where temperatures drop to 20°F. It is a fussy transplant; container plants are recommended.

Lady palm and slender lady palm *(Rhapis humilis)*, are tough and dependable but slow, maturing between 5 and 10 feet tall. They are delicate understory plants and can be used in darker locations.

Needle palm is a very hardy (surviving temperatures of 0°F), low-growing (2 to 3 feet high), clump-forming palm with fan-shaped leaves. It is a shade-loving understory accent plant that needs rich soil.

Pindo palm draws high marks for beach landscapes, withstanding both drought and cold weather easily as far north as Myrtle Beach. For a "small" palm, it needs room, as it reaches 20 feet high and 10 feet across.

Saw palmetto spreads to form low clumps (6 feet high, 10 feet across) of spreading palm leaves. This sturdy native is distributed widely from South Carolina south and appears at home under both live oaks and older pines.

maximum height. These two shrubs make excellent under-plantings to the taller shrubs mentioned earlier.

Both pampas grass, an Argentine import, and the durable Spanish dagger or mound lily yucca, *Yucca gloriosa,* deserve their 10-foot place in the sun. Neither is particularly friendly to the skimpily clad, but both are tough plants for a formidable location.

As for erosion control or holding sandy soil in place, aptly named shore juniper *(Juniperus conferta),* creeping rosemary (*Rosmarinus officinalis* 'Prostratus'), and memorial rose *(Rosa wichuraiana)* join the native Virginia creeper *(Parthenocissus quinquefolia)* and yellow jessamine *(Gelsemium sempervirens)* to spread rapidly.

The lee of such a planting is likely to provide greater opportunity for more-diverse plantings. There's still more work to be done to make this happen.

Diggin' In

The single most beneficial thing you can do for seashore plantings is to bring in topsoil, particularly if you are wrestling with planting behind the dunes. Beach sand is both poor and porous. If you intend to plant a lawn, a minimum of 4 inches of topsoil will be necessary; 6 inches or more is even better. This richer material may be tilled in with the existing soil to create the planting medium, which could be seeded or receive sodding.

Even if you bring in 6 to 8 inches of sandy loam for any shrubbery beds, adding additional organic material to the individual plant pits will facilitate rapid growth. Well-rotted sawdust or pine bark is usually available and very inexpensive, frequently sold in bulk. However, peat moss remains tried and true for sandy soils since it both adds organic matter and improves water retention.

Mulch heavily to retain moisture, and when watering, use a slow soaking method, which will encourage the plants' roots to penetrate deeper into the soil where temperatures are more constant. The obvious watering option, though costly, is a sprinkler system, which, owing to the porosity of the soil, rarely results in overwatering shrubbery.

Certainly, there's a lot to consider when installing a beachfront garden that makes it more than a casual challenge — winds, salt spray, moving sand. What's especially nice about this type of gardening is that the digging is easy, and you can walk off the job and go fishing.

The Northeast Shores

PATRICK CHASSE

The Northeast coastal region, stretching from New England's border with Canada to the Chesapeake Bay, contains some of America's most memorable seashore. From Maine's rock-bound shores and Cape Cod's rolling dunes to the out-stretched beaches of Maryland's Chincoteague Island, it is also subject to the greatest ranges of climatic change on the continental U.S. coast. The key to designing stable coastal plantings within this varying environment is studying the in-digenous ecology of the area.

The horticultural potential of a site is determined primar-ily by the type of plant communities that can most comfort-ably evolve there. Basic patterns of light, temperature, pre-cipitation, winds, and tides form the rhythms that guide the evolution of seaside plant communities, and are perhaps the most profound and variable influences brought to bear on Northeast coastal sites. Sun, wind, precipitation, tempera-tures, tides, and storms wash over the coast in both beneficial and excessive — even disastrous — amounts.

Tides, governed by the pull of the moon and the sun upon the earth, rise and fall daily along the coast. The average height difference between high and low tides is greater toward the earth's poles and diminishes toward the equator. Within the Northeast region, this difference varies from 18 feet in eastern Maine to 3.5 feet in the Chesapeake Bay. In salt marshes the growing zones of salt marsh cord grasses, *Spartina patens* and *Spartina alterniflora,* are determined by the amount of time they are inundated with salt water. Salt marshes and other areas of direct contact with the sea are harshly unsuitable for gardening. They are usually government-protected wetlands and shorelands and are best served by careful restoration and preservation.

Storms generate the push that washes salt water farther back over the coast, in the form of either storm tides or wind-borne salt spray. Hurricanes, gales, squalls, and other tumultuous combinations of high winds, heavy rain, and tidal surges are the most serious natural catastrophes on the Northeast coast, and they can wreak havoc in natural plant communities as well as built landscapes. Salt spray carried on incoming winds can travel several miles inland, where it dries — or "burns," as some describe it — and kills plant leaves. Pre-storm protection with an antidesiccant protective spray, such as the ones used to reduce winter windburn, can help reduce salt damage, and a thorough hosing down with fresh water after a storm will help as well. Excess salt buildup in the soil from storms can damge plants and must be flushed down below sensitive root zones with fresh water. As shallow coastal wells are sometimes contaminated with salt from storm washes, testing the level of salt in your well water after major storms is good insurance against watering your garden with salty water. Levels of salt contamination in water too small to taste can damage tender plants.

Native shore plants have evolved various mechanisms for repelling or eliminating excess salt, such as the waxy leaf coating of bayberry, *Myrica pensylvanica,* or the woolly insulation on the leaves of dusty miller, *Artemisia stelleriana,* but ornamental plants from other environments may find salt deadly. When selecting ornamental plants for a seaside garden, look for cultivated plants that share some of these natural defense mechanisms. As storms are relatively unpredictable, the best precaution to take against damage is to keep sensitive plants well away from the shore, or shield them physically from such an "assault" with a windscreen barrier, such as a wall, fence, or hedge. Buildings make good barriers, and the sheltered side of a house or cottage can protect more-delicate garden plants.

Wind alone, especially if it is dried by cold winter temperatures, can have the same desiccating or burning effect on plants as salt does. A great deal of winter damage to plant buds is due to desiccating winds — not to the low temperatures alone, as is commonly thought. Deciduous plants drop their leaves for winter and avoid some of this stress, and plants with natural waxy coatings can better withstand the drying effects. The worst of the drying winter winds come from the northeast, and protecting cold-tender plantings along their northwest sides with hedges, fences, or temporary winter wrapping will help. In summer, some beneficial wind patterns are caused by differential heating between the sea and the land, which causes convection of rising warm air over land that pulls in a cooling onshore breeze from the water. These cooling breezes are an asset to heat-weary people *and* plants and may allow you to grow some heat-sensitive plants in your garden that cannot be grown 10 miles inland.

Average precipitation in the region is fairly uniform, about 40 to 45 inches per year. In the colder areas this takes the form of snow during the coldest months (10 inches of snow when melted equals 1 inch of precipitation) and does not become available to plants until a significant thaw opens soil pores. The shallow soils blanketing the northern rocky shore and the sandy soils of most southerly sections drain off their moisture quickly, causing temporary drought stress for plants between rains — especially in the hotter summer months.

Although all new plantings require additional watering for strong establishment, supplemental watering with permanent irrigation systems can support a greater range of garden plants. The irrigated lawn or garden usually becomes *dependent* on the extra water, however, and cannot gracefully endure drought stresses should the system or the water source fail. With localized summer droughts more common, and many communities rationing water use, the lower priority of outdoor water uses can leave the garden disastrously dry. In the interest of water and energy conservation, using plants with low or flexible water requirements will help build a drought-resistant and lower-maintenance landscape. Other modest managed and natural sources of water can provide a welcome boost to coastal gardens. Adding commercial water-absorbing granules, called hydrogels, to soil before planting can help the soil retain natural moisture longer for plant use. On regularly foggy sections of the coast, especially islands, plants also benefit from the condensation of fog — called "fog drip" — on plant stems and leaves. And since water for gardening doesn't need to be potable quality, a shallow surface well, household graywater, and rainwater collection in a rain barrel or cistern can supplement household supplies.

Average minimum winter temperatures in the Northeast region range from 5°F (USDA Hardiness Zone 7) in the Washington, D.C., area to -20°F (USDA Hardiness Zone 5) on the upper Maine coast. Although most plants have fairly definite upper and lower limits of temperature tolerance or hardiness, different sections of the plant — such as the roots or the shoots — can be affected differently by excesses of heat or cold and patterns of temperature change. One such stressful combination particularly common along the Northeast coast is the tendency of rapid freeze-thaw cycles. Rapid changes between warm thawed conditions and freezing are traumatic for plants and are deadlier than long exposure to significantly lower temperatures. These thaw cycles also melt away the naturally insulating snow cover and expose plant roots to the full brunt of the next cold spell. Winter mulching of tender plants with salt marsh hay or evergreen boughs will help insulate roots against these sudden temperature shifts.

The extreme temperature gradient from the hottest summer days to the most bitter cold of winter provides a challenge for survival unparalleled in other regions of the country. A range of native plants, including the low bearberry, *Arctostaphylos uva-ursi,* or highbush blueberry, *Vaccinium corymbosum,* can tolerate the full range of low and high temperatures in the Northeast region, and these make a good structural planting for any coastal garden. If you want to insure against major damage from unpredictable changes in climate, stay clear of plants that are marginally heat- or cold-hardy in your area.

The Northeast region of our coast, a varied and beautiful habitat for gardeners and gardening, stretches directly about 700 miles from the Canadian border at Calais, Maine, to Washington, D.C., up the Potomac River from Chesapeake Bay. At the northern end, the glacially sculpted rocky coast of Maine winds a convoluted 5,200 miles in and out of coves and around more than 400 islands until it straightens out a bit above the New Hampshire border. The spruce fir forest blanketing these northern headlands and islands consists largely of salt-tolerant evergreens — white spruce *(Picea glauca),* and pitch pine *(Pinus rigida)* — along with balsam fir *(Abies balsamea),* red spruce *(Picea rubens),* white pine *(Pinus strobus),* red oak *(Quercus rubra),* white birch *(Betula papyrifera),* and red maple *(Acer rubrum).*

The nooks and crannies along the craggy granite coast of cliffs and cobblestone beaches provide a great variety of garden microclimates that allow different types of native vegetation to establish. A number of low plants such as wine-leaf cinquefoil *(Potentilla tridentata),* mountain cranberry *(Vaccinium vitis-idaea),* crowberry *(Empetrum nigrum),* and

American harebell *(Campanula rotundifolia)* have found a home similar to their usual arctic and mountaintop environs on the exposed tops of rocky headlands. More common wild seashore plants that also make good landscape plants include lowbush blueberry *(Vaccinium angustifolium)*, bearberry, Bar Harbor juniper *(Juniperus horizontalis)*, bayberry, sweet fern *(Comptonia peregrina)*, and beach rose *(Rosa rugosa)* — the last two originally brought to these shores from Japan. At the base of these rocky cliffs, or along the gravelly beaches found in the coves, more salt-tolerant plants such as blue flag *(Iris versicolor)*, sea lavender *(Limonium nashii)*, seaside golden-rod *(Solidago sempervirens)*, beach pea *(Lathyrus japonicus)*, and tufts of beach grass *(Ammophilia breviligulata)* make their home. Along the southern coast of Maine, through New Hampshire and Massachusetts, as sandy beaches are inter-spersed with rocky outcrops and headlands, some of these plants find another type of home growing among the dunes.

Dunes, spits, and barrier islands are formed by the action of wind and water and are held in place mostly with the help of plants, the most important of which is beach grass, which grows from Maine to Virginia. As in the desert, windblown sands can abrasively sandblast plants and structures, as well as bury them in shifting drifts. Additional herbaceous dune plants include dusty miller, beach heather *(Hudsonia tomen-tosa)*, and the familiar beach pea, seaside goldenrod, and bay-berry. One of the more unpopular plants common to North-east shores, poison ivy, *Rhus radicans*, appears in several forms, all virtually impossible to control without noxious chemicals. Below New York's Long Island, along the Jersey shore, through Pennsylvania, Delaware, and Maryland, bay-berry mixes with wax myrtle, *Myrica cerifera*, and is eventu-ally replaced by it on more southerly shores.

Barrier islands, which begin with Plum Island in north-eastern Massachusetts and are strung down the whole length of the Northeast coastal region, act as a sort of flexible bumper along the coast, shifting and moving in storms and absorbing much of the shock that would otherwise push far-ther into the shore. Disturbing plant soil-holding systems can result in an unraveling of this root network and the erosion or disintegration of the underlying landforms. Barrier beaches and the dunes behind them provide a more homogeneous, though shifting, environment than the rocky coast. Besides the plants that occur on rocky shores, additional native plants form the backbone of these plant communities. One of the loveliest small trees is the beach plum, *Prunus maritima*, long valued for its white spring blossoms and the delicious fruits borne in late summer. When protected from winds and salt spray by the dunes, beach plum and other woody plants such as bayberry, pitch pine, red maple, winterberry *(Ilex verticillata)*, black cherry *(Prunus serotina)*, Atlantic white cedar *(Chamaecyparis thyoides)*, and American holly *(Ilex opaca)* can form a maritime forest, such as the Sunken Forest on Fire Island, New York. At the lower end of the region, characteristic southern trees such as live oak *(Quercus virginiana)*, blackjack oak *(Quercus marilandica)*, and sweet-bay magnolia *(Magnolia virginiana)* creep into the maritime forest mix.

A key part of the development of maritime forests, and any other plantings on sandy shores, is adequate supplies of fresh water. The sand is so permeable that rain passes quickly through, and any advantage of extra moisture will help the plants. The troughs and pockets between dunes serve as catch basins and concentrate more moisture, giving a boost to plants established there. Designing a garden to capture fresh water in this way is a viable strategy to eliminate or reduce the need for irrigation.

Another important consideration is the need for shelter from the most severe weather. If you use many nonnative plants, most of which are less hardy to these elements, you will need to provide protection. If preservation of a panoranic view is a priority, a low foreground planting of tough native plants will serve best, and using or constructing natural landforms will help your garden blend into its setting, and look more expansive.

Most exisiting vegetation in shoreland settings plays a vital role in stabilizing the soil and sand, and its removal exposes the land to serious erosion. The best strategy is to replant quickly after site clearing and preparation, in an assembly-line fashion. On steep or sandy sites more vulnerable to wind and water erosion, extra protection in the form of soil-stabilization mats will help keep the soil in place until new plant roots can tie the soil together. New spray-on binding agents — somewhat like papier-mâché — have also been developed for this purpose.

Indigenous coastal sand and soils tend to be acidic and low in nutrients, organic matter, and water-holding capacity. Having your soil tested will give you the best idea of your soil conditions. New plants, especially those not native to the area, will greatly benefit from the addition of nutrients and organic matter to the soil. Good compost will add both nutrients and a water-holding buffer. Commercial fertilizers should be used carefully, in balance with the type of planting. The pH, or level of soil acidity/alkalinity, affects a plant's ability to absorb and use nutrients and must be seriously taken into account. Traditionally, peat moss has been added to make soil more alkaline. But as peat moss is basically a nonrenewable resource, many gardeners are looking to alternative materials, such as oak leaf mold or aluminum sulfate, for increasing soil acidity.

Which plants will do well on your site is a factor of their normal cultural preferences and adaptability to seaside conditions. Native plants found on or near the site have demonstrated survival power and would make a sound structural framework for your seaside garden. If you would like more unusual or showier plants than the natives, consider analog plants, or those that share basic preferences and tolerances with the natives and will bear the best survival potential. Japanese black pine, *Pinus thunbergiana*, and Austrian black pine, *Pinus nigra*, are good salt tolerant substitutes for pitch pine, while eastern red cedar, *Juniperus virginiana*, and northern white cedar, *Thuja occidentalis*, are almost as durable as Atlantic white cedar. Several desert plants find the seashore comfortably familiar, including species of prickly pear cactus, *Opuntia* spp., and yucca, *Yucca filamentosa*. Because the silver wool on fuzzy leaves helps keep salt droplets away from delicate leaf tissues, many non-shore plants with woolly leaves, such as snow-in-summer, *Cerastium tomentosum*, and species of *Artemisia*, can adapt to seaside life. Plants from other coasts are also good candidates, if they don't mind the cold, and many bear a sea- or beach-related name, such as sea kale, *Crambe maritima*, and sea holly, *Eryngium maritimum*. Plant cousins — others in the same genus — provide another good pool of possibly adaptable plants. The American holly, found along the coastal plain, has several related "cousins," such as the inkberry, *Ilex glabra*, that make good plants for coastal gardens. A certain amount of trial and error is inevitable in seaside gardening, but keeping an eye out for plants doing well in other gardens nearby and asking local nurseries for advice will quickly help you build a collection of successful plants.

No garden takes care of itself, though the maintenance requirements of a garden can vary from intensive to minimal. All gardens need the added boost of extra care just after planting, including supplemental watering, wind protection, and protection from marauding weeds while the new plants become adjusted to the site. Even if a garden is planted with low-maintenance natives, it will need some human help until it is fully established. Three years is about average for a new garden to settle in, and then one begins to worry about thinning and pruning and keeping it all in balance. Gardens, like all living things, bring with them a responsibility for aftercare — it's part of an implicit bargain with nature, for "improving" upon it.

How to Garden by the Sea

WILLIAM FLEMMER III

For countless generations seaside gardening was a very unimportant form of horticulture in this country. The seacoast in northern areas was rocky and wooded, and farther south the soil was very sandy and infertile; neither was suitable for profitable agriculture. Since farming was the occupation of most of the population in the 18th and early 19th centuries, the seacoast itself was sparsely settled. There were charming little fishing villages, picturesquely located around natural harbors, and these contained modest but colorful gardens full of flowers with the especially intense color that an ocean climate seems to create. All this started to change in the Victorian era as rapidly growing industry and commerce gave rise to wealthy families and a well-to-do middle class who could afford the luxury of vacation homes. Since these cottages or more impressive dwellings were inhabited during the summer months, it was natural that more-elaborate gardens began to be planted around them, and seaside gardening greatly increased.

In recent times there has been a further expansion of seaside horticulture. Careful studies of population trends show that while the agricultural portion dwindles as people leave the land to engage in other occupations, a second shift in the distribution of our population is taking place: away from the interior toward the coasts and also the warmer areas of the country. This trend is accompanied by the conversion of seaside vacation homes into all-year residences, especially for use as retirement homes by people from the city and inland suburbs. Formerly isolated barrier islands and sparsely inhabited coastal stretches are being built up. With this steady increase in seashore homes for both summer vacation and year-round use, gardening under coastal climate conditions will continue to expand and delight future generations of gardeners.

Seashore gardening has some special problems, but it has some important natural advantages as well. The most significant of these is the climatic modification caused by the ocean itself. Oceans operate as enormous thermostats, and an "oceanic" or coastal climate is temperate, with greatly reduced swings in temperature between winter and summer in contrast to the extremes of a "continental" or inland climate, which can be scorching hot in the summer and bitter cold in winter. The ocean is slow to warm up in summer, which cools the coastal area, and slow to cool down in winter, retaining its warming effect. This moderation of an oceanic climate is kind to plant life, and many more genera and species of plants will thrive near the coast than at exactly the same latitude far inland. The tremendous moderating effect of the oceans can be clearly seen in the hardiness zone map of North America (see p. 376). The warmer zones extend far to the north along both of the coastlines. Zone 8, for example, which scarcely extends north of Mexico in the central part of the United States, reaches up into Canada on the West Coast. Even in a small state such as New Jersey, the killing frosts of fall come a month earlier in the northern portion than along the coast. The southern tip of the state, with water on both sides, is actually the northern end of Zone 7, where warm-climate plants such as crape myrtles and English holly winter over without injury. Islands have an even more temperate climate. For example, it is possible to grow camellias on Nantucket Island off the coast of Massachusetts, although they will not survive on the mainland much north of Washington, D.C.

Because of its high humidity, the seashore in winter may feel much colder to us than the really cold but dry air of inland regions. However, for plants the actual temperature is what is most significant, and the raw winter day that we find acutely uncomfortable is much more beneficial than the more intense dry cold we would call "bracing." England, which has an oceanic climate because of its special position at the terminus of the Gulf Stream, is the despair of its inhabitants in winter, yet redwoods and rhododendron species, which would never survive at the same latitudes inland in Canada or central Europe, flourish there. The modifying effect of the ocean can be surprisingly limited. Windmill palms *(Trachycarpus fortunei)* will grow on the edge of the west coast of Scotland, while only a few miles inland even the native oaks are dwarfed and sere.

The moderation of the extremes of heat and cold is of major beneficial effect for seashore gardening. Other effects are definitely very adverse, and among these the impact of salt spray driven by onshore winds is of great importance. Many plants are particularly sensitive to the burning effect of salt on their foliage and are thus unusable close to salt water. Others that have evolved for growth right on the coast have become highly resistant to salt injury. Not surprisingly the "big three" shrubs for seashore planting — bayberry *(Myrica pensylvanica),* beach plum *(Prunus maritima),* and rugosa rose *(Rosa rugosa)* — are also the first choice for highway planting in the northern states where the roads are heavily salted in winter. The salt spray produced by high-speed traffic is just like that which results from the winds of ocean storms. It is interesting to note that species from the same genus can vary enormously in salt tolerance. For instance, the showy, tall inland forms of goldenrod are weak and sickly at the seashore, while the shorter, leathery seashore goldenrod *(Solidago sempervirens)* thrives even just above the high-tide mark on the beach, in soil frequently saturated with salt water. These two species are so closely related that they can be easily crossed — yet they have been completely separated by environmental adaptation.

Not all the effects of salt spray are harmful, however. There are situations in which it proves to be surprisingly beneficial — for example, in rose culture. Hybrid tea roses in the humid summer heat of the eastern states are severely checked in growth by black spot fungus and by several forms of mildew fungus that cause the leaves to drop off. Once this defoliation takes place, further growth and blooming virtually cease until the advent of cool weather in the fall, when fungal activity is suppressed. The ordinary garden rose hybrids do not grow well right out on the edge of the sea, but a little farther inland or behind barrier shrub or tree plantings, sheltered from the extreme impact of coastal storms, they grow beautifully. Gentle ocean spray drifting inland acts as a natural fungicide, mild enough not to burn the leaves but severely inhibiting the growth of leaf-attacking fungi. This improved leaf retention, plus some other factor not yet understood, accounts for the superior color and vigor of roses grown near the coast. Even the old-fashioned rambler roses, 'Dorothy Perkins' and 'Excelsa', which are mildewed and bedraggled-looking inland, are pictures of health and vigor on Nantucket and Martha's Vineyard islands, where they have unblemished foliage and richly colored flowers. Similarly, the glorious French hybrid lilacs, many of which are disfigured by mildew on the summer foliage inland, are not troubled at the shore.

A real problems exists in recommending plants and cultural methods for seashore gardening because seashore soils, like those inland, are anything but uniform. The nature of coastal soils results from the geological history of the area where they are found. One major type, typical of much of the Atlantic coast from Long Island south to the Florida Keys, is an extremely porous sandy soil. These soils were once the sandy floors of shallow seas and were raised up to become land by a gradual uplift following the Pleistocene era. What will grow in these regions is conditioned by the very sandy, quick-draining quality of this soil as well as by the effect of the sea itself. The coast of northern New England, especially of Maine and the Maritime Provinces of Canada, was formed by the subsidence of the land into the ocean; therefore, typical loamy and even clay inland soils are found at the very edge of the water. The soil can support a much larger variety of plant material, and the limiting factors, in addition to winter cold, are storms and salt spray. Many areas are dissected into deep fjords very much like those on the far side of the Atlantic in Norway. The coasts of Oregon, Washington, and British Columbia are similar to that of Maine. The sea has encroached upon a true upland terrain, gradually eroding the coastline into a fantastic jagged panorama of cliffs and rocky islets, still capped with soil indistinguishable from that occurring many miles inland. Change the tree and shrub list and it could be the west coast of Japan.

The eastern coastal strip has its own peculiar individuality and charm greatly enhanced by the special vegetation that has evolved there and that should be the backbone of any landscape planting in that area. Maine and Nova Scotia have very acidic, granitic soils and are characterized by forests of thick black spruce *(Picea mariana)* growing to the very edge of the ocean with an undergrowth of blueberries and other members of the heath family. The New Jersey and Delaware coasts have forests of pitch pine *(Pinus rigida)* and thickets of bayberry interspersed with American holly *(Ilex opaca)*, red cedar, and tupelo. From the Carolinas south, live oak and cabbage palmetto, with occasional southern magnolias, give the coast its special low-country beauty. On the West Coast the Monterey cypresses, clinging grimly to their relict peninsular station, and the towering Sitka spruce *(Picea sitchensis)* of the northern portion are landmarks. The local woody and herbaceous flora that accompany them have been fashioned by countless centuries of adaptation for just that place.

Planting at the Shore

In sandy areas of the coast, planting techniques should be the opposite of those used for wet soils, where planting on mounds is essential for root establishment. Here as everywhere, nature points the way for an intelligent observer. Wherever a beach plum or other seaside shrub has been uncovered by erosion of the sand dunes or a big excavation, the roots of the plant will be found to be enormously long, extending for many yards down into the sand to where permanent moisture is to be found. The great porosity of the sand, which retains moisture only at a considerable distance below the surface, also readily permits the penetration of oxygen necessary for the roots to grow deeply enough to find adequate moisture. When one plants for dune stabilization in such sandy conditions, the root mass should be set several times deeper than would be normal in soils more retentive of moisture (see fig. 1). Often, leggy shrubs that would be unacceptable for regular landscaping can be used for sand-dune planting with fine results.

In all planting in sandy soils, plenty of humus should be mixed with the natural sand. It will not last long, but it will encourage root growth by retaining moisture in the root zone.

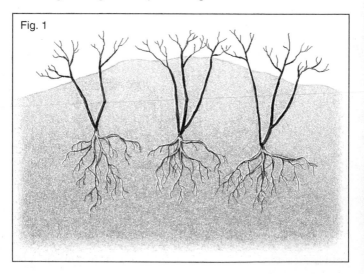

Fig. 1

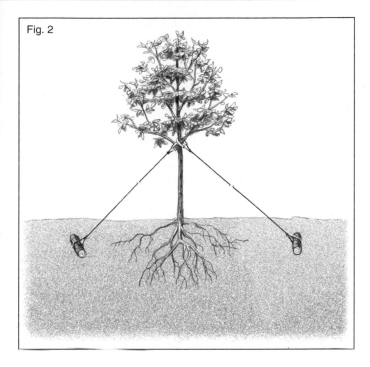

Fig. 2

Fresh water for irrigation is frequently limited and expensive at the seashore, so any effort to make it persist in the garden is very worthwhile.

A major objective when planting trees in a sandy location is to get the root system to spread as widely, deeply, and rapidly as possible in order to provide storm anchorage. Until a newly planted tree has had a chance to form a large enough root system for good support, staking or cable bracing is essential. The looseness of sand offers a poor root hold, and newly planted trees are easily upset. This same instability of sand allows the stakes normally used for cable-brace attachment to be easily loosened or pulled up by violent storms. Unless you can drive very long and strong stakes deeply into the soil, a much better method of attaching guying cables is to fasten them to small logs or 2x4 sticks buried in trenches crosswise to the line of pull (see fig. 2). If the trenches are also dug back to the planting pit in the form of a *T*, and a sand and humus mix is used to fill these connecting portions and the cross sections for the logs, roots will rapidly grow out along the lower portions of the trenches and form strong anchors for the trunk. By the time the supporting cables or wires have been removed or have rusted out from salt-air corrosion, the roots will have grown out widely into the surrounding soil. If a supporting stake is used, as is satisfactory

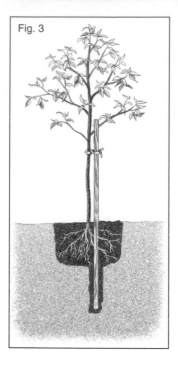

Fig. 3

for small trees, the hole for it should be dug deeper than the bottom of the planting pit and should be back-filled with humus and sand (see fig. 3). This extra encouragement will speed the formation of a deep taproot to provide strong bracing when the tree is larger and more susceptible to being uprooted by a storm. The tops, or "leaders," of shade trees planted in coastal gardens or along seaside residential streets should be shortened back. This encourages the formation of a low, spreading crown that will give good shade but escape the leverage of violent storms.

Adequate bracing or cable support is essential to the successful establishment of coastal shade trees or conifers. Far too often, however, the support is correctly installed but then forgotten. Even when protected by short lengths of hose where the cable or wire surrounds the trunk, neglected wires in later years can choke off the expanding trunk and kill the tree. Thousands of dollars' worth of easily prevented losses occur each year. Wire or cable supports should be carefully checked each spring and fall and removed or loosened where necessary. Even when several years of maintenance contracts for a landscape project are a part of the original planting contract, this essential checking can be overlooked. But there is even less excuse in a home planting where the homeowner is responsible for all maintenance after the landscape planting has been accepted.

The trunks and branches of coniferous and broad-leaved trees on exposed coastal sites are often bent back inland by the pressure of strong prevailing winds and the scorching of new growth on the exposed side that results from repeated deposits of salt spray. Planting trees, especially pines, with their trunks slanted back from the prevailing winds is a seldom used but very effective method of avoiding storm damage. Conforming already to the wind pressure, they do not require heavy bracing for security. Slanted plantings may look bizarre for the first two years, but with surprising rapidity the branches rearrange themselves into natural positions and the

Fig. 4

final effect is very picturesque. If the planting involves several or more specimens, the trunks should be set with angular variations of 10 degrees but which average out to the same natural angle from the perpendicular that is found in the local native vegetation (see fig. 4). It is only a convention that every tree should have an absolutely perpendicular trunk. One of the great characteristic appeals of trees both at the shore and at timberline in the mountains is their obvious shaping by powerful environmental forces. There are a number of plantings in Japanese gardens where the effect of this special orientation is extraordinarily handsome.

Seashore planting in areas where regular inland soils extend to the edge of the sea requires some but not all of the special techniques useful in very sandy areas. The soil is more fertile than in sandy coasts and does not require the addition of as much humus. Because of the extra velocity that winds develop sweeping in unhindered over miles of flat water, extra care in anchoring large shade trees and large conifers is essential. However, because the soil is much more dense and unyielding, the installation of buried cross sticks in trenches is not necessary; large stakes driven in the ground are adequate. Shortening the trees' tops also aids in getting them securely established and rooted fast before their crowns of foliage become large. Where there are sizable boulders as a natural landscape feature, trees planted as close to them as possible will be able to thrust their roots down beside and under them. Planting on the inland side of boulders or ledges gives added security. The worst uprootings occur when hurricanes or violent winds are preceded by heavy rains that soften the soil and loosen the grasp of roots. Roots wedged among or under rocks have much greater resistance to being pulled loose. If, after a planting pit is excavated, soil is dug away from under a rock and then replaced by a liberal mixture of soil and humus with a little fertilizer added, the roots of the new tree will grow rapidly in the desired direction (see fig. 5).

Nature's method can be used to establish trees and shrubs in crevices between rocks or ledges in which there is too little room to plant larger specimens. A smaller hole can be excavated and a young seedling can be planted in the small pocket of improved soil, just as though a seed had germinated there naturally. This method is also useful for establishing young creeping junipers even as small as 3-inch pot plants, which will later spread out to mantle a portion of the rock. Junipers are well adapted for such locations and require a surprisingly small volume of soil for good growth. Their roots will penetrate narrow cracks in rock structure to find moisture and thin sheets of soil. For interesting foliage patterns and flowers, house leeks (*Sempervivum* spp.), sedums, and creeping phlox can be planted in tiny but deep crevices an inch or two wide. There are many fascinating species that can be purchased from specialist growers.

In all situations where woody plants are to be planted in

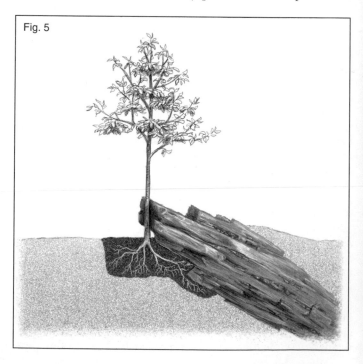

Fig. 5

windswept, exceptionally exposed locations, severe pruning back at planting time is important for survival during the first year, particularly where water for periodic soaking is limited or absent or the home is used only for vacation time. Wild plants start in such exposed locations from the germination of seed. The normal course thereafter is the production of a large root system before such top growth takes place. Thus the young plant has a favorable balance of root to top and can compensate for the extra water loss caused by strong winds. Plants growing in coastal sand dunes often have a much greater volume of plant tissue below the surface of the sand than above it. If newly set deciduous shrubs are cut back almost to the ground at planting time or if the branches of new trees are severely shortened and thinned out, they too will have more root than top and will regenerate much more vigorously than if every twig were left in place. Even coniferous evergreens benefit from selective shortening and thinning of the branches. The pruning has to be done carefully in the case of pines and spruces because these plants do not resprout readily from old wood as do deciduous shrubs and trees. One curious exception is the pitch pine, which will resprout from the trunk even after a serious forest fire. Twig shortening should remove only half of the previous season's growth — and that on a selective basis — leaving one out of three branches not trimmed at all.

In cooler climates such as the coastal strips from Connecticut north to the Maritime Provinces of Canada, screening or shelter plantings are often installed to break the force of ocean winds. Sheltering hedges protect flowering shrubs and herbaceous plants from shredding in windstorms and can extend the outdoor use of the garden earlier in the spring and later in the fall months. Windbreaks using dense plant material are much more effective than solid walls of wood or stone. Plant screens (40 percent density or more) absorb and greatly slow down the wind for a distance up to ten times the height of the hedge or screen. In contrast, a solid barrier creates strong turbulence on the leeward side of the screen and results in little or no protection. An outstanding demonstration of the value of hedges for plant protection occurs on the Scilly Islands off the southern tip of England. The Scilly Islands have long been famous for cut-flower production and notorious for violent windstorms. When the solid wooden walls erected to protect the flower fields blew down in the worst storms, they were replaced with tall, narrow hedges of evergreen escallonia that remain unaffected by the winds and do an excellent job of protecting the flowers.

Trees for the Seashore

WILLIAM FLEMER III

Any coastal garden, but especially a vacation garden, should emphasize those trees that are perfectly adapted to seashore conditions. Native coastal plants, of course, are well able to look after themselves and typify the special beauty of the wild littoral. But there are other trees that are also well suited to coastal planting sites.

Trees

Coastal wattle *(Acacia longiflora)* is one of several species of the very large Australian family of wattles that are highly resistant to salt spray and the battering of sea winds. This tough small tree or shrub is hardy in the coastal strip of Zone 8 and thrives along the California coast, at times growing in almost pure sand. It bears narrow olive green leaves and abundant spikes of canary yellow flowers in the early spring. It is a good barrier screening plant to protect less resistant species.

European sycamore maple *(Acer pseudoplatanus)* is the best of all the maples for the coast. It is hardy to Zone 5 and grows to 50 feet at the shore (taller in richer inland soils). It forms a very wide crown of large lobed leaves, and there are several selections with leaved tinted dark purple.

Downy shadblow *(Amelanchier canadensis)* is a small tree that thrives near salt water. It is hardy from Zone 4 south and is a lovely feature of the New England coast, especially in April when it is covered with nodding clusters of white flowers. One of the finest features of Long Island, New York, is a long-abandoned pasture full of mature shadblows on the tip of Montauk Point, beautiful in spring and again in fall when the leaves turn orange and red. Shadblows will not grow well on sand dunes, but in heavier or moister soils they are perfectly at home within sound range of the sea.

Pacific madrone *(Arbutus menziesii)* grows wild right out to the high-tide mark on the Pacific coast. It is an evergreen tree with clusters of small white flowers (6 to 9 inches) in May and colorful orange-red berries. Its special beauty is the striking, glossy red-to-orange bark, which is especially handsome in contrast with the glossy dark foliage. The madrone, hardy in Zone 8 from British Columbia south to California, reaches 60 feet in rich soil but will grow well even in poor soil.

Australian pine or horsetail beefwood *(Casuarina equiseti-folia)* is a tall tropical conifer from Australia, but it is in no way related to the true pines. Hardy to Zone 10, it is particularly happy in southern Florida and on the Caribbean islands. In both areas it reaches 70 to 80 feet in height and seeds itself abundantly along the coast, even in almost pure sand at the high-tide line. It can be sheared as a tall hedge or left untrimmed to form a tall, feathery evergreen tree.

Monterey cypress *(Cupressus macrocarpa)* has the smallest distribution of any American conifer — a minuscule 2-mile coastal strip from Cypress Point to Point Lobos, California. This limited stand is obviously the remnant of a much larger population in prehistoric times, perhaps occupying headlands long since gnawed away by the ceaseless battering of the Pacific. Fortunately the species is easy to propagate and takes kindly to cultivation, as it is one of the best conifers for seashore planting, both here and abroad. It is hardy to Zone 7 and grows very rapidly when young, slowing down and becoming increasingly picturesque with age.

English holly *(Ilex aquifolium)* is an excellent broad-leaved evergreen, the most beautiful of the tree-sized hollies, with glossy dark green foliage. Female trees bear abundant bright red berries, widely sold for Christmas decorations. It is very tolerant of salt spray and much used for seaside hedges in France and England. Although hardy to Zone 6, it is much more reliable on the West Coast, where the cool, foggy weather duplicates its native climatic conditions in western Europe. American holly *(Ilex opaca)* is much more cold-hardy than the English species and is hardy to Zone 5. It grows wild from coastal Massachusetts all the way down the coast to northern Florida.

Eastern red cedar *(Juniperus virginiana)* grows wild all down the Atlantic coast from southern Maine to South Carolina, even in almost pure dune sand. It reaches 20 to 40 feet at the shore and greater heights inland. Seaside trees become picturesquely twisted and molded by prevailing winds. Hardy to Zone 2, it is always a tough and reliable conifer for coastal gardens, and the blue berries of female trees are a most important staple for overwintering birds.

Southern magnolia *(Magnolia grandiflora)* looks so exotic and "tropical" that it is always a surprise to see how well it does beside the sea. Hardy from Zone 7 south, it is one of the glories of the primeval forests of Bulls Island and other Sea Islands below Charleston, South Carolina.

Tupelo or sour gum *(Nyssa sylvatica)* is predominantly a swamp tree from Maine to Florida, but it also grows right out to the shore in many areas. The northern races are hardy to Zone 3. Its rather leathery leaves are very spray-tolerant and turn an intense scarlet in the fall — a brilliance matched by only a handful of other big trees. The blue berries of female trees are important fall food for birds. Tupelo was formerly very rarely planted because its coarse and sparse root system made transplanting a risky procedure. It has proved to grow exceptionally well in containers and is now rapidly increasing in popularity because these container-grown plants are so easy to establish.

Black spruce *(Picea mariana)* is one of the hardiest of all spruces, thriving in Zone 2. It certainly has the widest native range of any spruce, growing from Newfoundland to Alaska. It does not grow as large as many other species, usually reaching 40 to 50 feet on the coast, where it is singularly tolerant of salt spray and fierce storms. It is the characteristic seaside conifer of the coast of Maine and the Maritime Provinces.

Sitka spruce *(Picea sitchensis)* is the preeminent coastal conifer of the West Coast from northern California up to Alaska. It makes an enormous tree on rich inland sites, but it also grows right out on the shore line unhurt by winter storms or salt spray. Although hardy to Zone 6, it demands a cool, humid climate and is not satisfactory on the East Coast.

Austrian pine *(Pinus nigra),* tolerant of air pollution, is also very resistant to salt spray and windburn. It has been planted by the millions to stabilize the great dikes that protect the Dutch bulb fields from the fury of the North Sea in winter. In these sterile dredged soils, trees 40 years old may be only 3 or 4 feet tall, but they hang on grimly — clear testimony to the tenacity of this species. Extensive groves of Austrian pine in inland parts of the American East are frequently killed by a slow-acting fungus that attacks the twigs. The slat-laden air of the seaside is apparently an effective fungicide, because trees planted right on the coast are seldom attacked. Stiffly upright in growth and having long, dark green needles, they are hardy from Zone 4 south to Zone 7.

Monterey pine *(Pinus radiata)* is a strictly coastal species from the Monterey peninsula in California and hardy from Zone 7 to warmer areas. It has an irregular, rather open habit of growth and bright green needles. Of rapid growth when young, it is singularly resistant to sea winds and salt spray and is much used along the southern coast of England for sheltering plantings, as well as being the most frequently planted tree for reforestation in Australia.

Japanese black pine *(Pinus thunbergiana)* is the first choice for coastal locations from Massachusetts south to North Carolina and along the Pacific coast because no pine exceeds its tolerance of extreme seaside conditions. It will grow right down to the high-tide line, and the roots have survived flooding with salt water for many days. It is a poor timber tree but a most picturesque ornamental. The trunk is usually twisted and bent, and frequently several trunks are developed from the same root system. The Japanese love the gnarled beauty of this pine. It clothes the innumerable rocky inlets and cliffs of the Japanese coast and is invariably a feature of their marvelous paintings of maritime landscapes. Even young trees indicate the direction in which their leaning trunks are going to grow, and if these are all oriented away from the sea when they are planted, a striking landscape design will result. The tree's lush dark green needles and prominent white buds are always attractive, and it looks healthy in even the poorest sandy soils in Zone 6 south. (In some areas, large *P. thunbergiana* have died from a canker stain disease for which no cure has yet been discovered. In such areas, our native pitch pine, *P. rigida*, is an excellent substitute.)

White poplar *(Populus alba)* is an unusual and very hardy poplar that thrives in the cold of Zone 3 in sandy soil and full exposure to sea air. The leaves are lobed like small maple leaves, dark green above and silvery white on the undersurfaces, creating a pretty effect on breezy days. The normal form makes a short-trunked but very wide-spreading tree — a habit of growth that gives it the advantage of being windfast.

Holly oak or Holm oak *(Quercus ilex)* is a rounded and broadly spreading evergreen with small glossy leaves. It is native to southern Europe and has a broad coastal distribution around the Mediterranean Sea. Hardy to Zone 7 of this country, it is an excellent seashore tree. The very leathery 2-inch leaves are not harmed by salt spray, and the tough-wooded branches are never wind-damaged. Being small-leaved and twiggy, it is well adapted to shearing and is much used in southern France and Italy for tall, windbreak hedges. It can reach 60 to 70 feet in locations with good soil but only 40 feet or so when exposed at the waterfront.

Live oak *(Quercus virginiana),* one of the most majestic of all broad-leaved evergreen trees, is normally associated with wide avenues, colonnaded antebellum mansions, and other stereotypes of Southern plantation life. It is also a first-rate tree for seashore planting. Live oak is hardy from Zone 7 south, with the northernmost outpost of native trees on the shore just north of Norfolk, Virginia. On the barrier islands of South Carolina and Texas, where violent hurricanes and drenchings with salt spray are yearly occurrences, it is an important forest tree. Waterfront specimens are bent and contorted by the force of prevailing winds, but they persist for centuries in the poorest soils and most exposed locations. Live oaks, unless container-grown, should be severely pruned at transplanting time, and even reduced almost to stakes, as the root systems of young trees are sparse. They resprout easily from adventitious buds and soon develop the broad spreading crowns characteristic of the species.

Cabbage palmetto *(Sabal palmetto),* the hardiest of our limited number of native palms, is a frequent associate of the live oak in coastal sites and on sea islands. It is found in Zone 9 from coastal North Carolina southward along the Atlantic coast, never far from salt water in the northern part of its range. It will stand any amount of salt spray, even salt water over the roots in hurricane high tides, without injury.

Chinese windmill palm *(Trachycarpus fortunei)* is the hardiest of all palm trees (Zone 8) and is very salt-tolerant indeed. It is planted up the Atlantic coast to Virginia and on the Pacific coast to Vancouver Island, allowing the unlikely statement that palms can be grown in Canada! It is very slow-growing, has a shaggy fibrous bark, and is effective when planted in clumps to amplify the effect of the trunks.

Roses at the Seashore

PETER SCHNEIDER

If it is a challenge to grow roses at the seashore, it is a challenge accepted happily by Nature. *Rosa rugosa* has naturalized throughout the Northeast, and rugosa colonies are so well established in coastal Maine that it is hard to believe that this Asian rose is not a native Yankee. Shrugging off wind and salt, sending their roots resolutely into the sand, and blooming throughout the summer, rugosas are the ideal rose to choose for seashore gardens.

R. rugosa is a variable species, with single-petaled blooms ranging from white through pink and purple and into maroon. The stunning white form, *R. rugosa alba,* is as stable as it is beautiful, and the gardener can order it with confidence from many reputable nurseries. However, both *R. rugosa* (which may be pink or purple) and its red form, *R. rugosa rubra,* are sometimes indiscriminately mixed up by commercial sources.

Rugosa blooms, which are larger than those of most other

species roses, are followed by tomato-like ornamental hips often reaching an inch in diameter. In the autumn, ripening hips and new flowers appear together, competing for attention against a background of shining, dark green rugosa foliage. Rugosa hips will commonly last well into the winter, although an unusually warm and rainy autumn will shorten their display.

Hybridization has expanded the rugosa color range into yellow (first with 'Agnes' and more recently, and satisfactorily, with 'Topaz Jewel') and added some excellent clear reds (such as the floriferous 'Linda Campbell' and the single-petaled 'Robusta'). Attempts to create apricot and orange-shaded rugosas have been less successful, and the "mauve" rugosas all range toward purple. Unfortunately, many recent creations are not as fragrant as the species rugosas and their early hybrids (of which the reddish purple 'Roseraie de l'Hay', introduced in 1901 — and often confused with the boring 'Rose à Parfum de l'Hay' — is an outstanding example).

Other renowned rugosas include the snow-white 'Blanc Double de Coubert'; the compact, pale pink, single-petaled 'Frau Dagmar Hastrup'; the stalwart purple 'Hansa'; and the crimson 'Mrs. Anthony Waterer', which offers good color and savory fragrance but less repeat bloom than we expect from a rugosa. The mauve-red 'Scabrosa', though saddled with one of the ugliest names ever given to a rose, provides more constant repeat bloom than any other rugosa. Plant a dozen 'Scabrosa' and you will get a uniform, useful, and very colorful hedge in return.

Most recent breeding work with rugosas has been focused on their arctic hardiness. That the results, such as the series of Explorer roses bred in Canada, thrive at the seashore as well as on the prairie may be taken as a bonus. The two Explorer roses best suited for seaside use may be 'Jens Munk', a carefree medium pink growing as wide as it does tall, and the spicily scented 'Henry Hudson', a semidouble white.

Rugosas are named for their rugose, or wrinkled, leaves. While these leaves boast greater disease resistance than those of many other kinds of roses, they will also be the first to demonstrate phytotoxic reactions to chemical sprays. Spraying rugosas with chemical fungicides or insecticides will always do more harm than good. Ways in which rugosas commonly react to garden chemicals include burned-looking leaves and defoliation. Rugosas are rarely troubled by insects, and when they do get black spot or powdery mildew, they are almost always vigorous enough to outgrow it.

Rugosas grown right by the sea will rarely achieve the 5 to 6 foot heights of those cultivated in more sheltered gardens. The species rugosas will usually grow to just 2 to 3 feet on exposed beach, but this growth will be healthy, vigorous, and lush.

Rugosa roses are not perfect. Some gardeners may find their growth coarse and their informal flowers lacking either the symmetry of the familiar hybrid tea or the perfect charm of the quartered petals of the old garden rose. They don't make good cut flowers. Most rugosas have abundant prickles. This makes them even more valuable as an impenetrable hedge, but it can also make them dangerous to work (or play) around. Leaves on many rugosas will yellow and drop as autumn approaches, while this is an annoying trait, it should not be mistaken for disease.

Beyond rugosas, the seashore rosarian has as many choices as there are roses. With enough effort, one can grow anything, but the easiest choices will be roses that stand up to the special conditions of seashore gardening: roses that are tolerant of sandy soils and have a growth habit that won't be beaten down by wind, colors that don't wash out in bright sunlight, and petals that will open normally and remain unspotted despite fog and heavy dew.

Sand

The best way to get non-rugosas to grow in sand is to get them budded onto *R. fortuniana* understock. Like *R. rugosa*, *R. fortuniana* is especially suited for growing in sand, but because it is less prone to suckering, it makes a much better rose understock than *R. rugosa* does. Long a favorite of Florida rosarians, *R. fortuniana* has recently won converts on Cape Cod and in the New Jersey Sand Belt. It is not, however, reliably winter-hardy so far north as Maine or around the Great Lakes.

Many garden centers in Florida offer roses budded onto *R. fortuniana*; Floridians should be sure to ask for this specifically. (They may also have better luck with the rugosas, which dislike extreme heat, if they are budded onto *R. fortuniana*.) Roses from the large mail-order houses are grown in California or Arizona and budded onto 'Dr. Huey' or 'Manetti' understock. The only retail mail order source for roses budded onto *R. fortuniana* is Giles Ramblin' Roses, 2968 State Road 710, Okeechobee, FL 34974, which offers a wide selection of varieties.

Wind

Windy conditions at the seashore make roses that grow bolt upright (such as the hybrid tea 'Folklore', the grandiflora

'Queen Elizabeth', and many of the Kordesii climbers) unsatisfactory choices. If a rose is much taller than it is wide,
the wind will work continuously to loosen its roots; with
sandy soil offering little anchor, the rose may never have a
chance to establish itself. When a naturally bushy variety
makes shorter growth, it still looks like a bush. When an upright variety makes shorter growth, it looks like a stick. Staking tall roses is a practical if not particularly attractive option; choosing bushy varieties is much better.

Despite the height they can achieve inland, many of the old
ramblers work beautifully at the seashore, either trained horizontally to a fence or some other structure, or allowed to
grow naturally into a large mound or clump. 'American Pil-
lar', a single-petaled carmine pink with a white eye, is a longtime favorite, as is the pink 'Dorothy Perkins'. 'Dorothy
Perkins' is often plagued by mildew on the West Coast, but
the brisk air circulation usually found in East Coast seashore
gardens will keep mildew well in check. The double-petaled
red rambler 'Chevy Chase' deserves special mention for its resistance to black spot.

While the ramblers do not offer repeat bloom, their month
of glory arrives after the modern roses have finished their first
flush of bloom. Gaps in the rose flowering season can be filled
with the late-blooming deep pink *R. setigera*. A native American also well suited to growing by the sea, this species rose
does not even begin to bloom until midsummer, when the
ramblers are almost done.

Ground-cover roses are simply ramblers bred by modern-
day nurserymen with no visions of arbors, arches, or pergo-
las dancing around in their heads. The idea of ground-cover
roses scrambling up and down sand dunes is appealing, but
the reality waits for ground-cover roses with growth as lush
as it is strong and with flowers large enough to be noticed
from a distance. For now, the best ground covers to try
around dunes would be the most rampant ones, especially
Kordes' light pink 'Immensee' and its white form 'Weisse Immensee'.

Sun

Intense sunlight reduces many yellow and apricot roses to an
unpleasant shade of muddy white. This problem is most noticeable with miniature roses, but it affects roses in all classes.
It is a particular problem with many of David Austin's English roses, bred and selected in overcast England.

One of the few truly colorfast yellow hybrid teas is 'Gina
Lollobrigida'. 'Summer Dream' is an apricot hybrid tea that
holds its color better than most, and the recent All-American

Rose Selection 'Singin' in the Rain' is a cinnamon-apricot floribunda that does not fade. At the other extreme, some bi-colored rose varieties, such as the hybrid tea 'Double Delight', require lots of sun to develop their best color. And, of course, seashore rosarians in northern California, Oregon, and Washington rarely have to worry about intense sunlight. Gardeners in these locales will find it easy to cultivate apricot and yellow roses in their true, best colors.

Fog and Dew

The heavy dew that often forms at the seashore makes it difficult to grow roses that have lots of petals. This is a special problem in areas of persistent fog along the Pacific coast. Under these conditions, buds of many of the true old garden roses (and their modern replicas) will simply refuse to open. Unless cut and taken to open indoors, an uncertain proposition in itself, buds will simply rot and fall off. The simplest solution to this is to grow single-petaled and semidouble roses; these light-petaled roses will open in any weather.

The pretty dogwoodlike blooms of the floribunda 'Betty Prior' give no hint of this variety's toughness. Widely available from general nurserymen as well as from specialist rose growers, 'Betty Prior' is as rugged a rose as you can find. It is ideally suited for seashore use. Like many early floribundas, 'Betty Prior' is most effective when planted in groups of three or six; in fact, Roy Hennessey, the eccentric Oregon rose nurseryman of the 1950s and 1960s, refused to sell 'Betty Prior' in anything but quantities of three. The single-petaled pink miniature 'Simon Robinson', bred from R. *wichuraiana* and inheriting much of its durability, is in some respects like a small-scale version of 'Betty Prior'.

Of course, there are some double roses that will open easily despite persistent dew; some examples among the hybrid teas are 'Elegant Beauty' (yellow), 'Forgotten Dreams' (dusky red and gloriously fragrant), 'Senator Burda' (blood red and also very fragrant), and the blush 'Pristine' as well as its white sport 'Fountain Square'.

The Kordes "Frühlings" series of roses are all single-petaled or nearly so and bred from R. *spinosissima* (the Scotch briar rose). 'Frühlingsgold' (which is actually creamy yellow) and 'Frühlingsmorgen' (pink with a pale yellow eye) are the best known and most widely available. Despite blooming only once a year, these are particular favorites in the Pacific Northwest, where spinosissima hybrids thrive. Other spinosissima favorites include the deep yellow 'Aicha', bred in Denmark; the pearlescent 'Kawka'; and David Austin's pale pink blend 'Robbie Burns'. 'New Face', a yellow blend bred by Ilsink of Holland, is a hybrid spinosissima that offers excellent repeat bloom.

Dew will also cause unsightly red or pink spots to appear on white or pale-colored roses. Few white, light pink, or light yellow roses are immune to this problem. 'Polarstem' is a white hybrid tea exception, and, in general, the thicker a rose's petals are, the more resistant it will be to weatherspotting. Therefore the ideal seashore rose would be one with thick petals, but not too many of them.

Other hybrid teas with special suitability for seashore gardening include the camellia pink 'Duet', the coral pink 'Silver Jubilee', the deep pink 'Peter Frankenfeld', and the red 'Precious Platinum'. These four are among the healthiest and sturdiest of all hybrid teas. While the Brownell "sub-zero" hybrid teas are overrated for their winter hardiness, they were bred and tested by the sea in Little Compton, Rhode Island, and make good choices for the seashore garden.

Among floribundas, some excellent choices beyond 'Betty Prior' include the scarlet and gold 'Playboy', 'Amber Queen', the red 'H.C. Anderson', and the pink 'Sexy Rexy'. Despite having very double petals, 'Sexy Rexy' will open well at the seashore. In order to guarantee repeat bloom on 'Sexy Rexy', it is essential that old flowers be cut off promptly, before any rose hips can form.

Most of the Meidiland roses should adapt well to seashore gardens (the possible exception being the perpendicular 'Pink Meidiland'), and the Meilland's dependable 'Carefree Wonder' shrub rose makes a kaleidoscopic low hedge of pink and white.

Culture

The task of improving sand to the point where it will grow a wide variety of roses can be endless — sand leaches every nutrient away, sometimes almost as soon as it can be added. Many seashore rosarians have found that it is simpler to plant their roses in large containers and sink these into the sand, rather than trying to change the sand itself. Peach baskets were used for this purpose in the past; today a 7- or 9-gallon biodegradable nursery pot will work just as well. In order to get the rose off to a less stressful start, this method is most successful in areas where some shade is available.

A container mix of one-third compost, one-third commercial potting soil, and one-third soilless mix (such as ProMix) together with a small amount of timed-release fertilizer works well. Drainage holes at the bottom of the pot are essential. To improve water retention, line the bottom of the planting hole with about half an inch of wet newspaper. In my experience, the highly touted, moisture-retaining polymers are not particularly effective.

Over a sandy base, it is impossible to overwater your roses. Frequent deep watering is important; light watering accomplishes nothing.

Rose pruning at the seashore should be restricted to the removal of obviously dead or diseased wood, and the light shaping of the plant. If you must prune vigorously, remember that ramblers and some ground covers bloom but once a year, and a harsh cutting back in spring will eliminate an entire year's display. As rugosa plants age, older shoots will begin to bow over as they are pushed aside by new growth. This bowed-over growth soon becomes unproductive, and it should be removed.

Organic feeding is especially important whenever growing conditions are less than ideal. Whether planted directly in ground that is sandy (or, as can be the case on the West Coast, gravelly, rocky, or adobe) or in sunken pots, roses will thrive on biweekly feedings of fish emulsion and liquid seaweed. If you are applying these organics directly to the foliage as a foliar spray, be sure the rose has been well watered at least 8 hours before spraying. The seashore gardener often has access to organic fertilizers — such as seaweed and fish scraps — that are considered exotic inland; taking advantage of locally available organic fertilizers will help your roses give their very best.

The sun and breeze at the seashore will dispel most rose diseases naturally, and choosing disease-resistant varieties helps ensure a healthy garden. By getting the right roses off to the right start, with plenty of organics, the seashore gardener can enjoy the color and fragrance that only roses can provide, against the incomparable backdrop of the sea.

Herbs for the Seashore

JUDITH KEHS

Herbs are ideal plants for the coastal garden. Along the shores of southern Europe, the oreganos, rosemaries, thymes, sages, lavenders, and santolinas have thrived for centuries within sight of the sea, adapted to constantly changing weather and inhospitable growing conditions. Herbs flourish in spite of (possibly because of?) barren rocky soils, long hours of direct sun, hot dry periods tempered by salty breezes, and the violent storms common to seashore locales.

Silvery-foliaged plants, such as the salvias, lavendulas, artemisias, achilleas, and santolinas, are uniquely equipped to endure and survive seaside climates. What we see simply as velvety silver or gray leaves are actually evidence of microscopic hairs that serve to hold precious droplets of nourishing moisture and help sustain plants in sunny, windy, hot environments. Besides the silvery-leaved herbs, many other herb plants have proved remarkably adaptable to seashore growing conditions. Perhaps their long history of adaptability and perseverance has given rise to the popular theory that the more herbs suffer, the richer their scents and the more pungent their flavors.

Broadly defined, herbs are plants that are useful histori-cally because of their flavor, fragrance, or magical or medic-inal properties, and also for such household applications as fabric preparation and dyeing (soapwort, indigo, calendula), insect repellents (pennyroyal, tansy, wormwood), and the making of brooms (Scotch broom, broom corn), furniture polish (lemon balm), and mattress stuffing (hops, bedstraw). A fascinating selection of herbs can be seen in historical restoration gardens and arboretums throughout this country and elsewhere. Most household herb gardens today, however, are created around a basic collection of fragrant and culinary plants, with an increasing interest in herbs for ethnic cuisines.

Light

Most herbs need sun — quite a lot of it — to thrive and to stimulate the oils that give them their distinctive flavors and aromas. Although a full day of sun is ideal, herbs will do rea-sonably well with 4 to 6 hours of direct sunlight. In fact, a little shade helps reduce plant stress from too-long exposure to intense summer sunshine.

Moisture

Herbs can tolerate much drier environments than other plants, but that doesn't mean they won't be stressed by the extreme drought conditions caused by the combination of sandy soil, hot sun, and steady winds. If your herb garden will be exposed to the strong winds and constant breezes that typify seashore locations, try to provide some form of fenc-ing or natural windbreaks, such as shrubbery or stands of tall perennials.

Even with windbreaks, you'll probably need to give your herbs supplemental water, at least when they are young. Water when the soil is dry to a depth of 3 inches, and water early in the day or in the evening, never in the full heat of the midday sun. Try to water the soil, not the plants. Large drops of water standing on tender leaves can burn them; in the evening, water standing on the leaves may give rise to disease spores (even though herbs are more resistant to disease than other plants are). And remember that it is better to water herbs too little than too much.

Soil

The sandy or rocky soils typical of most seashores provide the good drainage that is crucial to growing herbs. But de-spite their ability to survive in inhospitable environments, very arid sandy or rocky soil is not enough to nurture healthy herbs. You'll have to improve the soil or build the garden above the ground.

The classic solution is raised beds, filled with a mixture of equal parts of coarse builder's sand (not beach sand), good garden soil, and peat or sphagnum moss. If you have compost, add some from time to time. Build the bed 6 to 10 inches above ground level, and make it no wider than 4 feet so that you can reach into it from every side.

If you prefer a ground-level bed, remove existing soil to a depth of 12 inches and refill the area with the same soil mix as described above.

Planting and Maintenance

Regardless of what size they are when you plant them, space herbs 10 to 12 inches apart. The garden will look sparse at first, but the plants will grow quickly and will develop better if not crowded — you can always fill the early gaps with annuals that can be moved out when the herbs grow large.

As soon as the herbs are well established and of reasonable size (10 to 12 inches in most cases), they can be clipped and used. Judicious harvesting throughout the season helps stimulate new and fuller growth. You can divide flourishing perennials (French tarragon, chives, creeping thymes, balms, and mints) anytime with care, but division is best done at the beginning or end of the growing season.

If your garden needs frequent supplemental watering, mulching is the answer. Almost any organic, nonacidic mulch material will do — grass clippings, cocoa or barley hulls, or slightly aged sawdust. Applied no deeper than 1 inch, these materials help preserve reasonable, but not excessive, moisture. At the end of the season, work the mulch into the soil, and apply a new layer the following year.

Winter mulch is another matter. Salt marsh hay, readily available near the seashore, is the best possible mulch. A 2-inch layer, laid down *after* the ground is frozen, will adequately insulate your perennial herbs. It isn't the initial freezing that damages plants so much as the later thawing and refreezing that weakens their root systems. Where winter freezing is not a factor, but where you can expect high winds or driving rains, a layer of mulch will protect your plants against these seasonal conditions.

Herbs in Containers

Almost any herb can be grown in a container, and some herbs really need to be confined because they are invasive in the garden. All the mints, including lemon balm, increase rapidly by roots and runners and require constant policing if they are not contained. Plant these in good-sized containers, not terribly deep but broad enough to accommodate the plants' lateral growth. (Some people prefer to sink large pots of mint right into the ground.) Catnip, another mint, planted in the garden is an invitation to all the felines in the neighborhood to visit and wallow in your garden, destroying the other plantings. Sink a pot of it in the ground well away from the other garden areas.

Bay laurel, rosemary, lemon verbena, and pineapple sage are all desirable perennials that are not hardy north of Zone 7. Grow them in containers that can be moved indoors.

Harvesting

When culinary herbs are well established, you may start picking sprigs to use in cooking. A rule of thumb is to harvest no more than one-third of the plant at any time. Parsley, burnet, and sorrel leaves should be harvested from the base of the plants, not from the center of the crown where new growth originates. Also keep in mind that the flavor of herbs is best at midday when the heat of the sun has fully stimulated the aromatic oils and that when the plants bloom their flavor is slightly diminished — though still quite good. For as long as possible, prevent annuals from blooming by nipping out the buds as they appear, since after they flower they quickly go to seed and the life cycle ends.

At the end of the growing season, before frost in colder areas, harvest culinaries for winter use. Harvest during the warmest part of the day when all moisture on the leaves has dried. Among the several options for preserving herbs are hang-drying in bunches, freezing, and oven-drying (in a microwave or other oven). Some methods of preserving are better for certain herbs — freezing for basil and chives; hang-drying for thymes, rosemary, oregano, mints, and sages; and oven-drying for nearly all herbs. Fortunately, most microwaves today come with instruction pamphlets that include drying information for most common herbs. The herbs, once thoroughly dried to a brittle, papery consistency, should be stored in airtight containers out of the light, moisture, and heat or in sealed plastic bags in the freezer, ready to use when needed. The shelf life of dried herbs is 9 to 12 months; frozen herbs should be used within 6 months. Frozen herbs are about equal to fresh herbs in potency, but dried herbs are twice as strong as fresh ones. Using your own herbs fresh, dried, or frozen is preferable by far to relying on commercial products. They're more economical, flavorful, and enjoyable.

Landscaping a Vacation Home

CAROL STOCKER

Even the most beautiful landscape design for your vacation home will be very unsatisfactory if it grows to be high-maintenance. Whether you spend winters in Palm Beach, summers in Bar Harbor, or weekends in Malibu, you'll be even less able to coddle plants than the homeowner who lives full-time near the beach. And you may not want to try, since you're on vacation and relaxing when you're at the shore.

But there are thoughtful strategies for managing an easy but beguiling vacation-home garden near the sea. Culinary herbs and late-blooming shrubs that have been severely cut back, or stooled, earlier in the year can fill a beach garden with summer flowers and fragrance that fit happily into a natural setting. The greatest advantage to landscaping a vacation home is that you can concentrate on plants that bloom only for the few weeks or months that you are there, creating an intensified season of color without worrying as much about long sequences of bloom or winter interest. If you're at your beach house in July and August and that is when the rose of Sharon, hydrangea, and tamarisk are a mass of flowers, you needn't reject them simply because they look like sticks most of the rest of the year.

Start by looking around to see what does well for your neighbors and also what is in flower during your usual vacation period. You'll notice that near the sea plants can bloom at different times, and for longer periods, than farther inland. The lupine that finishes flowering in June in Boston will still be going strong in July in coastal Maine, and *Campanula persicifolia* will bloom there all summer thanks to cool nights that prolong the life of individual blossoms.

Keep It Natural

The trend toward naturalistic gardening and xeroscaping using native plants is even stronger in vacation colonies than among year-round homeowners. The further you move from the native landscape, the more maintenance headaches you risk creating. If the original landscape of your new beach house is something you can live with, please do. And if you don't like all that beach grass, bayberry, and black pine, live with it anyway for at least a couple of seasons before you make big adjustments. You may find that the biggest change is in your own sense of beauty after you've had time to "consult the genius of the place," as poet Alexander Pope put it. The elegant branches and red antlerlike blooms of staghorn sumac and the waxy glow of bayberries are an acquired taste.

Watering and Soil Preparation

The defining challenge for owners of vacation homes is watering, so select drought-resistant plants. To retain water add imported topsoil, compost, or sphagnum peat moss to your planting areas by digging the humus in to a depth of 12 to 18 inches for perennials or by building raised beds. The underlying sands will ensure good drainage. For planting trees and shrubs, add one-third mix of organic material to two-thirds original soil when refilling the planting hole. Polymers such as Water Grabber added to planting beds and especially pots will absorb water for plant roots to draw on later, decreasing watering needs.

Mulching is another way to help your planting beds retain moisture, with the bonus of reducing weeds. In windy sites choose heavy mulches such as pine bark over lightweights such as cocoa hulls.

An irrigation system on a timer is another option. The main drawback is that such systems can malfunction, and a timer stuck in the "on" position with no one to check it can drain your well or leave you with astronomical water bills before your next visit. This is less apt to happen with a top-notch professionally installed system than with an inexpensive do-it-yourself kit, but be prepared to pay $7500 an acre for one of these. If you choose such a system, consider one with spray heads set on 4- or 5-foot risers that can wash off salt deposited on vegetation while it waters.

It is, however, often cheaper and easier to hire someone to come in and water a new garden and wash salt off greenery when you're not around than it is to deal with electronic irrigation systems in absentia. Don't overlook the possibility of working out a quid pro quo with a neighbor who can water for you during spells of heat and drought.

Most plants that are going to be tough enough to survive over time will need regular watering only their first couple of years until they've established their root systems, anyway. Group your plantings according to their watering needs, with the thirstier plants in one spot if possible, near a spigot.

Maintenance

Spring is the big cleanup time for vacation gardens. You can hire a crew to do this, but it's better to make a special trip yourself so you can check winter damage. Depending on the location, March, April, and May are the months to remove debris, temporary wind buffers, and broken limbs. This is the time to cut down last year's perennial foliage, which has acted as a mulch over the winter. Be sure to renew soil and mulch that has been blown away.

This is also the time, when the buds are swelling, to prune shrubs that benefit from stooling (cutting back all stems to 6 inches from the trunk). Coastal favorites such as chaste tree *(Vitex agnus-castus)*, *Tamarix ramosissima*, Russian sage *(Perovskia* spp.), shrub bush clover *(Lespedeza thunbergii)*, *Indigofera decora*, *Hypericum claycinum*, *Hydrangea paniculata* and *H. arborescens*, caryopteris, callicarpa, *Buddleia davidii*, weigela, purple-leaf plum *(Prunus × cisterna)*, *Eucalyptus gunnii*, and purple smokebush *(Cotinus* spp.) will put on a better summer show of foliage, fruit, or flowers with this harsh early-spring pruning. It also will correct the sloppiness that results from heavy winter dieback where these shrubs are of borderline hardiness.

If you have a vegetable or cutting garden that's been mulched with seaweed, rototill or dig the seaweed in now. Give garden plots a good preemptive weeding. Order hanging baskets and planters of annuals now from local greenhouses that you can pick up when you return in the summer.

Consult with any help you're going to hire for the season, and work out a maintenance schedule.

The summer's primary chores are weeding, watering, harvesting, and deadheading to prolong bloom. Fertilizing should be done in smaller amounts than are generally recommended. It's especially important in sandy soil to grow the roots rather than the tops, so use low-nitrogen fertilizers. Do not fertilize after August 1, so plants won't start new growth as the off-season approaches and suffer winterkill. The exceptions are annual flowers and vegetables, which require ongoing fertilizing at 10-day intervals if you are doing foliar feeding.

Gardens can also be cleaned up in late fall, but most vacationers leave before perennial foliage has ripened enough to be cut away, so you are better off not getting too tidy when you depart. When you're finished with the vegetable garden, give it a good weeding and throw down a load of seaweed to rot on top until next spring's rototilling. Divide summer-blooming perennials just before Labor Day if you leave then so that they will have a full year to recover. Give everything lots of extra water for a week before you leave. Don't forget to take houseplants home with you.

Many gardeners start out rejecting the idea of hiring help for their vacation homes but change their minds with experience. Most vacation colonies have generated local business to fill this need. When you plug into the gardening community, you will hear through word of mouth who does good work. While the lawn-care and tree-pruning business has long been a male domain, many young women have recently started their own home businesses specializing in skilled garden maintenance, such as weeding and planting successions of annuals when you're not there to do it yourself. It's becoming increasingly common on large properties to hire one crew for general landscape maintenance and a different one for help with flower beds.

Shrubs and Trees

Shrubs are the bulwark of the vacation beach garden. But only a few varieties can both survive salt spray at the water's edge and provide the bonus of summer blooms. *Rosa rugosa* and tamarisk will thrive in the North. In Zones 8 to 10 include the graceful crimson-purple *Fuchsia magellanica* of Argentina, the white daisy bush (*Olearia* spp.), and hebes, a large family of showy evergreens from New Zealand.

Hedging or architectural barriers such as your house should provide some protection from wind and salt spray for other summer-blooming shrubs that like seaside conditions.

Among these the rose is the queen, but hydrangeas probably deserve knighthood.

Some of the toughest performers in the flower garden are shrublets, such as potentilla, hypericum, cinquefoil, caryopteris, and perovskia, which look like perennials but have the deep, anchoring roots of shrubs. Chaste tree and butterfly bush are full-size shrubs in warm coastal areas but often die back like perennials in Zone 6. Most of these should be cut back each spring as mentioned earlier.

Perennials

Start small when planning a perennial garden, for these plants need more water and care than shrubs do. A seaside setting quickly reduces the most intricately planned border to a test of survival of the fittest. Accept your losses gracefully, and plant more of the winners.

The fittest, such as thistles and legumes, often have deep roots to search for water and to anchor the plants. (Unfortunately, these roots can make the plants difficult or impossible to transplant or divide.) Other survivors frequently have silver leaves, such as artemisias, or fleshy leaves, such as sedums, or fleshy roots, such as daylilies, as protection from drought. Most prefer full sun, good drainage, and soil that is neither rich nor moist. Such game plants often bloom much longer than the tender spring flowers of the inland woods.

Bloomers for July and August for maritime gardens include yarrow (achillea), crocosmia, erigeron, geranium, gypsophila, obedient plant (physostegia), tritonia, stokesia, scabious, asters, kniphofia, campanula, *Malva moschata*, lavender *(Lavandula angustifolia)*, feverfew *(Chrysanthemum parthenium)*, fountain grass (pennisetum), polygonum, calluna, *Euphorbia corollata*, salvia, yucca, veronica, agapanthus, perennial sweet pea *(Lathyrus latifolius)*, sea lavender *(Limonium latifolium)*, and penstemon.

The possible combinations are endless. For a July garden of blue-grays and pinks that complement a seaside setting, try purple coneflower (echinacea) and lamb's ears (stachys) with sea holly (eryngium), *Tritonia rosea*, globe thistle (echinops), and *Lavatera olbia*.

Aster X frikartii with *Sedum* 'Autumn Joy', *Calamintha nepetoides*, miscanthus, buddleias, hydrangeas, and, south of Zone 6, powder blue ceanothus would be another soft combination, but later in the summer and longer lasting.

Rudbeckias, coreopsis, and gaillardia would create a long-blooming field of golden daisies under the summer sun.

Corner garden: Try gaillardia & yarrow

summer-blooming heathers

Avoid rigid taller perennials except in wind-sheltered locations. For instance, choose dwarf delphinium 'Blue Elf' over towering 'Pacific Hybrids'.

There are many low-growing summer perennials that can help substitute for part of a lawn. Snow-in-summer, dwarf speedwell, woolly yarrow, and woolly thyme will tolerate some foot traffic. For non-walking areas, consider cinquefoil, lamium, geraniums, summer-blooming heaths and heathers, daylilies, and potentilla for cold climates. Farther south also consider lavender, lilyturf, lantana, and verbena.

Annuals

Annuals are fast-growing and shallow-rooted, so they require more water, richer soil, more fertilizing, and more deadheading than other types of plants. When their needs are met, they provide many weeks of color since they don't have to pace themselves to ensure long-term survival. They are the colorful jewelry of the garden, easily added, easily discarded, so experiment with these bagatelles.

If planted in beds of rich soil and mulched, the more drought-resistant annuals such as portulaca, sweet alyssum, and nasturtiums will survive on weekend watering. If you do not visit your vacation home at least once a week during the summer, forget about annuals unless you have gardening help.

If you spend a couple of continuous months at your vacation home, consider growing pots of annuals in strategic locations such as on a deck. Pots don't require as much weeding or worrying about soil fertility or pests, but they do need daily watering in hot weather because moisture evaporates on all sides. You can water less frequently if you mix polymers in your potting soil, keep the pots out of the sun and wind, or use large pots — the bigger the pot, the longer it retains moisture.

For a casual country look, assemble clusters of pots in mixed sizes. For a more formal look, flank entrances with matched pairs. Ornate old terra-cotta pots have become collectibles, and it's fun to keep an eye out for them at flea markets. New ones can be instantly "aged" by spraying them with buttermilk, which will blacken the pots and encourage moss to grow on them.

If you get to your beach house late in the season, you can have a commercial greenhouse plant and water your pots until you can pick them up. At the end of the season, just dump the plants and soil in your compost pile.

Gardens
by the Sea

It takes a dramatic planting like this one to hold its own against the backdrop of the Pacific Ocean. This garden is at Monarch Beach, California.

Roses on a white picket fence are a typical and lovely sight on the islands off the coast of Massachusetts.

*A seashore garden at San Luis Obispo, California. The
shrubby sea lavender below the steps is* Limonium perezii.
The western tea myrtle in front of the umbrella is Melaleuca
nesophylla.

A riotous mass of old-fashioned, easy-care perennials, including hollyhocks and gloriosa daisies, makes a wonderful welcome at a vacation house.

Lush green lawns and perennial borders flourish along the many coves and inlets dotting the Atlantic shores.

Rosa rugosa, *a stowaway on a Japanese ship, has naturalized all up and down the northern Atlantic coast. It can tolerate cold, wind, drought, sandy soil, and salt spray — and has a heavenly fragrance as well.*

A profusion of Santolina chamaecyparissus *and* Erigeron Karvinskianus *grows in this Shell Beach, Cálifornia, garden.*

Roses, astilbes, campanulas, violas, and coralbells are all perennials that thrive near the ocean.

*With a hedge to define it and to shelter it from the elements,
a formal garden looks perfectly at home near the sea.*

*Deciduous
Trees*

Acer campestre   *Hedge maple*
Height: to 40 ft.
Good shade tree,
hedge, or screen
Zone 4

Full sun
Average soil
p. 239

Acer platanoides

Norway maple
Height: 50–60 ft.
Good for fall color
Yellow-green
flowers in spring
Zone 3

Full sun
Tolerates salt spray
p. 239

Acer rubrum

Red maple
Height: 40–60 ft.
Excellent fall color
Red flowers in
spring
Zone 3

Full sun
Good for damp
sites
p. 239

Betula nigra

River birch
Height: 40–70 ft.
Colorful peeling
bark
Yellow fall foliage
Zone 4

Full or part sun
Rich, moist soil
p. 252

Cercis canadensis

Eastern redbud
Height: 20–35 ft.
Blooms in early
spring
Zone 5

Full or part sun
Well-drained soil
p. 260

Diospyros
virginiana

Persimmon
Height: 30–40 ft.
Fruits ripen in late
fall
Colorful fall foliage
Zone 5

Full sun
Moist, sandy soil
p. 273

Fraxinus pennsylvanica

Green ash
Height: 50 ft.
Fast-growing
Good shade tree
Zone 2

Full or part sun
Almost any soil
p. 288

Gleditsia triacanthos

Honey locust
Height: 40–60 ft.
Lacy, fernlike foliage
Casts a light shade
Zone 4

Full or part sun
Average soil
p. 293

Koelreuteria paniculata

Golden-rain tree
Height: 30–35 ft.
Flowers
midsummer
Puffy pods in fall
Zone 5

Full sun
Well-drained soil
p. 305

Liquidambar styraciflua

Sweet gum
Height: to 60 ft.
Easy to grow
Excellent fall color
Zone 6

Full sun
Average soil
p. 311

Nyssa sylvatica

*Sour gum
Height: 30–60 ft.
Excellent fall color
Tolerates salt spray
Zone 3*

*Full or part sun
Tolerates damp soil
p. 320*

**Platanus
occidentalis**

*American sycamore
Height: to 100 ft.
Colorful flaking
bark
A large, majestic
tree
Zone 5*

*Full sun
Tolerates damp soil
p. 337*

Populus alba
White poplar
Height: 50–60 ft.
Shimmering foliage
Handsome pale
bark
Zone 3

Full sun
Tolerates poor soil
p. 339

Prunus serotina
Black cherry
Height: 60–75 ft.
Birds love the
small, tart cherries
Zone 3

Full or part sun
Average soil and
watering
p. 341

Quercus coccinea

Scarlet oak
Height: 50 ft.
Reliable fall color
Good tree for
lawns
Zone 5

Full sun
Light, sandy soil
p. 344

Quercus stellata Post oak Full sun
Height: 30–50 ft. Tolerates poor soil
Grows slowly p. 344
Often gnarled and
picturesque
Zone 6

Robinia pseudoacacia

Black locust
Height: 40–50 ft.
Very fragrant white
flowers in late
spring
Zone 4

Full sun
Grows in most
soils
p. 347

***Salix alba* 'Tristis'**

Weeping willow
Height: to 50 ft.
Grows quickly
A graceful
specimen
Zone 2

Full sun
Tolerates moist soil
p. 352

Sophora japonica

*Pagoda tree
Height: 50–60 ft.
Beanlike pods in
fall
Creamy white
flowers in
midsummer
Zone 5*

*Full sun
Average soil
p. 359*

Syringa reticulata

*Japanese tree lilac
Height: to 30 ft.
Fragrant white
flowers in summer
Zone 3*

*Full sun
Average soil and
watering
p. 363*

Evergreen
Trees

Agonis flexuosa

*Peppermint tree
Height: 30–35 ft.
Weeping branches
Peppermint-scented
foliage
Zone 10*

*Full sun
Drought-tolerant
p. 241*

Albizia distachya

*Plume albizia
Height: 20–25 ft.
Fast-growing
Blooms in late
spring
Zone 9*

*Full sun
Can grow in sand
p. 241*

Araucaria heterophylla

Norfolk Island pine
Height: to 100 ft.
Distinctive profile
Soft, curved needles
Zone 9

Full sun or part shade
Well-drained soil
p. 245

Arbutus menziesii

Pacific madrone
Height: 50–80 ft.
Colorful flaking bark
Showy flowers and fruits
Zone 8

Full or part sun
Needs dry summers
p. 246

Arbutus unedo   *Strawberry tree*   *Full or part sun*
                       Height: 20–30 ft.   *Well-drained soil*
                       Colorful, long-   *Needs dry summers*
                       lasting fruits   *p. 246*
                       Zone 8

Callistemon
viminalis

Weeping
bottlebrush
Height: to 30 ft.
Long bloom season
Slender, drooping
twigs
Zone 9

Full sun
Average or dry soil
p. 255

Ceratonia siliqua

Carob
Height: 30–40 ft.
As wide as it is tall
Casts a dense shade
Zone 9

Full sun
Can grow in sand
p. 259

Chamaecyparis lawsoniana

Lawson cypress
Height: to 60 ft.
Dozens of cultivars
A versatile evergreen
Zone 6

Full or part sun
Fertile, moist soil
p. 261

Cupaniopsis anacardiodes

Carrotwood
Height: 25–40 ft.
Abundant golden fruits
Easy to grow
Zone 9

Full sun
Almost any soil
p. 269

Cupressus sempervirens 'Stricta'

Columnar Italian cypress
Height: 30–40 ft.
Very distinctive narrow shape
Zone 8

Full sun
Well-drained soil
Drought-tolerant
p. 269

***Eucalyptus
ficifolia***

*Red-flowering gum
Height: 30–40 ft.
Blooms all summer
Red, orange, pink,
or white flowers
Zone 9*

*Full sun
Well-drained soil
p. 281*

***Eucalyptus globulus* 'Compacta'**	*Dwarf blue gum Height: 30–40 ft. Blooms winter and spring Aromatic foliage Zone 9*	*Full sun Well-drained soil p. 282*

Ficus microcarpa
var. *nitida*

*Indian laurel fig
Height: 25–30 ft.
Neat and shapely
Tolerates shearing
Zone 9*

*Part shade
Needs regular
watering
p. 287*

Ilex aquifolium

*English holly
Height: to 30 ft.
Red berries in
winter
Glossy, spiny leaves
Zone 6*

*Full or part sun
Average soil and
watering
p. 300*

Ilex opaca

American holly
Height: 20–30 ft.
Red berries in
winter
Leathery, spiny
foliage
Zone 5

Part sun
Tolerates damp soil
p. 301

Juniperus virginiana

Eastern red cedar
Height: to 30 ft.
Fast-growing
Good for screening
Zone 2

Full sun
Well-drained soil
p. 304

Laurus nobilis

Sweet bay, bay laurel
Height: 10–40 ft.
Dense, dark foliage
Leaves are fragrant
Zone 8

Full sun or part shade
Average soil and watering
p. 307

Ligustrum lucidum

Glossy privet
Height: 30 ft. or more
Fragrant white flowers in early summer
Zone 8

Full or part sun
Well-drained soil
p. 310

Lyonothamnus floribundus ssp. asplenifolius

Fernleaf Catalina ironwood
Height: 30–50 ft.
Attractive foliage
White flowers in late spring
Zone 9

Full sun
Well-drained soil
p. 314

Magnolia grandiflora

Southern magnolia
Height: 30–60 ft.
Large, glossy leaves
Fragrant flowers
Zone 7

Full or part sun
Well-drained, moist, organic soil
p. 314

Melaleuca quinquenervia

Cajeput tree
Height: 30–35 ft.
Multiple trunks
have attractive
bark
Blooms June to fall
Zone 9

Full sun
Fertile, well-
drained soil
p. 316

Olea europaea

Olive
Height: 25–30 ft.
Silvery foliage
Fast-growing
Zone 8

Full sun
Tolerates dry soil
p. 321

Picea glauca

White spruce
Height: 60-70 ft.
Forms a dense cone
Short, prickly
needles
Zone 3

Full sun
Well-drained soil
Regular watering
p. 332

Pinus canariensis

Canary Island pine
Height: 60–75 ft.
Slender and
graceful
Very long needles
Zone 9

Full sun
Well-drained soil
p. 333

**Pinus densiflorus
'Umbraculifera'**

*Japanese umbrella
pine
Height: 10–25 ft.
Broad, dense crown
Attractive bark and
plenty of cones
Zone 5*

*Full sun
Average soil and
watering
p. 334*

Pinus halepensis   *Aleppo pine
Height: 50–60 ft.
Multiple trunks
Gray-green needles
Zone 8*

*Full sun
Very tolerant of sea
salt and drought
p. 334*

Pinus mugo

Mugo pine
Height: to 15 ft.,
often shorter
Very dense, dark
green foliage
Zone 3

Full sun
Average soil and
watering
p. 334

Pinus nigra

Austrian pine
Height: 40–60 ft.
Stout and sturdy
Stiff, dark green
needles
Zone 4

Full sun
Tolerates poor soil
and sea spray
p. 334

Pinus pinea　　*Swiss stone pine*　　*Full sun*
　　　　　　　　　Height: 70–80 ft.　*Well-drained soil*
　　　　　　　　　Grows slowly　　　*p. 334*
　　　　　　　　　Glossy needles
　　　　　　　　　Large, edible seeds
　　　　　　　　　Zone 8

Pinus sylvestris

Scotch pine
Height: to 70 ft.
Orange bark
*Short, twisted
needles*
Very picturesque
Zone 3

Full sun
Tolerates sandy soil
p. 335

Pinus taeda

Loblolly pine
Height: 80 ft.
Fast-growing
Long needles
Prickly cones
Zone 7

Full sun
Wet or dry soil
p. 335

Pinus thunbergiana

Japanese black pine
Height: 20–40 ft.
Becomes gnarled
and picturesque
with age
Stiff, dark needles
Zone 6

Full sun
Very tolerant of sea
wind, salt, and
sand
p. 335

Pittosporum undulatum

Victorian box
Height: 35–40 ft.
Very fragrant
flowers
Fast-growing
Zone 9

Full sun
Average soil and
watering
p. 336

Podocarpus macrophyllus

Yew pine
Height: to 30 ft.
Needlelike leaves
Also good for
hedges
Zone 8

Full sun or part
shade
Well-drained soil
Tolerates drought
p. 338

**Prunus
caroliniana**

Carolina cherry
laurel
Height: to 30 ft.
Very fragrant
flowers
Fast-growing
Zone 7

Full or part sun
Rich, moist soil
Can't take drought
p. 340

| **Prunus**
laurocerasus | Cherry laurel
Height: 10–25 ft.
Very fragrant
flowers
Glossy foliage
Zone 7 | Sun or shade
Tolerates dry,
infertile soil
p. 341 |

Quercus agrifolia   *Coast live oak*   *Full sun*
Height: to 75 ft.   *Well-drained soil*
Forms a broad,   *p. 343*
spreading canopy
Zone 9

Quercus ilex   *Holly oak*   *Full sun*
Height: to 50 ft.   *Very tolerant of*
New growth is very   *wind, dry soil, and*
showy in spring   *salt*
Excellent for   *p. 344*
screens
Zone 7

**Quercus
virginiana**

*Live oak
Height: 60 ft.
Forms a broad,
open canopy
Small, glossy leaves
Zone 7*

*Full sun
Neutral or acidic
soil
Regular watering
p. 344*

Sabal palmetto

*Cabbage palmetto
Height: 20–60 ft.
Large, fanlike
fronds
Erect, shaggy trunk
Zone 9*

*Sun or shade
Almost any soil
Tolerates salt
p. 351*

Schinus molle

California pepper
tree
Height: to 40 ft.
Thick, gnarled
trunk
Rose-pink berries
in fall and winter
Zone 9

Full sun
Average soil
Tolerates drought
p. 354

Sequoia
sempervirens

Coast redwood
Height: 70–80 ft.
Fast-growing
Strong, erect trunk
Needlelike foliage
Zone 8

Full sun or part
shade
Almost any soil
Regular watering
p. 357

Syagrus romanzoffianus

*Queen palm
Height: 30–60 ft.
Fast-growing
Long, featherlike
fronds
Zone 9*

*Full sun
Average soil
Regular watering
p. 361*

| **Thuja plicata** | Western red cedar
Height: 50–70 ft.
Fast-growing
Forms a narrow
cone
Fragrant foliage
Zone 5 | Full sun or part
shade
Average soil and
watering
p. 366 |

Trachycarpus fortunei

Windmill palm
Height: to 20 ft.
Slow but easy to grow
Fan-shaped fronds
Zone 8

Full or part sun
Well-drained soil
Regular watering
p. 367

Tristania conferta

Brisbane box
Height: 40–60 ft.
Flowers in summer
Colorful peeling bark
Zone 9

Full or part sun
Average or dry soil
p. 368

**Umbellularia
californica**

*California bay,
Oregon myrtle
Height: 60–75 ft.
Very aromatic
foliage
Zone 7*

*Full sun
Well-drained soil
p. 368*

**Washingtonia
robusta**

*Mexican fan palm
Height: 75–90 ft.
Large, fan-shaped
fronds
Forms a thick shag
on trunk
Zone 8*

*Full sun
Well-drained soil
p. 373*

Deciduous Shrubs

Amelanchier laevis

Serviceberry
Height: 15–25 ft.
Blooms in early spring
Colorful fall foliage
Zone 4

Full or part sun
Well-drained soil
p. 242

Aronia arbutifolia   *Red chokeberry*
Height: 6–10 ft.
Red berries last all fall and winter
Red fall foliage
Zone 4

Full or part sun
Almost any soil
p. 248

Aronia melanocarpa

Black chokeberry
Height: 4–5 ft.
Birds eat the fruits
Showy white
flowers in late
spring
Zone 4

Full or part sun
Almost any soil
p. 248

Baccharis halimifolia

Groundsel tree,
saltbush
Height: 6–10 ft.
Blooms in late fall
Easy to grow
Zone 6

Full sun
Almost any soil
Tolerates salt spray
p. 251

***Berberis
thunbergii***
'Crimson Pygmy'

*Japanese barberry
Height: 1–2 ft.
Compact and
round
Red-purple foliage
Zone 4*

*Full sun
Well-drained soil
p. 252*

Buddleia davidii

*Butterfly bush
Height: 5–10 ft.
Fragrant flowers
can be purple, lilac,
pink, or white
Zone 5*

*Full sun
Prefers hot, dry
summers
p. 254*

***Caryopteris ×
clandonensis***

*Bluebeard
Height: 2–3 ft.
Blooms in late
summer
Combines well
with perennials
Zone 6*

*Full sun
Well-drained soil
p. 257*

Clethra alnifolia

*Sweet pepperbush,
summer-sweet
Height: 6–9 ft.
Pale pink or white
flowers are very
fragrant
Zone 4*

*Full or part sun
Damp soil
Tolerates salt spray
p. 264*

**Cotinus coggygria
'Royal Purple'**

*Smoke tree
Height: 12–18 ft.
Very colorful
foliage
Blooms last all
summer and fall
Zone 4*

*Full or part sun
Tolerates poor soil
p. 267*

**Cotoneaster
divaricatus**

*Spreading
cotoneaster
Height: 5–6 ft.
Red berries in fall
Red fall foliage
Zone 5*

*Full sun or part
shade
Well-drained soil
p. 268*

Cotoneaster multiflorus

*Many-flowered cotoneaster
Height: to 10 ft.
Red berries in fall
Spreads 15 ft. wide
Zone 3*

*Full sun
Well-drained soil
p. 268*

Cytisus × praecox 'Hollandia'

*'Hollandia' broom
Height: 3–5 ft.
Blooms for several
weeks in spring
Not invasive
Zone 6*

*Full sun
Tolerates poor, dry
soil and drought
p. 271*

Elaeagnus umbellata

*Autumn olive
Height: to 12 ft.
Very fragrant
flowers
Reddish brown
berries in fall
Zone 4*

*Full sun
Tolerates poor, dry
soil and salt spray
p. 276*

Erythrina crista-galli

*Cockspur coral tree
Height: 6–15 ft.
Blooms spring to
fall
Grows quickly
Zone 8*

*Full sun
Fertile soil
Dies back in severe
winters
p. 280*

Euonymus alatus *Burning bush*   *Sun or shade*
                    Height: 8–10 ft.   *Well-drained soil*
                    Vibrant fall color   *p. 283*
                    Easy to grow
                    Zone 3

Forsythia ×   *Forsythia*   *Full sun*
intermedia   *Height: to 8 ft.*   *Average soil and*
                   Blooms in early   *watering*
                   spring   *p. 288*
                   Gets quite large
                   Zone 4

Hippophae rhamnoides

*Sea buckthorn
Height: 6–10 ft.
Orange berries in fall
Silvery foliage
Zone 3*

*Full sun
Very tolerant of sandy soil and salt
p. 298*

Hydrangea macrophylla

*Garden hydrangea
Height: 3–6 ft.
Pink, blue, or white flowers in summer
Large glossy leaves
Zone 6*

*Full or part sun
Rich, moist soil
p. 299*

**Myrica
pensylvanica**

*Bayberry
Height: 8–10 ft.
Fragrant waxy
berries
Glossy foliage
Zone 4*

*Full sun or part
shade
Tolerates sandy soil
and salt spray
p. 318*

**Potentilla
fruticosa
'Katherine Dykes'**

*'Katherine Dykes'
bush cinquefoil
Height: 2–3 ft.
Blooms all summer
Very easy to grow
Zone 2*

*Full sun
Average soil and
watering
p. 340*

Prunus maritima   *Beach plum*   *Full or part sun*
                      Height: under 6 ft. *Thrives in sandy*
                      Blooms in spring   *soil*
                      Tasty plums in   *p. 341*
                      summer
                      Zone 3

Punica granatum   *Dwarf*   *Full sun*
'Nana'   *pomegranate*   *Average soil with*
                      Height: under 3 ft. *occasional watering*
                      Delicate foliage   *p. 342*
                      Abundant flowers
                      and small fruits
                      Zone 8

Rhus copallina

Shining sumac
Height: to 12 ft.
Colorful, glossy,
compound leaves
Forms a thicket
Zone 4

Full or part sun
Well-drained soil
p. 346

Rosa 'Betty Prior'

'Betty Prior' rose
Height: 2–3 ft.
Blooms from
summer through
late fall
Spicy fragrance
Zone 4

Full sun
Well-drained soil
p. 348

**Rosa
'Chevy Chase'**

*'Chevy Chase' rose
Height: to 15 ft.
Blooms in
midsummer
Healthy foliage
Zone 6*

*Full sun
Well-drained soil
p. 348*

Rosa 'Duet'

*'Duet' rose
Height: 3–4 ft.
A hybrid tea rose
Blooms abundantly
Healthy foliage
Zone 5*

*Full sun
Well-drained soil
p. 348*

Rosa 'Fruhlingsgold'

'Fruhlingsgold'
('Spring Gold') rose
Height: to 5 ft.
Blooms in spring
Vigorous and
healthy
Zone 4

Full sun
Well-drained soil
p. 349

Rosa 'Petite Pink Scotch'

'Petite Pink Scotch'
rose
Height: under 3 ft.
Blooms in early
summer
Dainty, glossy
leaves

Zone 5
Full sun
Tolerates poor,
sandy soil
p. 349

Rosa rugosa   *Rugosa rose, salt-*   *Full sun*
              spray rose   *Very tolerant of*
              Height: 2–5 ft.   *sand, salt, and sea*
              Very fragrant   *breezes*
              flowers   *p. 349*
              Virtually carefree
              Zone 4

Rosa rugosa   *White rugosa rose*   *Full sun*
'Alba'   *Height: 2–5 ft.*   *Very tolerant of*
              Very fragrant   *sand, salt, and sea*
              flowers   *breezes*
              Large round hips   *p. 349*
              Attractive foliage
              Zone 4

Rosa virginiana

Virginia rose
Height: 3–6 ft.
Blooms in summer
Forms a thicket
Red canes in winter
Zone 4

Full sun
Well-drained soil
p. 349

Rosa wichuraiana

Memorial rose
Height: to 1 ft.
Spreads 10 ft. or
more and makes a
good ground cover
Zone 5

Full sun
Average garden soil
p. 349

Salix discolor

*Pussy willow
Height: to 20 ft.
Blooms in early
spring
Narrow, glossy
leaves
Zone 3*

*Full sun
Average or damp
soil
p. 352*

**Spiraea ×
bumalda
'Anthony Waterer'**

*'Anthony Waterer'
spirea
Height: 2–3 ft.
Blooms for weeks
in midsummer
Forms a low
mound
Zone 3*

*Full or part sun
Well-drained soil
p. 360*

Syringa vulgaris

Common lilac
Height: 5–15 ft.
Dozens of cultivars
have lilac, purple,
pink, or white
flowers
Zone 4

Full or part sun
Average soil and
watering
p. 363

Tamarix ramosissima

Tamarisk, salt
cedar
Height: 6–10 ft.
Blooms in
midsummer
Fast-growing,
tough, and
adaptable
Zone 4

Full sun
Very tolerant of
sandy soil and salt
p. 364

Vaccinium corymbosum

*Highbush blueberry
Height: 6 ft. or more
Makes a colorful and productive hedge
Very tasty berries
Zone 3*

*Full sun or part shade
Moist, fertile, acidic soil
p. 369*

Viburnum carlesii

*Korean spice viburnum
Height: 4–5 ft.
Very fragrant flowers
Blooms in midspring*

*Zone 5
Full or part sun
Average soil and watering
p. 370*

Viburnum prunifolium

Black haw
Height: to 15 ft.
Blooms in spring
Colorful fall foliage
Blue-black berries
Zone 4

Full or part sun
Average soil and
watering
p. 370

Vitex agnus-castus

Chaste tree
Height: 10–20 ft.
Blooms in hot
weather
Aromatic foliage
Zone 7

Full sun
Average or dry soil
p. 372

Evergreen and Semievergreen Shrubs

Abelia × grandiflora

Glossy abelia
Height: 6–10 ft.
Blooms all summer
Makes a good
hedge
Zone 6

Full or part sun
Average soil and
watering
p. 238

Acacia longifolia

Sydney golden
wattle
Height: 15–20 ft.
Blooms in late
winter
Good for a coastal
windbreak or
screen
Zone 8

Full sun or part
shade
Tolerates poor,
sandy soil and salt
spray
p. 238

Acacia verticillata

*Star acacia
Height: 12–15 ft.
Blooms in spring
Dark, needlelike
foliage
Zone 8*

*Full sun or part
shade
Tolerates poor,
sandy soil and salt
spray
p. 239*

Callistemon citrinus

*Lemon bottlebrush
Height: 10–15 ft.
Blooms year-round
Fast-growing
Zone 9*

*Full sun
Average or dry soil
p. 254*

**Carissa
macrocarpa**

*Natal plum
Height: 6–8 ft.
Flowers are
fragrant
A good barrier
hedge
Zone 9*

*Full sun
Average soil
p. 256*

**Ceanothus
gloriosus**

*Point Reyes
ceanothus
Height: to 18 in.
Spreads 10 ft. wide
Blooms in spring
Zone 8*

*Full sun
Well-drained soil
p. 258*

Ceanothus griseus var. horizontalis

Carmel creeper
Height: 2–3 ft.
A good ground cover
Blooms in spring
Glossy foliage
Zone 8

Full sun
Well-drained soil
p. 258

Chamaerops humilis

European fan palm
Height: 6–20 ft.
Slow-growing
Forms a clump
Zone 8

Sun or shade
Average soil and watering
p. 261

**Cistus ×
purpureus**

*Orchid rock rose
Height: to 4 ft.
Blooms in late
spring and summer
Good bank cover
Zone 7*

*Full sun or part
shade
Average soil
Drought-tolerant
p. 263*

Coprosma repens

*Mirror plant
Height: to 10 ft.
Very shiny foliage
Fast-growing hedge
Zone 9*

*Full sun
Well-drained soil
p. 266*

Cordyline australis

Giant dracaena, cabbage tree
Height: to 25 ft.
Resembles a palm
Fragrant flowers
Zone 8

Full sun or part shade
Deep, rich, moist soil
p. 266

Cotoneaster lacteus

Red clusterberry
Height: 6–8 ft.
Berries last all winter
Makes a good hedge
Zone 7

Full sun
Average or dry soil
p. 268

Cycas revoluta

Sago palm
Height: under 4 ft.
Very slow-growing
An unusual
specimen
Zone 8

Part shade
Well-drained soil
p. 270

Dodonaea viscosa
'Purpurea'

Hopbush
Height: 12–15 ft.
Showy pink fruits
last all summer
Tough and carefree
Zone 8

Full sun
Tolerates poor, dry
soil
p. 274

Elaeagnus × ebbingei 'Gilt Edge'

No common name
Height: to 10 ft.
Glossy foliage
Very fragrant flowers
Zone 6

Full sun
Tolerates poor, dry soil
p. 276

Escallonia rubra

Red escallonia
Height: 10–12 ft.
Blooms summer to fall
An excellent hedge
Zone 8

Full sun
Needs good drainage and regular watering
p. 281

**Euonymus
japonicus
'Aureomarginatus'**

*Variegated Japanese
euonymus
Height: to 10 ft.
Smooth, glossy
leaves
Very easy to grow
Zone 7*

*Full or part sun
Well-drained soil
p. 283*

Fatsia japonica

*Japanese fatsia
Height: 6–8 ft.
Fast-growing
Bold, tropical
foliage
Zone 8*

*Part sun or shade
Average or dry soil
p. 285*

Feijoa sellowiana
    Pineapple guava
    Height: to 10 ft.
    Bicolored foliage
    Unusual flowers
    Edible fruits
    Zone 8

    Full or part sun
    Tolerates dry soil
    p. 286

Garrya elliptica
    Coast silk tassel
    Height: 8–10 ft.
    Long catkins are
    very showy in late
    winter
    Dark, leathery
    leaves

    Zone 8
    Full sun or part
    shade
    Fertile, well-
    drained soil
    p. 290

Hakea suaveolens   *Sweet hakea*   *Full sun*
                        Height: 10–12 ft.   *Well-drained soil*
                        Resembles a pine   *p. 294*
                        Fragrant white
                        flowers in fall
                        Zone 9

Hebe speciosa   *Showy hebe*   *Full sun*
                        Height: 2–5 ft.   *Light sandy soil*
                        Blooms   *and regular*
                        midsummer to fall   *watering*
                        Low, spreading   *p. 295*
                        habit
                        Zone 7

**Ilex cornuta
'Burfordii'**

*Burford holly
Height: 15–20 ft.
Abundant berries
Makes a good
hedge
Almost spineless
Zone 7*

*Full sun
Well-drained soil
p. 300*

**Ilex glabra
'Compacta'**

*Dwarf inkberry
Height: 4–6 ft.
Black berries
Small, glossy leaves
Zone 5*

*Full sun or part
shade
Wet or dry soil
p. 301*

Ilex × meserveae
'Blue Prince'

'Blue Prince' holly
Height: 8–12 ft.
Very dark foliage
Unusually hardy
Zone 5

Sun in summer, but
shade in winter
Well-drained soil
p. 301

***Ilex* 'Nellie R.**
Stevens'

'Nellie R. Stevens'
holly
Height: 15–25 ft.
Fast-growing
Good specimen or
hedge
Zone 7

Full sun or part
shade
Well-drained soil
p. 301

Ilex vomitoria

Yaupon holly
Height: 15–20 ft.
Fast-growing
Very small leaves
Prolific berries
Zone 7

Full or part sun
Almost any soil
p. 302

Juniperus chinensis 'Hetzii'

Hetz juniper
Height: to 10 ft.
Wide-spreading limbs
Blue-green foliage
Zone 4

Full sun
Well-drained soil
p. 303

Juniperus chinensis 'Maney'

'Maney' juniper
Height: to 6 ft.
Bushy, upright form
Blue-green foliage
Zone 4

Full sun
Well-drained soil
p. 303

Lantana camara

Lantana
Height: 2–4 ft.
Many cultivars with red, orange, pink, yellow, white, or bicolored flowers
Zone 9

Full sun
Average or dry soil
p. 306

Leptospermum scoparium

New Zealand tea tree
Height: 6–10 ft.
Pink, white, or red flowers all spring and summer
Zone 9

Full sun
Well-drained soil
p. 308

Leucothoe axillaris

Coast leucothoe
Height: 2–4 ft.
Foliage turns rich red-purple in winter
Small white flowers
Zone 5

Part sun or shade
Moist, fertile soil
p. 309

Ligustrum japonicum

*Japanese ligustrum
Height: 10–15 ft.
Fragrant flowers in
early summer
Dark berries in
winter
Zone 8*

*Full or part sun
Well-drained soil
p. 309*

Lycianthes rantonnetii

*Blue potato bush
Height: 6–8 ft.
Can climb or
sprawl
Blooms spring to
fall
Grows rapidly
Zone 9*

*Full sun or part
shade
Average soil and
watering
p. 313*

**Mahonia
aquifolium**

Oregon grape
Height: 6–8 ft.
Forms a clump of
erect stems
Glossy, spiny leaves
Zone 6

Sun in summer, but
shade in winter
Well-drained soil
p. 315

**Melaleuca
nesophila**

Pink melaleuca
Height: to 20 ft.
Blooms in summer
Develops a gnarled,
windswept profile
Zone 9

Full sun
Well-drained or dry
soil
p. 316

Myrica californica

*Pacific wax myrtle
Height: 20–25 ft.
Fragrant foliage
Dark berries in fall
Zone 7*

*Full sun or part
shade
Tolerates dry, sandy
soil and salt spray
p. 318*

Nerium oleander *Oleander
Height: 6–12 ft.
Blooms all summer
Flowers come in
many colors
Zone 9 or 8*

*Full sun
Almost any soil
Tough and
adaptable
p. 319*

Osmanthus fragrans

Sweet olive
Height: to 30 ft.
Very fragrant flowers
Needs plenty of space
Zone 9

Full or part sun
Average soil and watering
p. 322

Phoenix canariensis

Canary Island date palm
Height: to 50 ft.
Fairly slow-growing
Thick, erect trunk
Zone 9

Full sun
Tolerates dry soil
p. 330

Phormium tenax 'Variegatum'

*Variegated New Zealand flax
Height: to 5 ft.
Forms a bold clump
Zone 8*

*Full or part sun
Average soil and watering
p. 330*

Phyllostachys aurea

*Golden bamboo
Height: 15–25 ft.
Makes a grove
Must be confined
Zone 6*

*Full or part sun
Average soil and watering
p. 332*

Phyllostachys nigra

Black bamboo
Height: 15–25 ft.
Stems turn black as
they mature
Must be confined
Zone 7

Full or part sun
Average soil and
watering
p. 332

Pittosporum crassifolium
'Compactum'

Dwarf karo
Height: 3–5 ft.
Good for
foundation
plantings
Thick, leathery
leaves
Zone 8

Full or part sun
Average soil and
watering
p. 336

Pittosporum tobira 'Variegata'

*Variegated mock orange
Height: to 6 ft.
Very fragrant flowers
Dense, bushy habit
Zone 8*

*Part sun
Average soil and watering
p. 336*

Plumbago auriculata

*Cape plumbago
Height: 6–8 ft.
Blue or white flowers
Blooms through summer and fall
Zone 9*

*Full sun
Tolerates dry soil once established
p. 337*

Pyracantha 'Mohave'

'Mohave' firethorn
Height: to 10 ft.
Narrow and
upright
Thorny stems
Berries all winter
Zone 7 or 6

Full or part sun
Well-drained soil
p. 343

Rhaphiolepis indica 'Jack Evans'

'Jack Evans' Indian
hawthorn
Height: 2–5 ft.
Blooms in late
spring
Good for low
hedges
Zone 8

Full sun
Average soil and
watering
p. 345

Rhus integrifolia

Lemonade berry
Height: 10–12 ft.
Blooms in late
winter
Good coastal
windbreak or screen
Zone 9

Full sun
Average or dry soil
p. 346

**Rosmarinus
officinalis**

Rosemary
Height: 1–4 ft.
Very aromatic
foliage
Cultivars can be
upright or spreading
Zone 8

Full sun
Well-drained soil
p. 350

Sabal minor

Dwarf palmetto
Height: 4–10 ft.
Short, stubby trunk
Large fanlike
fronds
Zone 8

Sun or shade
Any soil, wet or dry
p. 351

Taxus cuspidata   *Japanese yew*   *Sun or shade*
                       Height: depends on   *Well-drained soil*
                       cultivar   *p. 364*
                       Dense, dark foliage
                       Females bear fruits
                       Zone 5

Tecomaria capensis

Cape honeysuckle
Height: 8–10 ft.
Can climb or
sprawl
Blooms in late fall
Zone 9

Full sun or part
shade
Well-drained soil
Water in summer
p. 365

Viburnum tinus

Laurustinus
Height: 6–10 ft.
Blooms in late
winter
Bright blue berries
ripen in summer
Zone 7

Full or part sun
Average soil and
watering
p. 371

**Yucca
elephantipes**

Giant yucca
Height: 20–25 ft.
Multiple trunks
Very showy
specimen
Blooms in late
spring or summer

Zone 9
Full sun
Average soil and
watering
p. 375

Yucca filamentosa

Bear grass, Adam's
needle
Height: 5–6 ft.
Blooms in early
summer
Forms a patch
Zone 5

Full sun
Average soil and
watering
p. 375

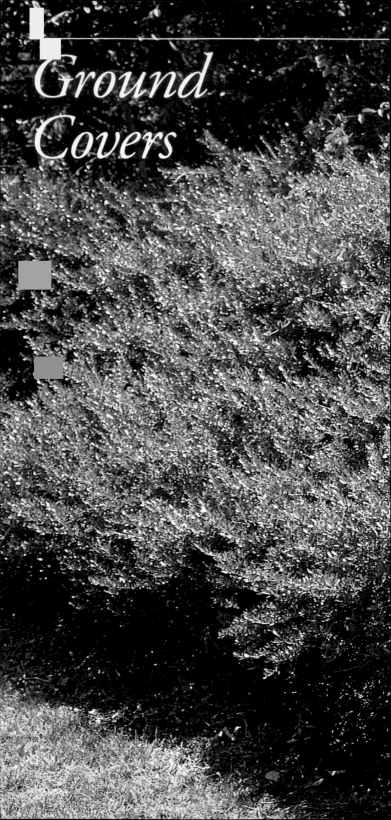

Ground Covers

Arctostaphylos uva-ursi

Bearberry, kinnikinick
Height: under 1 ft.
Spreads to 15 ft.
Small, shiny, evergreen leaves
Red berries in fall
Zone 3

Full or part sun
Well-drained soil
p. 246

Calluna vulgaris
'County Wicklow'

'County Wicklow' heather
Height: to 12 in.
Long bloom season
Evergreen foliage
Zone 4

Full sun
Sandy, acidic soil
p. 255

Carpobrotus edulis Ice plant
Height: under 18 in.
Thick, succulent
leaves and stems
Yellow-pink flowers
Zone 8

Full sun or part
shade
Good for sandy soil
p. 257

**Cerastium
tomentosum** Snow-in-summer
Height: to 6 in.
Woolly gray foliage
Blooms in summer
Spreads quickly
Zone 4

Full sun
Well-drained soil
p. 259

Coprosma × kirkii   *Creeping coprosma*   *Full sun*
Height: under 2 ft.   *Well-drained soil*
Trails down a bank   *p. 265*
Narrow, glossy
leaves
Zone 9

Drosanthemum   *Rosea ice plant*   *Full sun*
floribundum   *Height: to 6 in.*   *Well-drained soil*
Succulent foliage   *p. 274*
Blooms in late
spring
Trails down a bank
Zone 9

**Erica carnea
'Myretoun Ruby'**

*Winter heath
Height: 6–9 in.
Forms a dense mat
Blooms in late
winter and early
spring
Zone 4*

*Full or part sun
Well-drained,
acidic soil
p. 278*

**Erica ×
darleyensis**

*Hybrid heath
Height: to 2 ft.
Blooms fall to
spring
Lilac, pink, or
white flowers
Zone 4*

*Full or part sun
Average garden soil
with good drainage
p. 279*

***Euonymus fortunei* 'Emerald Surprise'**

'Emerald Surprise' euonymus
Height: 2–3 ft.
Small, leathery leaves
Forms an irregular, spreading mound

Zone 5
Sun or shade
Well-drained soil
p. 283

Juniperus conferta

Shore juniper
Height: 1–2 ft.
Spreads quickly
Soft-textured foliage
Zone 6

Full sun
Good for sandy soil
p. 303

Juniperus procumbens 'Nana'

*Dwarf Japanese garden juniper
Height: 1 ft.
Slow-growing
Good for small sites
Zone 5*

*Full sun
Well-drained soil
p. 304*

Lantana montevidensis

*Trailing lantana
Height: under 1 ft.
Evergreen foliage
Blooms all summer
Zone 8*

*Full sun
Well-drained soil
p. 306*

Liriope spicata

Creeping lilyturf
Height: 12–18 in.
Blooms in
midsummer
Evergreen, grassy
foliage
Zone 6

Part sun or shade
Well-drained soil
p. 312

**Myoporum
parvifolium**

Prostrate
myoporum
Height: 3–6 in.
Fills in very quickly
Evergreen foliage
Blooms in summer
and early fall

Zone 9
Full sun
Well-drained soil
Tolerates drought
p. 317

Opuntia humifusa

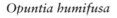

Prickly pear cactus
Height: under 1 ft.
Blooms in early
summer
Flat, spiny pads
Zone 4

Full sun
Tolerates poor, dry
soil and salt spray
p. 321

Osteospermum
fruticosum

Trailing African
daisy
Height: under 1 ft.
Blooms mostly in
winter
Evergreen foliage
Zone 9

Full sun
Well-drained soil
p. 323

Phlox subulata   Moss phlox   Full sun
                      Height: to 6 in.   Good for sandy
                      Blooms in spring   soil
                      Magenta, pink,   p. 329
                      lilac, or white
                      flowers
                      Zone 2

Phyla nodiflora   Lippia   Full sun to light
                      Height: to 6 in.   shade
                      Evergreen foliage   Good garden soil
                      Blooms spring to   with regular
                      fall   watering
                      Zone 9   p. 331

Satureja douglasii   Yerba buena
Height: 3–4 in.
Spreads quickly
Small, evergreen,
mint-scented leaves
Zone 8

Full sun or part
shade
Light, rich, moist
soil
p. 353

Sedum acre   Goldmoss sedum
Height: 4–6 in.
Spreads quickly
Bright green leaves
Blooms in late
spring
Zone 4

Full or part sun
Average soil
p. 355

Sollya
heterophylla

Australian bluebells
Height: 24–30 in.
Dense, evergreen
foliage
Blooms summer to
midfall
Zone 9

Full sun or part
shade
Well-drained soil
p. 359

Symphoricarpos
orbiculatus

Coralberry
Height: 2–3 ft.
Very easy to grow
Tremendous fruit
display in fall
Zone 3

Sun or shade
Well-drained soil
p. 362

**Verbena
tenuisecta**

*Moss verbena
Height: 3–6 in.
Blooms all summer
Thrives in hot
weather
Zone 9*

*Full sun
Well-drained soil
with occasional
watering*
p. 370

Vinca minor

*Periwinkle
Height: to 6 in.
Dense, evergreen
foliage
Blooms in spring
Zone 4*

*Sun or shade
Average soil and
watering*
p. 372

Vines

Ampelopsis brevipedunculata

Porcelain berry
Height: 20–25 ft.
Deciduous foliage
Blue berries in fall
Zone 5

Full sun or part shade
Average soil and watering
p. 244

***Bougainvillea* 'San Diego Red'**

'San Diego Red' bougainvillea
Height: to 20 ft.
Strong woody stems
Evergreen foliage
Long-lasting color
Zone 9

Full sun
Average or dry soil
p. 253

Campsis radicans

Trumpet vine
Height: to 30 ft.
Vigorous climber
Deciduous leaves
Blooms all summer
Zone 5

Sun or shade
Well-drained soil
p. 256

Clematis
maximowicziana

Sweet autumn
clematis
Height: to 30 ft.
Fragrant flowers in
late summer
Fast-growing
Zone 4

Full or part sun
Average soil and
watering
p. 264

**Distictis
buccinatoria**

Blood-red trumpet
vine
Height: to 30 ft.
Shiny evergreen
foliage
Blooms all summer
Zone 9

Full sun
Moist, fertile soil
p. 273

**Gelsemium
sempervirens**

Carolina jasmine
Height: to 20 ft.
Fragrant flowers in
early spring
Evergreen foliage
Zone 8

Full or part sun
Average soil and
watering
p. 292

Hardenbergia violacea

*Lilac vine
Height: 8–10 ft.
Blooms in early
spring
Evergreen foliage
Zone 9*

*Full sun
Well-drained soil
p. 294*

Hydrangea anomala ssp. **petiolaris**

*Climbing
hydrangea
Height: to 50 ft.
Flowers in summer
Large deciduous
leaves
Zone 5*

*Full or part sun
Rich, moist soil
p. 298*

***Lonicera ×
heckrottii***

*Gold-flame
honeysuckle
Height: 10–20 ft.
Fragrant flowers
Semievergreen
leaves
Not invasive
Zone 5*

*Full or part sun
Well-drained soil
p. 312*

*Lonicera
sempervirens*

*Trumpet
honeysuckle
Height: 10–15 ft.
Blooms in early
summer
Flowers are
scentless*

*Not invasive
Zone 4
Full or part sun
Well-drained soil
p. 312*

Parthenocissus quinquefolia

Virginia creeper
Height: to 25 ft.
Can climb or
sprawl
Scarlet fall foliage
Zone 2

Sun or shade
Almost any soil
with regular
watering
p. 325

Passiflora caerulea

Blue passionflower
Height: 20–30 ft.
Very fragrant
flowers
Evergreen foliage
Grows vigorously
Zone 8

Full or part sun
Average soil and
watering
p. 326

**Polygonum
aubertii**

*Silver fleece vine
Height: 25–35 ft.
Blooms in
midsummer
Very fast-growing
Zone 5*

*Full or part sun
Average or dry soil
p. 339*

Solandra maxima

*Cup-of-gold vine
Height: 12–15 ft.
Very large flowers
in fall and spring
A vigorous vine
Zone 9*

*Full or part sun
Rich, well-drained
soil
p. 358*

Trachelospermum jasminoides

Star jasmine, Confederate jasmine
Height: to 20 ft.
Very fragrant flowers
Evergreen foliage

Zone 8
Sun or shade
Average soil with water as needed
p. 367

Wisteria sinensis

Chinese wisteria
Height: to 30 ft.
Very fragrant flowers
A vigorous and substantial vine
Zone 5

Full sun or part shade
Average soil and watering
p. 374

Perennials

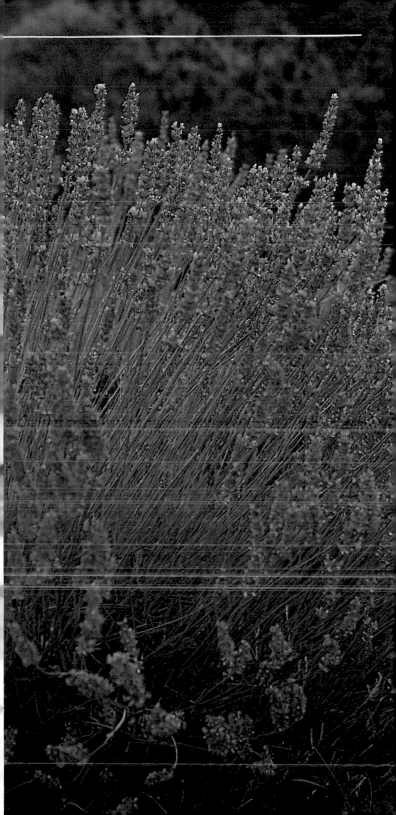

**Artemisia
ludoviciana
'Silver King'**

*'Silver King'
artemisia
Height: 2–3 ft.
Aromatic, silvery
foliage
Zone 3*

*Full sun
Tolerates poor, dry,
sandy soil and salt
p. 248*

**Artemisia
'Powis Castle'**

*'Powis Castle'
artemisia
Height: 3 ft.
Forms a loose,
bushy clump of
fragrant, silvery
foliage
Zone 6*

*Full sun
Tolerates poor, dry,
sandy soil
p. 249*

**Artemisia
stelleriana 'Silver
Brocade'**

*'Silver Brocade'
beach wormwood
Height: under 2 ft.
Makes a good
edging
Semievergreen
foliage
Zone 5*

*Full sun
Tolerates poor, dry,
sandy soil
p. 249*

Asclepias tuberosa

*Butterfly weed
Height: to 2 ft.
Blooms in summer
A good cut flower
Zone 3*

*Full sun
Good for sandy
soil
p. 249*

Asparagus densiflorus 'Sprengeri'

Sprenger asparagus
Height: to 2 ft.
Red berries in fall
Needlelike foliage
Forms a low mound
Zone 9

Full sun or part shade
Average soil and watering
p. 250

Baptisia australis

False indigo
Height: 3–4 ft.
Blooms in late spring
Attractive foliage
Zone 3

Full or part sun
Adapts to damp or dry soil
p. 251

Chrysanthemum maximum

Shasta daisy
Height: 1–3 ft.
Cultivars vary in
height and size
Blooms in early
summer
Zone 4

Full sun
Well-drained soil
Regular watering
p. 262

Chrysanthemum nipponicum

Nippon daisy,
Montauk daisy
Height: to 30 in.
Blooms in fall
Thick, smooth
leaves
Zone 5

Full sun
Well-drained soil
Regular watering
p. 263

Convolvulus sabatius

Ground morning glory
Height: to 18 in.
Blooms late spring to fall
Evergreen foliage
Zone 8

Full sun
Well-drained soil
p. 265

Delphinium × elatum hybrids

Hybrid delphiniums
Height: 3–6 ft.
Blue, purple, lavender, pink, or white flowers
Zone 3

Full sun
Fertile, moist soil
p. 271

Dianthus barbatus *Sweet William*   *Full sun*
Height: 1–2 ft.   *Well-drained soil*
Spicy-scented   *with regular*
flowers   *watering*
Excellent for cutting *p. 272*
Usually biennial
Zone 3

Echinops ritro   *Globe thistle*   *Full sun*
Height: 2–4 ft.   *Average or dry soil*
Spiny foliage   *p. 275*
Blooms in summer
Forms big clumps
Zone 3

Echium fastuosum

Pride of Madeira
Height: to 6 ft.
Grows very fast
Blooms late spring
to early summer
Zone 9

Full sun
Tolerates dry soil
p. 275

Erigeron glaucus

Beach aster
Height: 12–15 in.
Forms a low clump
Long bloom season
Fast-growing
Zone 3

Full sun or part
shade
Well-drained soil
p. 279

Eriogonum grande 'Rubescens'

*Red buckwheat
Height: to 1 ft.
Tends to sprawl
A good cut flower
Zone 8*

*Full sun or part
shade
Well-drained soil
p. 280*

Euphorbia myrsinites

*Myrtle euphorbia
Height: 8–12 in.
Trailing stems
Semievergreen
leaves
Blooms in early
spring
Zone 5*

*Full or part sun
Tolerates poor, dry
soil and salt spray
p. 284*

Euryops
pectinatus

Golden shrub daisy
Height: 4–6 ft.
Large and shrubby
Blooms year-round
Attractive foliage
Zone 9

Full sun
Well-drained soil
p. 284

Felicia amelloides

Blue marguerite
Height: 12–18 in.
Forms a low,
spreading mound
Long bloom season
Zone 9

Full sun
Good garden soil
and regular
watering
p. 286

Fuchsia
'Gartenmeister
Bonstedt'

*'Gartenmeister
Bonstedt' fuchsia
Height: to 3 ft.
Upright and bushy
Long bloom season
Zone 9*

*Full sun
Fertile, moist soil
with regular
watering
p. 289*

**Gaillardia ×
grandiflora
'Goblin'**

*Dwarf blanket
flower
Height: to 1 ft.
A good cut flower
Long bloom season
Zone 4*

*Full sun
Tolerates poor soil
and drought
p. 290*

Gaura
lindheimeri

White gaura
Height: 3–5 ft.
Graceful stems
Long bloom season
Zone 6

Sun or shade
Almost any soil
p. 291

Gazania hybrids

Treasure flower
Height: 12 in.
Large, colorful
flowers
Can be grown as
annuals
Zone 9

Full sun
Well-drained soil
p. 292

Gypsophila repens

*Creeping baby's breath
Height: to 6 in.
Blooms in early summer
Zone 4*

*Full sun
Well-drained soil
with plenty of lime
p. 293*

Helenium autumnale

*Helen's flower
Height: 4–5 ft.
Many cultivars,
with yellow,
orange, red, or
bronze flowers
Zone 3*

*Full sun
Tolerates damp soil
p. 295*

Hemerocallis
hybrid

Hybrid daylily
Height: 1–6 ft.
Easy to grow
Countless cultivars
Many flower colors
Zone 4

Full sun
Average soil and
watering
Most daylilies do
well by the sea
p. 296

Hemerocallis
'Stella d'Oro'

'Stella d'Oro'
daylily
Height: to 1 ft.
Flowers abundantly
over a long season
Zone 4

Full sun
Average soil and
watering
p. 296

Heuchera hybrids

*Coralbells
Height: 12–24 in.
White, pink, or red
flowers last for
weeks in early
summer
Evergreen foliage
Zone 4*

*Full sun or part
shade
Well-drained soil
Water during dry
spells
p. 297*

**_Hibiscus
moscheutos_**

*Rose mallow
Height: 4–6 ft.
Very large red,
pink, or white
flowers in late
summer
Zone 5*

*Full sun
Average or moist
soil
p. 297*

Iberis
sempervirens

Evergreen candytuft
Height: 6–12 in.
Forms a spreading
mat of evergreen
foliage
Blooms in spring
Zone 3

Full or part sun
Well-drained soil
p. 299

Kniphofia hybrids

Torch lilies
Height: to 6 ft.
Vivid yellow,
orange, gold, or red
flowers
Form large clumps
Zone 5

Full or part sun
Average or dry soil
p. 304

Kosteletzkya virginica

Seashore mallow
Height: 4–6 ft.
Forms an open,
bushy clump
Long bloom season
Zone 5

Full sun
Average or damp
soil
p. 305

Lavandula angustifolia

English lavender
Height: 1–3 ft.
Very fragrant
flowers
Grows as a shrub
in mild climates
Zone 5

Full sun
Well-drained soil
p. 307

Limonium perezii   Sea statice, sea lavender
Height: to 2 ft.
Showy flower clusters
Fast-growing
Zone 9

Full sun
Well-drained soil
p. 310

Nephrolepis cordifolia

Sword fern
Height: 30–36 in.
Evergreen foliage
Spreads quickly
Zone 9

Sun or shade
Average soil and watering
p. 319

Paeonia hybrids

*Herbaceous peonies
Height: to 3 ft.
Large red, rose,
pink, or white
flowers in late
spring;
Very long-lived
Zone 3*

*Full sun or part
shade
Well-drained, fertile
soil with regular
watering
p. 323*

Papaver orientale

*Oriental poppy
Height: to 3 ft.
Vivid flowers in
late spring
Goes dormant in
summer
Zone 2*

*Full sun
Average soil and
watering
p. 325*

Perovskia atriplicifolia

_Russian sage
Height: 3–5 ft.
Forms a large but
airy clump
Silver-gray foliage
Blooms in late
summer
Zone 5_

_Full sun
Well-drained soil
p. 327_

Phlomis fruticosa   _Jerusalem sage
Height: to 4 ft.
Rounded and
bushy
Blooms off and on
from spring to fall
Zone 7_

_Full sun
Average or dry soil
p. 329_

Phlox paniculata   Garden phlox
Height: 2–4 ft.
Blooms in late
summer, with
fragrant flowers in
many colors
Zone 4

Full sun or part
shade
Fertile, well-
drained soil and
regular watering
p. 329

Romneya coulteri   Matilija poppy
Height: to 8 ft.
Forms a large patch
Blooms late spring
to late midsummer
Zone 8

Full sun
Well-drained,
sandy soil
p. 347

Rudbeckia fulgida | *Black-eyed Susan* | *Full sun*
'Goldsturm' | *Height: 18–30 in.* | *Average soil and*
 | *Blooms* | *watering*
 | *midsummer to fall* | *p. 350*
 | *Easy to grow* |
 | *Zone 3* |

Santolina | *Lavender cotton* | *Full sun*
chamaecyparissus | *Height: to 2 ft.* | *Well-drained soil*
 | *Forms a low* | *p. 353*
 | *mound* |
 | *Aromatic foliage* |
 | *Small yellow* |
 | *flowers* |
 | *Zone 6* |

Santolina virens

*Green santolina
Height: to 2 ft.
Aromatic, rich
green foliage
Blooms in summer
Zone 6*

*Full sun
Well-drained soil
p. 353*

**Sedum
'Autumn Joy'**

*'Autumn Joy'
sedum
Height: 2–3 ft.
Blooms for weeks
in late summer and
fall
Forms a clump*

*Zone 3
Full or part sun
Average garden soil
p. 355*

Sempervivum tectorum

Hen-and-chickens
Height: 1–4 in.
Clumps multiply fast
Evergreen leaves
Zone 4

Full or part sun
Well-drained soil
p. 356

Senecio cineraria

Dusty miller
Height: under 2 ft.
Silvery foliage is semievergreen
Leaves deeply lobed
Zone 8

Full sun
Average soil and watering
p. 356

Solidago sempervirens

Seaside goldenrod
Height: 2–6 ft.
Forms a vase-
shaped clump of
stems
Blooms in fall
Zone 5

Full sun
Almost any soil
p. 358

Stachys byzantina

Lamb's ears
Height: 12–18 in.
Fuzzy gray leaves
Makes a good
edging
Upright flower
stalks
Zone 5

Full or part sun
Well-drained soil
Water during
droughts
p. 361

Grasses

Ammophila
breviligulata

Beach grass,
marram
Height: 3–4 ft.
Spreads by
rhizomes
Turns tan in winter
Zone 3

Full sun
Grows in pure sand
Used to stabilize
dunes
p. 243

Chasmanthium
latifolium

Northern sea oats
Height: 3–5 ft.
Flat seed heads
Forms upright
clumps
Zone 4

Sun or shade
Grows in most soils
p. 262

Cortaderia selloana

Pampas grass
Height: 8–10 ft.
Forms giant clumps
Plumelike seed
heads
Sharp-edged leaves
Zone 8

Full or part sun
Average soil
p. 267

Elymus arenarius

Blue lyme grass
Height: to 3 ft.
Spreads by
rhizomes
Unusual blue-green
color
Zone 4

Full sun
Well-drained soil
Stabilizes loose soil
p. 277

Eragrostis curvula *Weeping love grass*
Height: 3–4 ft.
Delicate, airy look
Blooms in late
summer
Zone 7

Full sun
Well-drained soil
Stabilizes loose soil
p. 277

***Erianthus
ravennae***

Ravenna grass
Height: 8–12 ft.
Forms upright
clumps
Blooms in fall
Zone 5

Full sun
Tolerates poor, dry
soil
p. 278

**Festuca ovina
var. *glauca***

*Blue fescue
Height: 6–12 in.
Semievergreen
foliage
Forms dome-
shaped clumps
Zone 4*

*Full sun
Tolerates dry,
sandy soil and salt
spray
p. 287*

**Miscanthus
sinensis
'Variegatum'**

*Variegated maiden
grass
Height: 5–8 ft.
Forms a large
clump
Graceful foliage
Zone 5*

*Full or part sun
Average garden soil
p. 316*

Panicum virgatum   *Switch grass*   *Full or part sun*
                         Height: 3–6 ft.   *Tolerates most soils*
                         Forms upright   *p. 324*
                         clumps
                         Blooms in summer
                         Zone 4

Pennisetum   *'Hameln' fountain*   *Full sun*
alopecuroides   *grass*   *Average soil and*
'Hameln'   *Height: to 2 ft.*   *watering*
                         Blooms for months   *p. 327*
                         Colorful fall foliage
                         Zone 5

***Pennisetum
setaceum*
'Burgundy Giant'**

*Crimson fountain
grass
Height: 2–3 ft.
Purple-bronze
foliage
Long bloom season
Zone 8*

*Full sun
Average soil and
watering
p. 327*

***Phalaris
arundinacea*
'Picta'**

*Ribbon grass
Height: 2–3 ft.
Bright striped
leaves
Very easy to grow
Zone 4*

*Full or part sun
Almost any soil
p. 328*

Encyclopedia
of Plants

Abelia

A-beel'ee-a
Caprifoliaceae. Honeysuckle family

Description

Evergreen or deciduous shrubs with fine-textured foliage and small bell-shaped flowers. About 30 species, native to Asia and Mexico.

How to Grow

Full or part sun. Ordinary soil and watering. Can be pruned anytime and will continue to bloom. Renew old plants by cutting some stems to the ground.

■ × *grandiflora* *p. 148*
Glossy abelia. A rounded semievergreen shrub, 6–10 ft. tall, with graceful arching branches. Opposite leaves are oval, 1 in. long, glossy dark green in summer, turning purplish or dropping in winter. Small white or pale pink flowers are borne continuously from early summer to fall. Makes a good hedge. *A.* 'Edward Goucher' stays under 5 ft. tall and has showier, rosy lavender flowers. Zone 6.

Acacia

A-kay'sha
Leguminosae. Pea family

Description

Evergreen trees or shrubs, often bearing exceptional displays of yellow flowers. Many have feathery compound leaves; some are thorny. About 1,200 species, most native to hot, dry regions, particularly Australia.

How to Grow

Full sun or part shade. Acacias can grow in poor, sandy soil. They need good drainage to prevent leaf yellowing and weak growth and are fairly drought-tolerant once established. Prune off old flowers in early summer to prevent mess. Nearly pest-free. Very tolerant of wind and salt spray. Propagate by seed.

■ *longifolia* *p. 148*
Sydney golden wattle. Rounded evergreen shrub or small tree, 15–20 ft. tall, with olive green foliage. Rich golden yellow flowers last from late winter into spring. Grows quickly and retains its lower branches, making a good screen or windbreak. Zone 8.

■ *verticillata* p. 149

Star acacia. Spreading evergreen shrub or small multitrunked tree, 12–15 ft. tall, with whorls of dark green, needlelike leaves. Light yellow flowers form 1-in. spikes in spring. Makes a good background, bank cover, or barrier hedge. Shear periodically to keep it dense. Zone 8.

Acer

Ay′sir. Maple
Aceraceae. Maple family

Description

Deciduous trees or shrubs with palmately lobed or compound leaves, often turning brilliant colors in fall. More than 110 species, native to the north temperate zone.

How to Grow

Full sun. These maples grow well in average garden soil but need regular rainfall or watering during the growing season. Their roots are too aggressive and shallow to allow underplanting with grass or ground covers. Use a 3-in. layer of chipped bark or other mulch to cover the soil. Prune to shape young trees and to remove storm-damaged limbs, but avoid pruning in late winter and spring when sap flow is profuse.

■ *campestre* p. 88

Hedge maple. A neat, shapely deciduous tree up to 40 ft. tall, with a dense crown that reaches to the ground. The small 5-lobed leaves are dark green in summer, yellow in fall. Tolerates heavy pruning and can be used for hedging, but also makes an excellent shade tree. There are variegated, weeping, and compact cultivars. Zone 4.

■ *platanoides* p. 88

Norway maple. A fast-growing deciduous tree, 50–60 ft. tall, that tolerates sea wind and salt spray better than most shade trees do. Rounded clusters of yellow-green flowers are conspicuous in spring. Large 5-lobed leaves are green in summer, turning yellow in late fall. 'Crimson King' has dark reddish purple leaves. Zone 3.

■ *rubrum* p. 89

Red maple. A deciduous tree, 40–60 ft. tall. Native to swampy sites throughout the eastern United States, but tolerates average soil. Showy clusters of small red flowers open in early spring; 3-lobed leaves turn brilliant red, orange, or

pink in fall. 'October Glory' and other cultivars have especially vivid and long-lasting fall foliage. Zone 3.

Achillea

A-kil-lee′a. Yarrow
Compositae. Daisy family

Description

Perennials with pungent gray or green leaves, often finely divided, and flat clusters of small flowers. About 80 species, native to the north temperate zone. Hybridization has produced
many excellent garden varieties.

How to Grow

Full or part sun. Tolerates poor soil and dryness; may flop
over in rich or moist soil. Divide in spring or early fall if a
clump gets too big or has been infiltrated by grass or weeds.
Plant at least 18 in. apart in flower beds. For ground cover,
plant 12 in. apart and mow occasionally to keep it low and
neat.

■ *millefolium* p. 202 *Pictured below*

Yarrow. A hardy perennial with pungent, gray-green, fernlike
foliage that looks fresh all year in mild climates. Small
flowers are crowded in flat clusters 2–6 in. wide atop stiff
stalks 2–3 ft. tall. Old-fashioned types have plain white or
dull crimson flowers in early summer. Modern cultivars and
hybrids such as 'Paprika' bloom from early summer to late
fall in shades of red, pink, orange, yellow, salmon, and cream.
These make excellent cut flowers. Other yarrows, such as *A.*
'Coronation Gold' and *A.* 'Moonshine', are also good seaside
plants. Zone 3.

Agonis

A-gon´iss
Myrtaceae. Myrtle family

Description
Evergreen trees or shrubs with alternate leaves and dense round heads of small flowers. Only 12 species, native to Australia.

How to Grow
Full sun. Tolerates a wide range of soils from sandy to heavy clay. Water deeply during establishment to discourage surface roots. Drought-tolerant once established. Stake and train when young to develop a straight trunk, especially in windy locations.

■ *flexuosa* p. 100
Peppermint tree. A small evergreen tree, 30–35 ft. tall, with weeping branches and narrow willowlike leaves that release a peppermint fragrance when crushed. It resembles a weeping willow. Small white flowers are abundant in late spring and early summer. Zone 10.

Albizia

Al-bizz´ee-a
Leguminosae. Pea family

Description
Trees or shrubs with pinnately compound leaves and flower clusters like tassels or pincushions. About 150 species, native to South America, Asia, Africa, and Australia.

How to Grow
Full sun. Thrives in pure sand. Grows fastest with abundant water, but survives on minimal watering once established. Naturally develops several strong-growing stems. Prune hard annually to rejuvenate. Propagate by seed.

■ *distachya* p. 100
Plume albizia. A fast-growing evergreen tree, 20–25 ft. tall, good for rapid screening or temporary use. Has a light, airy appearance with fine-textured compound leaves. Silky, greenish yellow flowers form 2-in. spikes in late spring. Recently renamed *A. lophantha*. Zone 9.

A more familiar tree, the silk tree or mimosa, *A. julibrissin*, is hardy to Zone 7 or 6 and has showy pink flowers all summer, but it is less tolerant of coastal conditions and suffers from salt spray.

Alcea
Al-see´a. Hollyhock
Malvaceae. Mallow family

Description
Biennials or perennials with rough or felty leaves and tall un-branched stems bearing large stalkless flowers. About 60 species, native to Eurasia.

How to Grow
Full sun. Ordinary soil and watering. Tall stalks may need staking. Start seeds indoors, sow them direct, or buy started plants in small pots. Once planted, hollyhocks often self-sow. Destroy leaves infected with rust or other fungal diseases.

■ *rosea* p. 202
Hollyhock. An old-fashioned favorite that makes a clump of several flower stalks 4–8 ft. tall. The large, rough, gray-green leaves are rounded or lobed. Flowers are single or double, 3–5 in. wide, in shades of white, yellow, apricot, pink, red, and near-black. Most hollyhocks are biennials, but some flower the first year and some live for 3 or more years. Zone 5.

Amelanchier
Am-e-lang´ki-er. Serviceberry, shadbush, Juneberry
Rosaceae. Rose family

Description
Deciduous shrubs or trees with white flowers in early spring, small edible fruits, and brilliant fall color. Only 6 species, native to North America.

How to Grow
Full or part sun. Well-drained acidic soil; tolerates dry soil and heat. Prune to a single trunk if desired; rarely needs other pruning. Susceptible to various insects and diseases but not badly damaged by them.

■ *laevis* p. 126 *Pictured opposite*
Serviceberry. A deciduous shrub or small tree, 15–25 ft. tall, that provides 3-season interest. Dangling clusters of white or

pinkish flowers are one of the first signs of new life in early spring. Clusters of berrylike, dark purple fruits make a tasty treat (for you or the birds) in June or July. The small leaves turn superb yellows, oranges, or reds in fall. *A. arborea* is similar; *A. × grandiflora* is a hybrid between the two. (Even professionals have trouble telling which is which.) Selected cultivars offer upright habit, abundant bloom and fruit, and/or outstanding fall color. Native throughout the eastern United States. Zone 4.

Ammophila
Am-mof´-i-la. Beach grass
Gramineae. Grass family

Description
Tough grasses that spread by underground stems. Only 2 species, native to the northern Atlantic coast and northern Africa.

How to Grow
Full sun. Needs well drained soil and tolerates drought. Can grow in pure sand and is often used for stabilizing dunes. Space nursery-grown plants 12–18 in. apart and apply small amounts of balanced fertilizer in spring and fall to encourage dense, vigorous growth.

■ *breviligulata* p. 230
Beach grass, marram. A spreading grass with slender leaves and flower stalks 3–4 ft. tall. New growth is bright green in spring and summer; old shoots persist but turn tan in winter. Grows wild along the East Coast. 'Cape' and 'Hatteras' are nursery-propagated cultivars selected for soil-conservation use. Zone 3.

Ampelopsis

Am-pel-op′sis
Vitaceae. Grape family

Description
Deciduous vines with compound leaves and small blue berries. Tendrils are branched but don't have suction-cup disks. Only 2 species, native to North America and Asia.

How to Grow
Full sun or shade (the more sun, the more berries). Ordinary soil and watering. Tolerates heat. Provide support and allow plenty of room; prune as needed to keep it in bounds. Japanese beetles will strip it bare, but it has few other problems.

■ *brevipedunculata* p. 192
Porcelain berry. A vigorous woody vine that climbs by tendrils, reaching 20–25 ft. tall. Large leaves are deciduous, with 3 coarsely toothed lobes, dark green in summer and red in fall. Small berries ripen to a bright turquoise color in fall. Good for decorating a stone or masonry wall or shading an arbor. Zone 5.

Amsonia

Am-sown′ee-a
Apocynaceae. Dogbane family

Description
Perennials forming clumps of upright stems containing milky sap, with slender shiny leaves and star-shaped flowers in spring. About 20 species, native to North America and Japan.

How to Grow

Full or part sun. Average soil. Tolerates constant moisture in fresh but not brackish wetlands. Increase by division in fall or early spring. Cut off the tops of the stems after bloom to encourage a flush of compact fresh growth.

■ *tabernaemontana* *p. 203 Pictured opposite*
Bluestar, willow herb. A carefree, long-lived perennial that forms a clump of stems 2–3 ft. tall. Clusters of starry, pale blue flowers top the stems for 3–4 weeks in early spring. The slender, smooth, pale green leaves turn yellow in fall. Dies back in winter. Native along the mid-Atlantic coast. Zone 3.

Araucaria

Ar-a-kay′ree-a
Araucariaceae. Araucaria family

Description

Evergreen conifers with stiff needlelike leaves and large rounded cones. About 18 species, native to the Southern Hemisphere.

How to Grow

Full sun or part shade. Tolerates a wide range of soils from sandy to clay but needs good drainage. Water regularly during dry spells. Stake and train when young for straight trunk development.

■ *heterophylla* *p. 101*
Norfolk Island pine. A pyramidal conifer, up to 100 ft. tall, with a distinctive silhouette. Looks striking on the skyline but grows too large for many home landscapes. Whorls of 5–7 branches are arranged in tiers. Both branches and twigs are covered on all sides with soft curved needles about $\frac{1}{2}$ in. long. Zone 9.

Arbutus

Ar-bew′tus
Ericaceae. Heath family

Description

Evergreen trees or shrubs with leathery leaves, conspicuous red bark, small pink or white flowers, and orange berries. About 14 species, native to western North America and Europe.

How to Grow
Full or part sun. These trees tolerate poor, dry soil and should
not be irrigated in summer; excess summer water leads to root
rot that can be fatal. They grow best along the Pacific coast.
Seedlings grow quickly but don't transplant well; sow seed in
place or buy container-grown specimens. Established plants
are pest-free and need no care, but they shed a lot of litter.

■ *menziesii*   p. 101
Pacific madrone. A beautiful broad-leaved evergreen tree,
50–80 ft. tall. Makes a picturesque specimen with an irregular oval crown. The bark is outstanding — tan twigs, maroon
branches, and peeling patches of buff and cinnamon on the
trunk. Drooping clusters of small creamy flowers cover the
tree for 3 weeks in May; fleshy orange-red fruits last from
early fall into winter. Native along the northern Pacific coast.
Zone 8.

■ *unedo*   p. 102
Strawberry tree. A small tree or large shrub, 20–30 ft. tall,
with a rounded crown, reddish twigs, and shiny, leathery,
evergreen leaves. Drooping clusters of small white to pinkish
flowers appear in October, blooming alongside the pebbly-
textured, bright red, strawberry-sized fruits. Zone 8.

Arctostaphylos
Ark-toe-staff´i-los
Ericaceae. Heath family

Description
Evergreen shrubs with crooked stems, small leathery leaves,
waxy bell-shaped flowers, and fruits like tiny apples. About
50 species, most native to western North America, and several hybrids and cultivars.

How to Grow
Full or part sun. Needs well-drained soil. Buy container-
grown plants, and set the top of the root ball slightly above
grade. Space 2 ft. apart for ground cover and use mulch to
control weeds until it fills in. Needs rain or irrigation until
it's established; can tolerate drought later. Branches root
where they touch the ground.

■ *uva-ursi*   p. 178   *Pictured opposite*
Bearberry, kinnikinick. A low evergreen shrub that stays
under 1 ft. tall but can spread to 15 ft. or more. An excellent

ground cover for gardens along the northern Pacific and Atlantic coasts, where it grows wild. Hardy to cold but can't take extreme heat and humidity. The small leathery leaves are glossy green in summer, bronzy reddish purple in winter. Small white or pale pink flowers in spring; shiny red fruits like tiny apples in fall. 'Point Reyes', 'Vancouver Jade', and 'Massachusetts' are especially attractive and healthy cultivars. Zone 3.

Armeria

Ar-meer´ee-a. Thrift
Plumbaginaceae. Plumbago family

Description
Low-growing perennials with small evergreen leaves and dense flower heads on stiff stalks. About 80 species, native to the Northern Hemisphere.

How to Grow
Full sun. Needs well-drained soil and grows well in sand. Prefers cool summers. In hot, humid weather or in rich, moist soil, the foliage is subject to rot. Easily propagated by seed or division.

■ *maritima p. 203*
Thrift, sea pink. A low-growing perennial that makes a grassy mat of evergreen foliage, good as a low edging for walkways or flower beds. Bears 1-in. heads of white, pink, or magenta flowers on stalks 6–10 in. tall. Blooms most heavily in spring, but may continue off and on through fall. Cultivars and hybrids have especially large flower heads. Zone 4.

Aronia

A-rone´ee-a. Chokeberry
Rosaceae. Rose family

Description
Deciduous shrubs that form a thicket of stems with blossoms
like pears, bright red fall foliage, and red or black berries.
Only 2 species, both native to the eastern United States.

How to Grow
Full or part sun. These adaptable, easy-to-grow shrubs tolerate poor soil, wet or dry, and spread slowly by suckers. Space
4–6 ft. apart for casual hedges or mass plantings that provide
food and shelter for songbirds.

■ *arbutifolia* *p. 126*
Red chokeberry. A deciduous shrub, 6–10 ft. tall, with many
upright stems and narrow leaves that turn bright red in fall.
Covered with clusters of small white flowers in late spring.
Small red berries ripen in fall and last all winter. Zone 4.

■ *melanocarpa* *p. 127*
Black chokeberry. A deciduous shrub, 4–5 ft. tall, more
rounded and less erect than red chokeberry. Glossy oval
leaves are dark green. White flowers are showy in late spring.
Birds eat the shiny, purple-black berries as soon as they ripen
in late summer. Zone 4.

Artemisia

Ar-te-miss´ee-a
Compositae. Daisy family

Description
Evergreen or deciduous shrubs or perennials. Most have aromatic foliage, often silver or gray. Flowers are small, rarely
conspicuous. About 300 species, native to dry regions in the
Old and New World.

How to Grow
Full sun. Most artemisias thrive in infertile sandy soil and tolerate drought and salt spray, but they can't tolerate wet soil
or humid climates. Cut back old stalks in late winter to encourage bushy new growth.

■ *ludoviciana* 'Silver King' *p. 204*
'Silver King' artemisia. A fast-growing perennial that spreads
to form a patch of slender stems 2–3 ft. tall. Both the stems

and the foliage are silvery gray and pleasantly aromatic. May get floppy in late summer, when sprays of tiny flowers top each stem. Let it naturalize along a roadside or in a meadow garden. If combined with other perennials, it should be confined in a pot or bottomless bucket or it will run all over the bed. 'Silver Queen' has prettier (more deeply cut) leaves but weaker stems than 'Silver King' and usually needs support. Sometimes listed as *A. albula*. Native to the Great Plains states. Zone 3.

■ **'Powis Castle'** *p. 204*
'Powis Castle' artemisia. A bushy perennial that makes a loose mound of fine-textured silvery foliage. Grows about 3 ft. tall and 4 ft. wide. Small flowers are inconspicuous. Use as a specimen in flower beds or foundation plantings or as a low hedge. Not invasive. Zone 6.

■ *stelleriana* *p. 205*
Beach wormwood. A low-growing perennial, under 2 ft. tall, with silvery, woolly foliage that resembles dusty miller (*Senecio cineraria,* p. 226). Dense clusters of small yellow flowers last from mid- to late summer. The silvery foliage makes a beautiful accent or edging. 'Silver Brocade' has nearly white leaves. Spreads slowly but is not invasive. Native along the New England coast. Zone 5.

Asclepias
As-klee´pee-us. Milkweed
Asclepiadaceae. Milkweed family

Description
Perennials with upright stems, milky sap, simple leaves, clusters of waxy flowers, decorative pods, and silky-plumed seeds. About 120 species, most native to North America.

How to Grow
Full sun. Tolerates dry, sandy soil. Buy container-grown plants in spring or sow fresh seeds in fall for bloom in 2–3 years. Choose a site and leave it there; old plants have large brittle roots, which makes transplanting difficult. Subject to aphids and powdery mildew, which disfigure the foliage and may weaken the plant for a season but do no permanent damage.

■ *tuberosa* *p. 205*
Butterfly weed. A hardy native perennial, 2 ft. tall. Forms a clump of upright stems surrounded with narrow green leaves

and topped with flat clusters, 2–5 in. wide, of bright orange flowers in summer. Makes a long-lasting cut flower, and cutting often induces a second round of bloom. The 'Gay Butterflies' strain bears flowers in shades of orange, yellow, and red. Native throughout the eastern United States. Zone 3.

Asparagus

As-pair´a-gus
Liliaceae. Lily family

Description
Perennials, sometimes woody or thorny, with thick or tuberous roots. Stems branch repeatedly to make a fluffy mass of green, but the true leaves are inconspicuous dry scales. The starry flowers, often fragrant, are followed by plump colored berries. About 100 species, native to the Old World, including the vegetable asparagus.

How to Grow
Full sun or part shade. Foliage color is usually darkest green in part shade, especially in hot locations. Does well in most soils. Withstands dry periods by using water stored in swollen root tubercles, but looks best with regular watering and fertilizing. If tops freeze or get shabby, prune to the ground in spring. Propagate from seed or divide old clumps in spring.

■ *densiflorus* 'Sprengeri' *p. 206*
Sprenger asparagus. A carefree perennial for mild climates, usually grown in containers or as a ground cover. Arching stems make a mound about 2 ft. high, up to 5 ft. wide, covered with shiny needlelike foliage. Fragrant, creamy white, star-shaped flowers open in spring. Bright red berries attract birds in fall and winter. Zone 9.

Baccharis

Bak´a-ris
Compositae. Daisy family

Description
Evergreen or deciduous shrubs, some with leafless green stems. Separate male and female plants; females sometimes have showy white seed heads. About 350 species, native to North America.

How to Grow
Full sun. These coastal natives tolerate poor soil, wet or dry, and salt spray. Prune or shear as often as once a year to control shape or height. Overgrown plants can be cut back by half to rejuvenate.

■ *halimifolia* p. 127
Groundsel tree, saltbush. A semievergreen shrub with many slender upright stems 6–10 ft. tall. Its light gray-green leaves persist into winter, and the large clusters of white fruiting heads on female plants are very showy in late fall, especially when planted in front of dark green pines or junipers. Native along the East Coast from Massachusetts to Texas. Zone 6.

Baptisia
Bap-tiz´ee-a
Leguminosae. Pea family

Description
Perennials forming bushy clumps of upright stems with trifoliate leaves, pealike flowers, and inflated pods. About 17 species, native to eastern North America.

How to Grow
Full or part sun. Prefers fertile, organic soil but tolerates poor soil, wet or dry. Easily raised from seed but won't flower for a few years. Set purchased plants in their permanent location; they develop big root systems and don't transplant well. Established plants are long-lived and carefree.

■ *australis* p. 206
False indigo. A hardy perennial wildflower that forms a clump 3–4 ft. tall and 4–6 ft. wide. The blue-green foliage is attractive all season. Stems are topped with foot-long racemes of indigo blue flowers for several weeks in late spring and unusual gray pods in fall. Excellent for borders or meadow gardens. Zone 3. *B. alba* grows slightly taller and has long spikes of white flowers. Zone 3.

Berberis
Ber´ber-iss. Barberry
Berberidaceae. Barberry family

Description
Evergreen or deciduous shrubs, usually spiny. Most have

abundant yellow flowers and persistent red, yellow, or black berries. About 450 species, native to Eurasia and Africa.

How to Grow
Full sun is necessary for best foliage color and fruit set. Tolerates infertile soil but needs good drainage. Established plants tolerate drought but not severe heat. Can be pruned into formal shapes or to control size, but the stems have fierce spines. Unpruned plants are upright, spreading, or rounded, depending on cultivar.

■ *thunbergii* p. 128 *Pictured above*
Japanese barberry. A deciduous shrub often used for hedges or foundation plantings. Grows 2–6 ft. tall and wide, depending on cultivar. All forms have dense twiggy growth and bright red berries in fall. The small teardrop-shaped leaves can be bright green, crimson-purple, or golden yellow in summer; all turn bright red in fall. Zone 4.

The evergreen barberries, such as *B. julianae* and *B. verruculosa*, also do well in protected sites along the Atlantic and Pacific coasts.

Betula
Bet´you-la. Birch
Betulaceae. Birch family

Description
Deciduous trees or shrubs, most fast-growing but short-lived. About 60 species, most native to cool northern climates in the Old and New World.

How to Grow
Full or part sun. Prefers fertile, organic, acidic soil with constant moisture but tolerates average soil with regular watering. Tolerates heat and humidity better than other birches do. Roots are shallow, so don't plant it near walks or driveways. Transplant when dormant.

■ *nigra* p. 89 *Pictured opposite*
River birch, black birch. A deciduous tree, 40–70 ft. tall, with

single or multiple trunks and attractive pink, beige, or salmon-colored bark that peels off in large curly sheets. Shimmering leaves are bright green in summer, yellow in fall. 'Heritage' has especially conspicuous pale bark. Native throughout the eastern United States. Zone 4.

Bougainvillea

Boo-gan-vil'ee-a
Nyctaginaceae. Four-o'clock family

Description

Evergreen woody vines, often spiny, sometimes shrublike. The actual flowers are small, but the bright-colored papery bracts are long-lasting and very showy. About 14 species, from Central and South America, and many hybrid cultivars.

How to Grow

Full sun. Ordinary soil. Plant in spring, taking care not to disturb the root ball. Water and fertilize regularly for the first year or two, but reduce summer watering once established to promote more abundant flowering. Provide a strong support for vining types. Prune heavily in spring to control size and to stimulate the growth of new flowering wood.

■ hybrids *p. 192*

Bougainvillea. These tough woody vines can sprawl or climb up to 20 ft. or be pruned and trained to grow like shrubs. They can be used to cover a bank or hillside or to scale a trellis or wall. The smooth, dark green, triangular-shaped leaves are evergreen in mild winters but drop at the slightest frost. Masses of papery bracts keep their bright colors for months. 'San Diego Red' is a vigorous climber with deep red bracts. 'Rosenka' is a shrub form with flowers that open gold and mature to pink. Zone 9.

Buddleia

Bud´lee-a. Butterfly bush
Loganiaceae. Buddleia family

Description
Deciduous or evergreen shrubs or small trees with clusters or spikes of small flowers, often fragrant and quite popular with butterflies. About 100 species, native to tropical and subtropical regions in the Old and New World.

How to Grow
Full sun. Ordinary or poor soil. Needs good drainage; tolerates considerable dryness. Looks best if you prune it to the ground each spring to force a fountain of fresh shoots, which will grow at least 5 ft. tall by midsummer. Thrives in long hot summers.

■ *davidii* *p. 128 Pictured above*
Butterfly bush. A deciduous or semievergreen shrub, 5–10 ft. tall. Arching stems are lined with slender leaves and tipped with long clusters of fragrant flowers that attract many butterflies. Blooms on new wood from midsummer to fall. Different cultivars have purple, lilac, pink, or white petals, almost always with a bright orange eye in the center of the flower. Zone 5.

Callistemon

Kal-i-stee´mon. Bottlebrush
Myrtaceae. Myrtle family

Description
Evergreen shrubs or trees with leafy stems and distinctive bottlebrush-like spikes of red or yellow flowers. About 20 species, native to Australia.

How to Grow
Full sun. Ordinary or dry soil. The following species are fast-growing and carefree. Prune in winter.

■ *citrinus* p. 149
Lemon bottlebrush. An evergreen shrub, 10–15 ft. tall. Bright red flowers make 6-in. "bottlebrushes" near the ends of the long, arching branches. Blooms off and on all year. The slender lemon-scented leaves are silky and pink at first, turning dark green and firm as they mature. Can be used in several ways. Set 4–5 ft. apart for a hedge or screen. Fasten to a wire frame or trellis to shape an espalier. Zone 9.

■ *viminalis* p. 102
Weeping bottlebrush. A small evergreen tree, up to 30 ft. tall, with an upright trunk and slender branches that hang straight down. Bright red 8-in. bottlebrushes dangle in the breeze. The narrow leathery leaves are light blue-green. To train young trees, provide a stake and remove lower branches until a head is formed. Zone 9.

Calluna

Ka-loo′na. Heather
Ericaceae. Heath family

Description

Evergreen shrubs that form a low mound of flexible stems with tiny scalelike leaves, tipped with spikes of small flowers in late summer and fall. Only 1 species, native to Europe and Asia Minor, but hundreds of cultivars.

How to Grow

Best in full sun. Needs excellent drainage and grows well in sandy soil amended with peat moss. Thrives in cool climates but can't tolerate hot summers, wet or dry. Set 1 ft. apart for mass plantings. Grows slowly for the first few years, then thrives for decades with no care. Lightly prune to shape after flowering, if desired.

■ *vulgaris* p. 178
Heather. Evergreen shrub, usually under 2 ft. tall. Heathers form low mounds of wiry branches clothed with minute overlapping leaves. Many change color from summer to winter, ranging from shades of pale to dark green, gold, and gray to bronze and reddish purple. Thousands of tiny flowers cover the plants with a cloud of white, pink, lavender, or rosy purple. Bloom season extends from midsummer to late fall. There are dozens of fine cultivars. 'County Wicklow' has green foliage, a mounding habit (12 in. by 20 in.), and pink flowers. Zone 4.

Campsis

Kamp´sis
Bignoniaceae. Trumpet creeper family

Description
Deciduous woody vines with pinnately compound leaves and large, showy, red or orange flowers. Only 2 species, one from the eastern United States and the other from eastern Asia, and their hybrid.

How to Grow
Sun or shade. Grows in any soil and needs no special care. Choosing an appropriate site is the only concern; the aerial rootlets cling tight and can damage roofs, masonry, or window screens. May spread underground, but the suckers are easily removed or controlled.

■ *radicans* p. 193
Trumpet vine, trumpet creeper. A vigorous vine that climbs to 30 ft. or more. Good for covering fences, stumps, or old buildings. Large deciduous leaves are compound with many toothed leaflets. Orange blossoms 3–4 in. long are borne continuously from June to fall in clusters at the tips of shoots. Hummingbirds love them. Dry woody pods hang on all winter. 'Flava' has dark yellow flowers. Native to the eastern United States. Zone 5.

Carissa

Ka-ris´sa
Apocynaceae. Dogbane family

Description
Spiny shrubs with leathery evergreen leaves, pink or white flowers, and fleshy fruits. About 37 species, native to Africa and Australia.

How to Grow

Full sun. Average soil. Tolerates ocean wind, salt spray, and moderate drought. Often used as a barrier hedge, because of its dense growth and abundant spines. Prune as needed to control size and shape.

■ *macrocarpa* p. 150
Natal plum. A fast-growing evergreen shrub, usually 6–8 ft. tall, but there are compact and prostrate cultivars that stay under 2 ft. Glossy oval leaves, fragrant white star-shaped

flowers, and edible red cherry-sized fruits give year-round interest. Formerly known as *C. grandiflora*. Zone 9.

Carpobrotus

Kar-po-bro'tus
Aizoaceae. Carpetweed family

Description
Low shrubby succulents with plump, curved, opposite leaves and large round flowers with many petals. About 30 species, most from South Africa.

How to Grow
Full sun or part shade. Does very well in sandy soil, where it is excellent for reducing erosion. To plant, space rooted cuttings 12–15 in. apart. For best color and rapid growth, water and fertilize during the growing season. Drought-tolerant in coastal sites once established. Watch for scale insects.

■ *edulis* p. 179
Ice plant. A succulent evergreen ground cover, under 18 in. tall, spreading nearly 6 ft. from the crown. Stems root at the nodes. Dull green leaves, usually curved, reach 5 in. long. Showy daisylike flowers open yellow and mature to pink. Fruit is edible but not tasty. One of the most reliable ground covers for windy, sandy, coastal sites, and moderately fire-resistant. Zone 8.

Caryopteris

Kare-ee-yop'ter-is
Verbenaceae. Verbena family

Description
Deciduous shrubs or perennials with simple leaves and abundant clusters of tiny blue, violet, or white flowers. About 6 species, native to eastern Asia, and a few hybrids.

How to Grow
Full sun. Prefers sandy loam with excellent drainage. Tolerates heat and drought. Cut back drastically in spring to promote shapely new growth. Pest-free.

■ × *clandonensis* p. 129
Bluebeard, blue mist. A small deciduous shrub, 2–3 ft. tall,

that combines well with perennials. Cut to the ground each spring, it quickly sends up new shoots with neatly spaced pairs of downy gray leaves. Fluffy clusters of lavender-blue flowers tip each shoot in August and September and attract butterflies. 'Blue Mist', 'Longwood Blue', and other selected cultivars have especially showy and abundant flowers. Zone 6.

Ceanothus
See-a-no´thus
Rhamnaceae. Buckthorn family

Description
Deciduous or evergreen shrubs or small trees, usually with dense branching. Clusters of tiny blue, violet, or white flowers can hide the foliage for weeks on end. About 55 species, all native to North America.

How to Grow
Full sun. The species below grow in nearly any well-drained soil. Water deeply during establishment, but refrain from watering established plants, especially during the summer, to avoid root rot. Plant in fall. Space 4–5 ft. apart for good coverage. Pinch tips to encourage branching.

■ *gloriosus* *p. 150*
Point Reyes ceanothus. A low evergreen shrub, native to coastal California, that forms a broad, dense mat only 18 in. high but up to 10 ft. wide. Dark green leaves about 1 in. wide are thick and leathery. Makes a spectacular display of light blue flowers in mid- to late spring. A good ground cover for preventing erosion on banks and hillsides. The cultivar 'Emily Brown' has darker blue flowers and grows 2–3 ft. tall. Zone 8.

■ *griseus* var. *horizontalis* *p. 151* *Pictured above*
Carmel creeper. A low evergreen shrub, usually under 2–3 ft. tall, native to the California coast and planted there as a ground cover. Prized for its tremendous display of fragrant, tiny, pale blue flowers, borne in dense 1-in.-long clusters from March to April. The small evergreen leaves are glossy and leathery. 'Yankee Point' (to 10 ft. wide) has deeper blue

flowers. 'Santa Ana' (to 15 ft. wide) has tiny dark green leaves and rich deep blue flowers. Zone 8.

Cerastium
See-ras´tee-um
Caryophyllaceae. Pink family

Description
Low-growing annuals or perennials, mostly weedy, with opposite leaves and small white flowers. About 60 species, native worldwide.

How to Grow
Full sun. Easy to grow in any well-drained soil, even pure sand. Spreads fast to make large patches. Useful as a ground cover but invasive in flower beds. Shear after flowering. Propagate by division or seed.

■ *tomentosum* p. 179
Snow-in-summer. A spreading perennial, 6 in. tall and 2–3 ft. wide. Forms mats of woolly gray foliage, topped with masses of white flowers about $1/_2$ in. wide in early summer. Zone 4.

Ceratonia
Ser-ra-tone´ee-a. Carob
Leguminosae. Pea family

Description
Evergreen trees with pinnate leaves and pods filled with sweet edible pulp. Only 2 species, native to Arabia and Somalia.

How to Grow
Full sun. Tolerates sandy soil and drought. Plant 6–8 ft. apart for a hedge or screen. To grow as a tree, shorten the lower branches and remove them only after a head is formed at the proper height. Don't plant close to a sidewalk or patio; the roots will lift pavement.

■ *siliqua* p. 103
Carob, St.-John's-bread. A broad shrub or tree, reaching to 30–40 ft. tall and as wide as it is tall. Makes a dense crown of shiny, leathery, evergreen, compound leaves. Blooms in spring, with 6-in. clusters of small red flowers. If pollinated, female trees produce long, woody, dark brown pods with sugary pulp and hard seeds inside. Zone 9.

Cercis

Sir'sis. Redbud
Leguminosae. Pea family

Description
Deciduous small trees or shrubs with stalkless clusters of pink or white pealike flowers sprouting directly from the branches or trunk in early spring, before the leaves open. Only 6 or 7 species, native to North America, southern Europe, and China.

How to Grow
Full or part sun. Needs good drainage and does well in sandy soil. Fairly fast-growing but sometimes short-lived, as the leaves, wood, and roots are all subject to fungal diseases. Remove dead branches and prune to shape after blooming. Often self-seeds but isn't weedy.

■ *canadensis* *p. 90 Pictured above*
Eastern redbud. A small deciduous tree, 20–35 ft. tall, with one or more trunks and a spreading crown. Small, pealike, rosy pink or purplish flowers line the twigs for 2–3 weeks in early spring, before the leaves develop. The heart-shaped leaves start out with a maroon cast, darken to green, and then turn gold in fall. Selected cultivars have clear white or true pink flowers. Native to eastern North America. Zone 4.

   The western redbud, *C. occidentalis,* has similar flowers and leaves but is shrubbier and usually has multiple trunks. It is very drought-tolerant. Native to California. Zone 8.

Chamaecyparis

Kam-ee-sip'ar-is. False cypress
Cupressaceae. Cypress family

Description
Evergreen conifers with needlelike juvenile foliage and scaly adult foliage. Wild trees grow huge and yield important timber, but hundreds of dwarf forms are better suited for gardens. About 7 species, native to North America and eastern Asia.

How to Grow
Full or part sun. Prefers fertile soil with constant moisture but tolerates poor soil. Does best along the Pacific coast, where it grows wild. Needs little if any pruning, but hedges can be sheared if desired. Shear in summer and cut only into green wood.

■ *lawsoniana* p. 103
Lawson cypress. A slender conifer, up to 60 ft. tall and 20 ft. wide. The shiny green foliage has a fine texture and is arrayed in flattened fanlike sprays. The cones are marble-sized, and the reddish brown bark forms long vertical strips or plates. 'Fraseri' is a popular selection with gray-green foliage. There are many other cultivars, varying in size, growth rate, foliage color, and hardiness. Dwarf forms make good hedges. Zone 6.

Chamaerops
Ka-mee´rops
Palmae. Palm family

Description
A fan palm that usually forms low clumps. Only 1 species, native to the Mediterranean region.

How to Grow
Sun or shade. Tolerates average or sandy soil with regular rainfall or watering. Needs little care; just remove tattered fronds. Separate suckers from older plants if the clump gets too dense. Can also be grown in containers.

■ *humilis* p. 151
European fan palm. A slow-growing, clump-forming palm that eventually reaches 6–20 ft. tall. The bright green leaves spiral around the trunk and fan out into long slender leaflets. Flowers and fruits are inconspicuous. Zone 8.

Chasmanthium
Kaz-man´thee-um
Gramineae. Grass family

Description
Perennial grasses that form clumps or small patches, with uniquely flat seed heads that dangle over the broad leaf blades. Only 5 species, native to eastern North America.

How to Grow

Sun or shade. Prefers moist, fertile soil but tolerates poor or dry soil. Sow seed or increase by division in spring; space 2 ft. apart for mass plantings to cover rough ground or slopes. Cut back to the ground in early spring.

■ *latifolium* p. 230 *Pictured above*

Northern sea oats. A perennial grass that makes a clump 3–5 ft. tall. The close-set leaves are broad for a grass, green in summer and fall and warm tan in winter. The flat drooping clusters of oatlike seed heads sway above the leaves in the slightest breeze; they form in summer and stay attractive all winter. Frequently listed as *Uniola latifolia*. Zone 4.

Chrysanthemum

Kri-san´thee-mum
Compositae. Daisy family

Description

Annuals, perennials, or subshrubs, usually with daisylike blossoms and lobed or divided leaves. Taxonomists have reclassified these plants several times, and the status of the genus is uncertain. There are about 100 species, nearly all from the Old World.

How to Grow

The following species all need full sun, well-drained soil, and regular watering during prolonged dry spells. Propagate by division in early spring. Pinch tips to encourage branching. Cut flower stalks to the ground after bloom fades.

■ *maximum* p. 207

Shasta daisy. A hybrid perennial daisy developed by Luther Burbank. There are several cultivars, differing in flower size and stem height. Most form a low mat of shiny, smooth, coarsely toothed, dark green leaves that are nearly evergreen.

The daisies are 2–5 in. wide, borne singly on erect stalks 1–3 ft. tall. Blooms most in early summer. Often listed as *C. × superbum*. Zone 4.

■ *nipponicum*   *p. 207*

Nippon daisy, Montauk daisy. A shrubby perennial with leafy stems up to 30 in. tall. Doesn't bloom until fall, with typical white daisies about 2 in. wide, but earns its place all summer with a show of particularly handsome foliage. The rich green leaves, borne all the way up and down the stems, are thick, smooth, and lustrous. Zone 5.

Cistus

Sis´tus. Rock rose
Cistaceae. Rock rose family

Description

Mostly evergreen shrubs of low spreading habit with simple opposite leaves and wide, open flowers. Some yield fragrant resins. About 17 species, native to the Mediterranean region, and a few cultivated hybrids.

How to Grow

Full sun or part shade. Best in ordinary soil but tolerates loose, dry, and sandy soils. Drought-tolerant once established. Pest-free and easy to grow. Pinch tips to encourage branching, and thin out the oldest stems periodically.

■ × *purpureus*   *p. 152*

Orchid rock rose. An evergreen shrub that makes a dense mound about 4 ft. tall and 4 ft. wide. Narrow, dull green leaves have a rough surface and 3 distinct veins. Reddish purple flowers are 3 in. wide, with a dark spot at the base of each petal. Blooms abundantly in late spring and summer. Makes a low screen or bank cover and combines well with other Mediterranean shrubs such as lavender and rosemary. Zone 7.

Clematis

Klem´a-tis
Ranunculaceae. Buttercup family

Description

Most clematis are deciduous or evergreen vines with showy flowers, small or large, and fluffy clusters of feathery-tailed seeds. About 250 species, nearly all native to the north temperate zone, and hundreds of hybrid cultivars.

How to Grow
Full or part sun. Ordinary soil and watering. Sweet autumn clematis is fast-growing and aggressive, but you can let it run through a hedge or climb a conifer if you cut it back hard every few years. Extremely vigorous in mild climates, it's more restrained where winters are cold. Cut back frozen shoots to healthy wood in spring. Blossoms on new growth.

■ *maximowicziana* p. 193
Sweet autumn clematis. A tough, carefree, deciduous vine that quickly climbs or spreads up to 30 ft. Let it sprawl over a fence or climb into shrubs or trees, or use it as a ground cover. Compound leaves have 3 small oval leaflets. Fluffy clusters of fragrant white flowers, about 1 in. wide, cover the vine for several weeks in late summer. Also sold as *C. paniculata*. Zone 4.

Clethra
Kleth'ra
Clethraceae. Summer-sweet family

Description
Deciduous or evergreen shrubs or trees with terminal clusters of fragrant white or pink flowers. About 60 species, most native to tropical climates.

How to Grow
Full or part sun. Grows wild in swampy or poorly drained soil and needs regular watering if planted in average garden soil. Tolerates salt spray well. Makes a good hedge; plant 5–6 ft. apart. Needs little pruning.

■ *alnifolia* p. 129
Sweet pepperbush, summer-sweet. A deciduous shrub native to the Atlantic coast and valued for the sweet, penetrating fragrance of its flowers. Spreads slowly to form a clump of upright stems 6–9 ft. tall, topped in midsummer with 5-in. spikes of small white or pink flowers. Attractive glossy leaves appear in late spring, turn gold in fall. Two new dwarf cultivars are good for foundation plantings or mixed borders. 'Hummingbird' has white flowers and grows only 4 ft. tall. 'Rosea' has pink flowers and grows only 4–6 ft. tall. Zone 4.

Convolvulus
Kon-vol'vu-lus. Bindweed, morning glory
Convolvulaceae. Morning glory family

Description
Twining vines, perennials, or shrubs, sometimes weedy, with alternate simple leaves. Bell- or funnel-shaped flowers usually open in early morning and close by noon. About 250 species, native worldwide.

How to Grow
Full sun. Any well-drained soil. Moderately drought-tolerant once established. Makes a superb ground cover for coastal sites. Space 24–30 in. apart. Prune out the oldest woody stems in early spring to encourage vigorous new growth and abundant flowering.

■ *sabatius p. 208*
Ground morning glory. A sprawling perennial with semi-woody stems; forms a low mat 18 in. high and 3 ft. across. Rounded evergreen leaves are covered with soft hairs and are gray-green in color. Pale blue flowers, 2 in. wide, cover the plant in late spring and appear intermittently until fall. Formerly known as *C. mauritanicus*. Zone 8.

Coprosma
Ko-proz'ma
Rubiaceae. Madder family

Description
Evergreen shrubs or small trees with opposite leaves, dense heads of small flowers on separate male and female plants, and small fleshy fruits. About 90 species, native mostly to Australia and New Zealand.

How to Grow
Full sun. Coprosmas need well-drained, neutral to slightly acidic soil and are moderately drought-tolerant once established. Prune as needed to keep plants dense and to maintain desired size.

■ × *kirkii p. 180*
Creeping coprosma. A low evergreen shrub or ground cover, under 2 ft. tall and often shorter if subjected to strong coastal winds. Grows quickly and makes a low spreading mat of

prostrate branches that will trail down a bank or over a wall. Glossy light green leaves are narrow, 1 in. long. Flowers and fruits are inconspicuous. Trouble-free. Zone 9.

■ *repens* p. 152

Mirror plant. An evergreen shrub, up to 10 ft. tall and 6 ft. wide, but easily kept smaller by pruning. Useful as a fast-growing hedge or screen. Leathery oval leaves are dark green and very lustrous; few plants have such shiny leaves. Female plants bear small orange fruits. 'Marble Queen' has showy variegated foliage and grows only 3 ft. tall. Zone 9.

Cordyline

Kor-di-ly´ne
Agavaceae. Agave family

Description

Evergreen woody plants with sparsely branching stems, each branch ending in a cluster of long narrow leaves. About 15 species, most native to India and Australia.

How to Grow

Full sun or part shade. Grows best in deep, rich, well-drained soil with abundant water but survives on minimal water once established. For an attractive multitrunk effect, plant several in a group or prune out the tip of individual plants when young. Remove older leaves as they wither.

■ *australis* p. 153

Giant dracaena, cabbage tree. A picturesque palmlike shrub or small multistemmed tree, up to 25 ft. tall. Sword-shaped leaves up to 3 ft. long and 4 in. wide form a dense cluster atop each branch. Bears large clusters of waxy, cream-colored, fragrant flowers in late spring and summer. Used for a bold, tropical effect. Several varieties are available, varying in leaf color and pattern. Zone 8.

Cortaderia

Kor-ta-dee´ree-a. Pampas grass
Gramineae. Grass family

Description

Perennial grasses that form huge clumps. About 24 species, native to South America and New Zealand.

How to Grow

Full or part sun. Grows anywhere; not fussy about soil or watering. Space 10 ft. apart for mass plantings. Remove old plumes in spring. Cutting back old foliage is a major chore every few years; burning it off is an easier solution if allowed in your area. Seedlings can be invasive; watch for and destroy them.

■ *selloana* p. 231

Pampas grass. A tough perennial grass that forms a dense clump, up to 8 ft. tall and wide, of slender, arching leaves. The foliage is nearly evergreen in frost-free zones, turns tan when frosted in colder areas. Cotton-candylike flowering plumes on stiff stalks lift 2 ft. or more above the foliage in late summer and remain intact through midwinter. Female plants are showier than the males. Most often used as a single specimen in mid-lawn but better suited for a barrier hedge or wind screen, because it gets quite big and the leaf edges are dangerously sharp. There are pink-flowered and dwarf forms. Zone 8.

   C. jubata looks similar but has become a weed in California, where it spreads by seed and crowds out more desirable plants. Avoid it.

Cotinus

Kot'i-nus, ko-ty'nus. Smoke tree
Anacardiaccac. Sumac family

Description

Deciduous shrubs or small trees with a bushy upright habit, rounded leaves that turn bright colors in fall, and showy flower stalks. Only 3 species, one each from the southeastern United States, Asia, and China.

How to Grow

Full or part sun. Tolerates poor soil, salt spray, wind, and summer dryness. Blooms on new growth, so prune in early spring. Cutting the stems back to the ground each year forces tall straight shoots with larger, brighter-colored leaves. No serious pests or diseases.

■ *coggygria* p. 130

Smoke tree. A tough, trouble-free deciduous shrub that can grow 12–18 ft. tall but is usually kept shorter by pruning. The leaves, shaped like Ping-Pong paddles are smooth and healthy, bright green or purple in summer and turning orange, scarlet, or maroon in fall. The fluffy clouds of beige, pink, or purple "smoke" that cover the foliage all summer are wiry, much-branched flower stalks; the actual flowers are small and drop quickly. 'Royal Purple' and other purple-leaved cultivars are especially popular. Zone 4.

Cotoneaster
Ko-to´nee-as-ter
Rosaceae. Rose family

Description
Evergreen or deciduous shrubs with white or pink flowers and red or dark fruits that last from fall to spring. Most branch repeatedly; some grow upright, while others spread sideways. About 50 species, native to Europe and Asia.

How to Grow
Full sun. Most cotoneasters do well in seaside conditions. They prefer fertile, amended soil but tolerate poor, dry sites. Once established, they are fairly tolerant of droughts. Choose only container-grown plants, and don't attempt to transplant established specimens. Can be afflicted by fire blight, leaf spots, and spider mites, but normally trouble-free in seaside conditions.

■ *divaricatus* p. 130
Spreading cotoneaster. An open, airy, deciduous shrub with graceful spreading limbs, 5–6 ft. tall and 10–12 ft. wide. Tolerates some shade and makes a mounded understory under tall trees. The small shiny leaves turn red in fall. Pink flowers in May are followed by bright red berries that last into early winter. Zone 5.

■ *lacteus* p. 153
Red clusterberry. An arching, fountain-shaped, evergreen shrub, 6–8 ft. tall and wide. Makes a good informal screen or clipped hedge. Red berries in clusters 2–3 in. wide last nearly all winter. The distinctly veined, oval leaves are thick and leathery, dark green above and silvery beneath. Often listed as *C. parneyi*. Zone 7.

■ *multiflorus* p. 131
Many-flowered cotoneaster. A large deciduous shrub, up to 10 ft. tall and 15 ft. wide. One of the most ornamental cotoneasters, with showy clusters of small white flowers in spring, refreshing gray-green foliage, abundant red fruits in

fall, and a spreading fountainlike habit that's attractive in the winter months. Give it plenty of room to develop, and use it as a focal point or specimen. Zone 3.

Cupaniopsis

Kew-pan-i-op′sis
Sapindaceae. Soapberry family

Description
Evergreen trees or shrubs with handsome pinnately compound leaves. About 60 species, native to Australia and the South Pacific islands.

How to Grow
Full sun. Grows in almost any soil, wet or dry, and tolerates heat, wind, and ocean spray. Grows easily from seed and self-sown seedlings can be a nuisance. Prune to shape as desired. Pest-free.

■ *anacardiodes* *p. 104*
Carrotwood, tuckeroo. A neat and handsome evergreen tree, reaching 25–40 ft. tall and wide. The compound leaves have 4–12 oblong leaflets that are smooth, leathery, and dull dark green. The tiny clustered flowers are inconspicuous but lightly fragrant in spring and are sometimes followed by yellow-orange fruits. Zone 9.

Cupressus

Kew-pres′sus. Cypress
Cupressaceae. Cypress family

Description
Evergreen conifers with round woody cones and fragrant scalelike leaves that hug the twigs. About 13 species, native to warm regions in the Northern Hemisphere.

How to Grow
Full sun. Well-drained soil. Irrigate during dry spells in the first few years. Older trees are quite drought-tolerant. Excess water and fertilizer stimulate too-fast growth.

■ *sempervirens* 'Stricta' *p. 104*
Columnar Italian cypress. An unusually skinny tree, 30–40 ft. tall but only 6–10 ft. wide, that makes a narrow column of

dense, dark, dull green, scalelike foliage. It's very conspicuous in a garden because of its distinctive shape; use one or two at a gate or doorway, or plant a row at measured spacing to emphasize a formal drive or property line. Plants often have multiple leaders. Let them spread apart for an irregular, interestingly shaped specimen, or tie them together to make a neatly columnar tree. Zone 8.

Cycas
Sigh´kas
Cycadaceae. Cycad family

Description
Palmlike plants with unusual stiff-textured fronds that radiate from a short trunk. About 30 species, native to the Old World.

How to Grow
Best in partial shade, even along the coast. Average well-drained soil. Water and fertilize regularly during the growing season to promote deep green, healthy foliage. Do not prune except to remove old lower leaves. Very slow-growing. Does well in containers. Watch for scale insects.

■ *revoluta* p. 154
Sago palm. A distinctive evergreen shrub, normally under 4 ft. tall. Starts with one stubby trunk but eventually develops multiple trunks, each topped with a rosette of glossy, dark green, fernlike leaves, 3–4 ft. long, divided into many slender segments. Old, well-established specimens occasionally produce rounded woody cones. Zone 8.

Cytisus
Sigh´ti-sus. Broom
Leguminosae. Pea family

Description
Bushy shrubs with prolific displays of pealike flowers. Some are deciduous, some evergreen, some nearly leafless with bright green twigs. More than 30 species, native to the Mediterranean region, and several hybrids.

How to Grow
Full sun. Notably tolerant of dry, rocky, poor soils and windy coastal sites. Does well in ordinary garden soil but needs

good drainage. Drought-tolerant once established. Prune annually to reduce seed formation and to encourage new flowering stems, but don't cut into wood more than 1 year old. Use a single specimen in a mixed border, or mass several to cover a bank or slope.

■ × *praecox* *p. 131*
Hybrid broom. A deciduous shrub, usually 3–5 ft. tall. Short narrow leaves appear in spring but drop quickly. Most of the year the bush is a compact mound of wiry gray-green twigs. Brooms are very showy for several weeks in spring when the branches are covered with masses of yellow, gold, cream, red, or purple flowers that resemble pea blossoms. 'Hollandia' has two-tone flowers, pinkish red and white. These hybrid brooms are not invasive. Zone 6.

C. scoparius, Scotch broom, is a fast-growing shrub with stiff upright branches and fragrant golden yellow flowers. It's considered a weed along the Pacific coast, where it self-sows aggressively, but it's fairly uncommon and generally welcome along the East Coast. Zone 6.

Delphinium
Del-fin´ee-um
Ranunculaceae. Buttercup family

Description
Annuals, biennials, or perennials with palmately lobed or divided leaves and upright stalks of bright blue, pink, white, scarlet, or yellow flowers with distinct spurs. About 250 species, native to the north temperate zone.

How to Grow
Full sun. Delphiniums require well-prepared organic soil, frequent light fertilization, and constant moisture. Tall forms need staking; short forms are more carefree. Cut back after first bloom and fertilize to encourage reblooming in fall. Delphiniums are short-lived, but new plants are easily raised from seed. Space seedlings 2 ft. apart, planting in fall for bloom the following year.

■ × *elatum* hybrids *p. 208*
Hybrid delphiniums. Dramatic perennials with branching flower stalks 3–6 ft. tall. There are many types, differing in overall height and flower size and form. Flowers are single or double, 2–3 in. wide, in shades of blue, purple, lavender, pink, or white. All have deep green, palmately divided leaves. The

Giant Pacific hybrids reach 5 ft. or more and usually have double flowers. The Connecticut Yankee hybrids are short (under 3 ft.) and bushy and have single blossoms. Zone 3.

Dianthus

Dy-an'thus. Pink
Caryophyllaceae. Pink family

Description
Low-growing annuals, biennials, or perennials with slender opposite leaves and showy flowers, often with a sweet or spicy fragrance. About 300 species, most from Europe and Asia.

How to Grow
Full sun. Well-drained garden soil with occasional watering during dry spells. Although classified as biennials, sweet Williams may hang on like perennials, blooming every summer for 2 or 3 years. The normal practice is to sow seeds in early summer and transplant to their final location by late summer. The bigger the rosette of foliage in fall, the more flowers in spring. Cut flowering stems to the ground after bloom unless you want to encourage self-sowing.

■ *barbatus* *p. 209*
Sweet William. A favorite old-fashioned cut flower, with spicy-scented flowers borne in flat clusters up to 4 in. wide on stiff stalks 12–24 in. tall. Colors include white, pink, rose, dark red, and bicolors. Blooms for about a month in late spring and early summer. Forms a broad mat of dark green, oblong leaves. Foliage is evergreen where winters are mild. Zone 3.

Other species and hybrids of *Dianthus* also thrive in seaside gardens. Most are very hardy and have slender, grassy leaves in shades of gray-green or blue-green and fragrant pink, white, rose, or red flowers.

Diospyros

Dy-os'pie-rus
Ebenaceae. Ebony family

Description
Most members of the genus are large tropical trees harvested for their hard, dark wood, called ebony. Some, called persimmons, are valued for their sweet, rich, pulpy fruits. About 475 species, almost all native to the tropics.

How to Grow

Full sun. Prefers moist, sandy soils but tolerates dry soil once established. Difficult to transplant, so choose container-grown or balled-and-burlapped trees, or sow seeds in place in fall for spring germination. Needs minimal pruning or care.

■ *virginiana* p. 90

Persimmon. A deciduous tree native to eastern North America, usually only 30–40 ft. tall and having a single trunk and neat oval crown. Makes a good small specimen or shade tree. Leaves are glossy green in summer, often turning yellow or purple in fall. Dark blocky bark is handsome in winter. Plump orange fruits turn soft and sweet after a few frosts in fall. 'Meader' is a self-pollinating strain with large tasty fruits. Zone 5.

Distictis

Dis-tick´tis
Bignoniaceae. Trumpet creeper family

Description

Tender woody vines with showy clusters of trumpet-shaped flowers. About 9 species, native to Mexico and the West Indies.

How to Grow

Full sun. Needs well-amended, fertile soil and constant moisture. Use it to cover a wall or fence, to hide a dead tree, or to shade an arbor. Provide a sturdy support and tie the young plant to it; it will soon climb on its own by tendrils and adhesive pads. Thin from time to time to restrict growth, to prevent tangling, and to remove dead twigs beneath the canopy.

■ *buccinatoria* p. 194 *Pictured above*

Blood-red trumpet vine. A woody vine that climbs or spreads to 30 ft., with shiny, dark, evergreen foliage. Compound leaves have just 2 large oval leaflets. Blooms off and on all summer, displaying big clusters of trumpet-shaped 4-in. flowers, orange-red to purple-red with yellow throats. Zone 9.

Dodonaea

Do-don´ee-a
Sapindaceae. Soapberry family

Description
Tropical evergreen shrubs or trees, often with sticky resinous secretions that have some medicinal properties. About 50 species. Most are native to Australia, but the species below is from Arizona.

How to Grow
Full sun. Tolerates poor, dry soil. Good for informal hedges or screens. Space 6–8 ft. apart. It usually grows as an erect multitrunked shrub but can be trained into a single-trunked tree. Trouble-free.

■ *viscosa* 'Purpurea' *p. 154*
Hopbush. A tough shrub, 12–15 ft. tall and wide, with narrow, leathery, evergreen leaves. 'Purpurea' has purplish leaves and is more commonly grown than the wild green-leaved form. The flowers are inconspicuous, but the flat, winged, pink fruits hang in showy clusters all summer. Zone 8.

Drosanthemum

Dros-an´thee-mum
Aizoaceae. Carpetweed family

Description
Low spreading shrubs with succulent leaves and showy flowers. About 90 species, native to South Africa.

How to Grow
Full sun. Grows in any soil, including rocky, barren sites. Drought-tolerant once established, especially near the coast. Stems root where they touch the ground, helping protect soil against erosion. Prune off straggly stems and plant them for propagation, spacing 12–15 in. apart for quick cover.

■ *floribundum* *p. 180*
Rosea ice plant. A succulent ground cover that forms a spreading cushion only 6 in. tall. Trails over rocks and walls. Fleshy, light green, cylindrical leaves are $1/2$–$3/4$ in. long and covered

with glistening spots that look like crystals. Small, many-petaled, pink flowers completely cover the plant from late spring through early summer. A low-maintenance plant, good for stabilizing steep banks and windy, sandy sites. Zone 9.

Echinops

Ek´i-nops
Compositae. Daisy family

Description

Perennials or biennials with prickly, thistlelike foliage and round flower heads with stiff, bristly bracts. About 120 species, native to the Old and New World.

How to Grow

Full sun. Ordinary or dry soil; tolerates drought. Easy to grow. Rarely needs staking or dividing — a good thing, since the leaves are quite prickly and unapproachable. Insects may damage the foliage, but they rarely hurt the flower heads.

■ *ritro* *p. 209*
Globe thistle. A robust perennial that makes big, slowly spreading clumps 2–4 ft. tall and wide. Leaves are pinnately dissected into spiny-toothed segments. Upright, branched stalks end in tightly packed globes of tiny metallic blue flowers. 'Taplow Blue' is floriferous, with steel blue 2–in. globes. 'Veitch's Blue' has smaller, darker flower heads. Zone 3.

Echium

Ek´ee-um
Boraginaceae. Borage family

Description

Biennials or perennials with rough, hairy foliage and funnel-shaped blue flowers. About 35 species, native to Eurasia.

How to Grow

Full sun. Well-drained soil of average or low fertility. Tolerates drought. Grows very rapidly, sometimes reaching full size in only a year. Prune after flowering to remove faded blooms and to keep plants bushy. Resistant to deer damage.

■ *fastuosum* *p. 210*
Pride of Madeira. A coarse-textured perennial, becoming woody in mild-winter areas, up to 6 ft. tall. Forms a rounded

mound of many-branched stems. Narrow, gray-green leaves up to 8 in. long are crowded near the branch tips. Very showy from late spring to early summer, when it bears dozens of thick spikes of blue-purple flowers. Zone 9.

Elaeagnus

Eel-ee-ag´nus
Elaeagnaceae. Oleaster family

Description
Deciduous or evergreen shrubs or small trees. Most have thorny stems, silvery foliage, and clusters of small but fragrant flowers followed by heavy crops of berries. About 40 species, most native to Europe and Asia.

How to Grow
Full sun. The species below tolerate poor, dry soil and coastal salt and winds. They are all fast growing, vigorous, and adaptable, good for windbreaks, screens, or wildlife habitat. Prune hedges regularly, at least once a year, to increase branching. Prune trees as desired.

■ × *ebbingei* p. 155
No common name. An evergreen shrub, up to 10 ft. tall and wide, with an irregular angular profile. The oval leaves have wavy margins and are glossy dark green above, silvery gray below. Tiny flowers in fall release a wonderful fragrance. Birds eat the small orange fruits in spring. 'Gilt Edge' has leaves with a narrow yellow border. Zone 6. Thorny olive, *E. pungens,* is similar but grows somewhat larger and has thorny twigs. There are many popular cultivars, most with variegated leaves. Zone 7.

■ *umbellata* p. 132
Autumn olive. A bushy, spreading shrub, usually about 12 ft. tall and wide, with dense thorny twigs. The leaves are dark green above, silvery below. Small creamy white flowers are very fragrant in spring. Reddish brown berries attract birds in fall. 'Cardinal' is an especially tough and attractive cultivar that bears abundant crops of berries. *E. commutata,* silverberry, is a smaller shrub with especially bright silvery leaves. *E. angustifolia,* Russian olive, is a larger shrub or small tree, up to 20 ft. tall, with slender silvery leaves, fragrant flowers in spring, and silvery fruits in fall. Windswept specimens develop a striking gnarled silhouette. These species are all hardy to Zone 4.

Elymus

El′i-mus
Gramineae. Grass family

Description

Perennial grasses with flat slender leaves and dense terminal flower spikes. About 50 species, native to temperate regions.

How to Grow

Full sun. Well-drained soil. Foliage color is best in hot, dry sites. Spreading rhizomes are good for erosion control, but invasive in flower beds. Cut or mow off the old foliage in late winter. Divide in early spring.

■ *arenarius p. 231*
Blue lyme grass. A distinctive perennial grass about 3 ft. tall that spreads to form a patch. Narrow leaves have a cool blue-green color that combines well with dark evergreens. Blue wild rye, *E. glaucus,* native to the Pacific Northwest, has similar foliage but forms clumps and doesn't spread. Zone 4.

Eragrostis

Air-a-gros′tis
Gramineae. Grass family

Description

Annual or perennial grasses with slender, arching leaf blades and delicate, airy flower spikes. About 250 species, native worldwide.

How to Grow

Full sun. Well-drained, sandy soil. Extensive root systems serve to bind loose soil and reduce erosion. Propagate by division in spring. Set 2 ft. apart for ground cover. Mow in late winter, leaving stubs 8–12 in. high. May self-seed.

■ *curvula p. 233*
Weeping love grass. A perennial grass with a clump of slender dark green leaves that turn tan in winter. Loose spikes of flowers top 3–4 ft. stalks in late summer. Zone 7. *E. trichodes,* sand love grass, is similar but has wider leaves and larger flower spikes and is hardy to Zone 5.

Erianthus

Air-ee-an′thus
Gramineae. Grass family

Description

Perennial grasses with tall reedy stems, flat spreading leaf blades, and silky flowering plumes. About 20 species, native to temperate and tropical climates.

How to Grow

Full sun. Best in relatively infertile, dry soil, where it stays upright and strong; requires staking in fertile or moist conditions. Cut old stalks to the ground in early spring. Although big, this plant is not invasive — it forms a clump and doesn't spread. A row of them makes a good screen or backdrop for a border.

■ *ravennae* p. 232
Ravenna grass, plume grass. A large, dramatic grass that makes a clump 8–12 ft. tall and 5–6 ft. wide. Fluffy silvery flower plumes last from late summer through winter. The stiff reedy stalks hold the plumes well above the mound of foliage. Leaves are 1 in. wide, dark green in summer, tan in winter. Zone 5.

Erica

Air´i-ka. Heath
Ericaceae. Heath family

Description

Evergreen shrubs or small trees whose branching twiggy stems are crowded with needlelike leaves and tipped with nodding clusters of small bell-shaped flowers. About 665 species, the majority native to South Africa, with some from the Mediterranean region and Europe.

How to Grow

Full or part sun. Heaths need well-drained, slightly acidic soil; amend neutral or slightly alkaline soil with plenty of peat moss. Space 18 in. apart for ground cover. Cut back hard after bloom for dense growth and a tidy appearance. Heaths don't tolerate hot summers, dry or humid. Cover with pine boughs, salt hay, or other light, porous, mulch for winter protection in cold zones.

■ *carnea* p. 181
Winter heath. A low-growing evergreen shrub, 6–9 in. tall, that spreads to form a dense mat and makes an excellent ground cover for sandy or acidic soil. The whorled leaves are short and pointy, bright to dark green. Tiny bell-shaped

flowers in long slender clusters at the branch tips last for weeks from winter to spring, in shades of white, pink, or red. 'Springwood White' has light green foliage and white flowers, 'Springwood Pink' has bright green foliage and pink bloom, and 'Myretoun Ruby' has dark green foliage and ruby red flowers. *E. cinerea* is similar, but has a more upright habit and flowers in spring. Both species are hardy to Zone 4 with winter protection.

■ × *darleyensis* *p. 181*
Hybrid heath. An evergreen shrub, like winter heath but larger and more vigorous, up to 2 ft. tall, and adapted to a wider range of soil conditions. Lilac, pink, or white flowers open over a long season from September to May. Zone 4 with winter protection.

Erigeron
Air-ij´er-on. Fleabane
Compositae. Daisy family

Description
Perennials, biennials, or annuals with hairy leaves and composite flowers. About 200 species worldwide, most native to North America.

How to Grow
Full sun or part shade. Needs well-drained soil; rots out in wet sites but tolerates drought once established in dry sites. Fast-growing. Remove faded flowers to encourage more blooms, and trim away withered leaves and old shoots. Propagate by division.

■ *glaucus* *p. 210*
Beach aster. A low perennial, 12–15 in. tall and 24 in. wide. Forms a clump of dark green, spoon-shaped leaves. Lilac to purplish daisylike flowers, $1\frac{1}{2}$ in. wide, are held slightly above the foliage on stout stems. Blooms off and on from late spring to fall. Combines well with other drought-tolerant plants in flower beds or rock gardens. Native to coastal Oregon and California. Zone 3.

Eriogonum
Air-ee-og´o-num
Polygonaceae. Buckwheat family

Description
Perennials or shrubs, some forming low mounds, often with silvery foliage. Showy yellow, white, pink, or red flowers are borne in clusters. About 150 species, native to the southern and western United States.

How to Grow
Full sun or part shade. Needs well-drained soil and tolerates drought once established. Fast and easy to grow. Cut off old flower stalks to encourage more blooms. Propagate by seed. Sometimes self-sows but doesn't become a pest.

■ *grande* 'Rubescens' *p. 211*
Red buckwheat. A sprawling perennial that forms a mound about 1 ft. high and 2 ft. wide. Oval gray-green leaves are clustered near the stem tips. Branched clusters of rose-red flowers are held above the foliage on stiff, upright stalks. Blooms from summer to early autumn and makes a good cut flower. Other species of *Eriogonum* are also good seaside plants. Zone 8.

Erythrina
Air-i-thry'na. Coral tree
Leguminosae. Pea family

Description
Evergreen or deciduous trees or shrubs with trifoliate leaves and large clusters of showy flowers. About 100 species, native to tropical climates.

How to Grow
Full sun. Needs well-drained soil of average or better fertility. Water deeply and infrequently during the dry season. Stems may freeze back in cold weather, but it usually re-sprouts in spring and grows very rapidly in warm weather. Prune heavily soon after flowering. Remove damaged, crowded, or overlapping stems, opening the plant somewhat so it will withstand wind.

■ *crista-galli* *p. 132*
Cockspur coral tree. A deciduous small tree that grows 20–25 ft. tall in frost-free climates. In Zones 8 and 9 it dies back in winter and makes a dense multistemmed shrub 6–15 ft. tall. The stems are somewhat thorny. The leaves have 3 large oval leaflets. Long clusters of very showy large scarlet flowers have an exotic, tropical look. Blooms most heavily in late spring, continuing through summer and fall. Zone 8.

Escallonia

Es-ka-low'nee-a
Grossulariaceae. Gooseberry family

Description

Evergreen shrubs or trees with showy clusters of white, pink, or red flowers. About 40 species, native to South America.

How to Grow

Full sun. Prefers moist but well-drained soil and needs regular watering during dry spells. Tolerates wind and salt. Needs little maintenance; just remove spent blooms after flowering. Makes an excellent coastal hedge or windbreak and tolerates heavy pruning or shearing.

■ *rubra* p. 155
Red escallonia. A vigorous evergreen shrub that can reach 10–12 ft. or be kept shorter. Leaves are 2–3 in. long, glossy green above, rough below, with a toothed margin and a slightly sticky surface. Loose clusters of pink to reddish tubular flowers, each $1/2$ in. long, appear from summer through fall. Zone 8.

Eucalyptus

You-ka-lip'tus
Myrtaceae. Myrtle family

Description

Evergreen trees, small or large, with leathery foliage that is sometimes very aromatic, bright-colored flowers, and woody pods. About 450 species, almost all from Australia.

How to Grow

Full sun. Any well-drained soil. Moderately drought-tolerant once established. Excess watering causes yellow leaves and weakens the tree. Plant from containers, buying the smallest plants available to avoid tangled roots. Stake well and tie loosely so the trunk can sway some; such movement helps strengthen the trunk. Prune lightly if needed to thin the top and to develop an open framework.

■ *ficifolia* p. 105
Red-flowering gum. An evergreen tree, usually with a single trunk and round head, 30–40 ft. tall. The smooth, thick, dark green leaves often have pink to purplish petioles and edges. Showy flowers in clusters up to 12 in. wide are typically

bright red but may be orange, pink, or dusty white. Blooms most during the summer, again in winter, and intermittently year-round. An excellent street or specimen tree for coastal gardens but unsuitable for planting in irrigated lawns. Nurseries can't specify the flower color of seedling trees, but deep pink petiole (leafstalk) color normally indicates red or scarlet flowers. Zone 9.

■ *globulus* 'Compacta' *p. 105*
Dwarf blue gum. A naturally compact form of the tall eucalyptus so common in coastal California, this cultivar grows only 30–40 ft. tall and can be kept much shorter with pruning. It forms an upright oval of extremely dense growth with branches nearly to the ground and makes a fast-growing screen or windbreak. The leaves are blue-gray when young, dark green on adult growth, and have a strong medicinal odor. Creamy white flowers, 1 in. wide, in winter and spring are followed by round, woody, blue-gray seedpods. Like the full-size form, this tree drops a steady litter of pods, leaves, and bark, and it has shallow roots that don't allow underplanting. Zone 9.

Euonymus
You-on´i-mus
Celastraceae. Spindletree family

Description
Deciduous or evergreen shrubs, creeping vines, or small trees. Most have simple opposite leaves and inconspicuous flowers. Bright-colored red, orange, or pink fruits open in fall to reveal even brighter seeds, edible to birds but poisonous to humans. More than 170 species, native mostly to Asia.

How to Grow

Full sun, part sun, or shade. Any well-drained soil. Moderately drought-tolerant once established. The species below tolerate salt spray and summer wind. Dry winter winds and winter sun can discolor the foliage, but the damage is soon replaced by new growth in spring. These plants need little pruning, but they can be sheared or clipped if you choose. Euonymus scale, a common pest inland, is less troublesome along the coast.

■ *alatus* p. 133 *Pictured opposite*
Burning bush. A very adaptable deciduous shrub, usually about 8–10 ft. tall and 10 ft. wide. The simple opposite leaves slowly turn from dark green in summer to pale greenish pink and finally brilliant scarlet in fall. It's one of the most vivid and reliable plants for fall color. Also interesting in winter, when the corky winged twigs are revealed. Looks best when unpruned, as the branches spread horizontally into graceful overlapping tiers. Makes a good single specimen or a showy mass planting or hedge. 'Compacta' is smaller (to 6 ft.), with even more intense red-pink fall color and slender wingless twigs. Zone 3.

■ *fortunei* selections p. 182
Winter creeper. A diverse group of evergreen vines and low shrubs with leathery, oval, green, green and gold, or green and white leaves. Vining forms make good ground covers or can climb a fence or tree. Include the shrubby forms in mixed borders and foundation plantings. 'Coloratus' is a vining form with dark green leaves that turn maroon in cold weather. 'Emerald Surprise' is shrubby and has variegated green, gold, and cream leaves. 'Kewensis' is a climbing vine with tiny dark green leaves. Var. *radicans* grows as a vine or shrub and has thick glossy leaves. Var. *vegetus* is rather shrubby and especially cold-hardy. Zone 5.

■ *japonicus* selections p. 156
Japanese euonymus. Evergreen shrubs, up to 10 ft. tall and 6 ft. wide, but often kept smaller by pruning. Oval leaves 1–3 in. long are smooth and glossy. The species has plain green leaves, but variegated forms are more popular. Different cultivars have leaves dotted or edged with gold, cream, or silvery white. 'Aureomarginatus' has leaves edged with gold. 'Microphyllus' has tiny dark green leaves spaced close together and makes a good substitute for boxwood. Zone 7.

Euphorbia

You-for'bee-a
Euphorbiaceae. Spurge family

Description

A giant and diverse group of herbaceous annuals and perennials, succulents, shrubs, and trees. All have a milky sap that causes a skin rash in some people. The actual flowers are usually small but may be surrounded with large, colorful, showy bracts. About 1,600 species, native worldwide.

How to Grow

Full or part sun. Tolerates poor, dry soil; salt spray; wind; and heat. Remove old or straggly stems at any time. Propagate by division in spring.

■ *myrsinites* p. 211
Myrtle euphorbia. A carefree perennial with stems 8–12 in. tall, sprawling up to 24 in. wide. Close spirals of stiff, fleshy, blue-green leaves crowd the stems; the leaves are evergreen in mild climates. Flat clusters of chartreuse or yellow flowers open in early spring. Looks good trailing down banks or over rock walls. Most other species of *Euphorbia* are also good seashore plants. Zone 5.

Euryops

Yur'yops
Compositae. Daisy family

Description

Evergreen shrubs with yellow daisylike blossoms. About 97 species, many from South Africa.

How to Grow

Full sun. Needs good drainage and tolerates dry soil once well established. Cut off old flowers to prolong bloom. Prune after heaviest bloom in early summer to control size. Combines well with shrubs or perennials in borders, makes a low-maintenance cover on banks, and does well in containers.

■ *pectinatus* p. 212
Golden shrub daisy. A shrubby evergreen perennial, 4–6 ft. tall and wide, that blooms almost continuously, with bright yellow daisies 1–2 in. wide, held on long stalks above a mound of furry, deeply cut, silvery gray-green foliage. The cultivar 'Viridis' is identical but has smooth, bright green leaves. Zone 9.

Fatsia

Fat′si-a
Araliaceae. Aralia family

Description
An evergreen shrub, grown for its bold foliage. Only 1 species, native to Japan.

How to Grow
Part sun or shade; protect from hot afternoon sun. Not fussy about soil or watering. Does well under eaves, in entryways, or in other dry, shady spots. Tolerates salt spray, but leaves can be scorched by too much sun or wind. Hard to shape by pruning; tends to grow as it chooses. Propagate by seed.

■ *japonica p. 156 Pictured above*
Japanese fatsia. A fast-growing evergreen shrub, 6–8 ft. tall, with coarse, glossy, palmately lobed leaves, often 12 in. wide and long. Sometimes makes rounded clusters of tiny white flowers on branched stalks, followed by small dark fruits. Leaves are usually dark green, but they can be edged or marked with white or gold stripes or blotches. Zone 8.

Feijoa

Fee-jo′a
Myrtaceae. Myrtle family

Description
Evergreen shrubs with opposite leaves, ornamental flowers, and edible fruits. Only 2 species, native to South America.

How to Grow
Full or part sun. Ordinary well-drained soil; tolerates dry soil but not wet sites. Space 10 ft. apart for a hedge. Branch tips may freeze back in severe winters, but it recovers with bushy new growth. Pest-free.

■ *sellowiana* p. 157

Pineapple guava. A dense, erect, evergreen shrub, to 10 ft. tall. Oval leaves are dark green above and gray below. Showy flowers in spring have waxy white petals and lots of bright red stamens; round yellow fruits ripen in fall and are very fragrant and tasty. Suitable for hedges, left unpruned for a casual mounded profile or sheared into formal shapes. Grows well in containers, and a single specimen makes a good patio plant. If you want to eat the fruit, look for 'Coolidge', 'Nazemeta', or 'Pineapple Gem' — all are self-pollinating and have good flavor. Zone 8.

Felicia

Fe-liss′ee-a
Compositae. Daisy family

Description

Annuals, perennials, or small shrubs with composite flowers on long stalks. About 83 species, most from South Africa.

How to Grow

Full sun. Ordinary or better soil and regular watering. Cut flowers often; prune to control shape. Looks good spilling from window boxes or over walls, or spreading along the front of a bed or border. Where grown as a perennial, prune hard in late summer to encourage renewed bloom.

■ *amelloides* p. 212

Blue marguerite. A shrubby evergreen perennial, often grown as an annual in cold climates. Grows 12–18 in. tall and spreads 3–4 ft. wide. The long-stalked daisylike blossoms, pure bright blue with yellow centers, open 1–2 in. wide and bloom almost continuously in mild weather. The leaves are oval and dark green and have a somewhat rough texture. 'San Gabriel', 'San Luis', and 'Santa Anita' are vigorous forms with larger-than-average blooms. Zone 9.

Festuca

Fes-too′ka. Fescue
Gramineae. Grass family

Description

Annual or perennial grasses, most forming clumps of slender leaves. Some species are used as turfgrasses, and others are ornamental. About 300 species, most of them from temperate regions.

How to Grow

Full sun. Needs well-drained soil; tolerates dry, sandy sites and salt spray. Often used as a specimen, edging, or ground cover. Space 8–10 in. apart for ground cover. Cut back once a year, in fall or spring. Can go years without division.

■ *ovina* var. *glauca*   *p. 233*

Blue fescue. A small clumping grass with very slender, almost threadlike, leaves. Forms a dense mound 6–12 in. tall and wide. The foliage is evergreen where winters are mild. Narrow spikes of flowers appear in summer; remove them before seeds develop to focus the plant's energy on foliage production. Seedling plants are commonly sold but vary considerably in blueness. The best bright blue forms, such as 'Elijah's Blue' and 'Sea Urchin', must be propagated by division. Large blue fescue, *F. amethystina,* looks similar but grows 12–24 in. tall and wide. Zone 4.

Ficus

Fy'kus. Fig
Moraceae. Mulberry family

Description

Trees, shrubs, or clinging vines, nearly all with thick evergreen leaves. All figs have sticky milky sap and bear flowers and seeds inside a fleshy receptacle — the fig. About 800 species, from tropical and warm climates worldwide.

How to Grow

Part sun, with shade from the hot afternoon sun or winter sun. Well-drained soil with regular watering; these plants do not recover well from wilting. Prune anytime to control size or shape.

■ *microcarpa* var. *nitida*   *p. 106*

Indian laurel fig. A neat, shapely, evergreen tree, usually 25–30 ft. tall. It has an erect trunk with smooth, pale gray bark and a dense crown of glossy, thick, bright green, oval leaves, 2–4 in. long. Can be sheared into formal shapes or used for hedges. The tiny fruits are dry and inedible, small enough not to be messy. The species, *F. microcarpa,* has similar leaves but is weeping in form, with branches trailing nearly to the ground unless trimmed. Severe freezes can disfigure or kill these trees. Zone 9.

Forsythia

For-sith´ee-a
Oleaceae. Olive family

Description
Deciduous shrubs with showy, yellow, 4-petaled flowers in early spring before the leaves appear. Just 7 species, native to Europe and Asia.

How to Grow
Full sun. Ordinary soil. Needs watering during dry spells. Tolerates pruning but looks better if you give it room to spread naturally into a graceful mound or broad hedge or let it scramble into adjacent trees or tumble down a rough bank. Renew periodically by cutting some of the oldest shoots to the ground, immediately after flowering.

■ × *intermedia* *p. 133*
Forsythia. A vigorous and adaptable deciduous shrub, to 8 ft. or taller, with long arching shoots. Cheerful yellow flowers cover the stems in early spring, before the leaves expand. (Don't be surprised to find scattered blooms again in late fall.) Oval leaves with toothed margins are dull green in summer, turning maroon in fall. Selected cultivars have more compact growth and bigger or brighter flowers. Zone 4.

Fraxinus

Frax´in-us. Ash
Oleaceae. Olive family

Description
Deciduous or evergreen trees with opposite leaves, usually pinnately compound. Trees produce small flowers in early spring, winged fruits in summer or fall. Many species are harvested for their strong resilient timber. About 65 species, most native to the north temperate zone.

How to Grow
Full or part sun. Grows in almost any soil and tolerates moderate drought once established. Easy to transplant and needs only routine pruning. Makes a good shade tree and roots aren't bothered by cultivation, so you can underplant with shrubs and perennials.

■ *pennsylvanica* *p. 91*
Green ash. A deciduous tree that grows quickly (2 ft. or more a year) and reaches about 50 ft. tall. The compound leaves

cast a medium shade and turn gold in fall. Plant only nursery-propagated cultivars, which have neat symmetrical
branching and don't produce seeds; seedlings are a nuisance
and grow into irregular, weedy trees. Look for 'Bergeson',
'Marshall's Seedless', 'Newport', 'Patmore', or 'Summit'.
Sometimes listed as *F. pennsylvanica* var. *lanceolata* or *F.
pennsylvanica* var. *subintegerrima*. Native throughout the
eastern United States. Zone 2.

Fuchsia
Few'sha
Onagraceae. Evening primrose family

Description
Most are tender evergreen shrubs or small trees, with simple
leaves and showy flowers that dangle like earrings from the
stems. About 100 species, most native to Central and South
America.

How to Grow
Full sun along the coast, part shade inland. Avoid dry, windy
locations. Best in fertile soil amended with plenty of organic
matter. Water regularly and fertilize every 2 weeks during the
growing season. Pinch tips often to promote branching. Of
the many fuchsias available, the cultivar below is one of the
easiest to grow in most conditions. It is very resistant to the
fuchsia bud mite, a serious pest.

■ **'Gartenmeister Bonstedt'**   *p. 213*
'Gartenmeister Bonstedt' fuchsia. An evergreen shrub, usually
treated as an annual, with vigorous upright shoots up to 3 ft.
tall. Can be trained as a standard (tree form) or pinched into
a bushy mound. Opposite oval leaves are dark green with
purple veins. Drooping clusters of narrow, coral-red flowers
are borne from summer to fall (continuing nearly all year in
mild climates) and attract hummingbirds. Zone 9.

Another relatively easy-to-grow fuchsia is the hardy fuchsia, sold as *F. magellanica* or fuchsia 'Riccartonii'. It dies to
the ground after hard frost but recovers in spring, bearing
red-purple flowers on upright stems that reach 3 ft. or more
in a season. Zone 7.

Gaillardia
Gay-lar'dee-a
Compositae. Daisy family

Description

Annuals, biennials, or perennials with hairy leaves and showy daisylike blossoms, usually in various combinations of dark red and yellow. About 28 species, most native to North America.

How to Grow

Full sun. Tolerates poor soil and drought. Very adaptable and easy to grow. Propagate from seed (seedlings may bloom the first year) or by division. Deadheading improves appearance and prolongs bloom.

■ × *grandiflora* *p. 213*

Blanket flower. A perennial prairie wildflower that forms a mound 2–3 ft. tall and wide. Blooms all year in mild areas and throughout the summer and fall months in colder regions. The daisylike blossoms are 3–4 in. wide; red to yellow with orange, red, or maroon banding; and good for cutting. The basal foliage is rough-textured and gray-green. 'Goblin' is a dwarf cultivar, with large flowers on stems only 1 ft. tall. *G. aristata* and *G. pulchella,* the parents of this hybrid species, are also popular wildflowers. Zone 4.

Garrya

Gar′ee-a. Silk tassel
Garryaceae. Silk tassel family

Description

Evergreen shrubs or small trees, with simple opposite leaves and showy dangling catkins. Only 13 species, most native to western North America.

How to Grow

Full sun or part shade. Fertile, well-drained soil. Once established, survives on minimal water in coastal sites but requires supplemental watering if planted inland. Can be used as a specimen or hedge. If desired, shape by pruning immediately after flowering. Catkins are borne on the tips of the previous season's growth.

■ *elliptica* *p. 157*

Coast silk tassel. An evergreen shrub, usually 8–10 ft. tall but sometimes grown as a small tree up to 20 ft. tall. Has multiple trunks and a dense, rounded crown of leathery dark green leaves. Silvery clusters of pendulous male catkins, 3–10 in. long, are borne in winter and early spring and look very showy against the dark foliage. 'James Roof' has unusually long catkins, up to 12 in. long. Native along the coast from central California through Oregon. Zone 8.

Gaura
Gaw´ra
Onagraceae. Evening primrose family

Description
Perennials or annuals with plain leaves and small white or pink flowers. About 20 species, native to North America.

How to Grow
Sun or shade. Not fussy about soil or watering. Prune old shoots to the ground in spring. Propagate by seed. May self-sow but isn't weedy. Don't try to divide or transplant old plants; they have big, deep roots.

■ *lindheimeri* *p. 214*
White gaura. A perennial wildflower that forms a sprawling clump of graceful arching stems 3–5 ft. tall. The reddish color of the stems shows through the sparse slender foliage. New flowers open continually at the tips of the stems from mid-spring to hard frost. Individual blossoms are starlike, about 1 in. wide, opening white and aging to pink. Native to Louisiana and Texas. Zone 6.

Gazania
Ga-zay´nee-a
Compositae. Daisy family

Description
Perennial herbs with a basal rosette of variably lobed leaves, and composite flowers borne singly on long stalks. About 16 species, most native to South Africa.

How to Grow
Full sun. Any well-drained soil. Maintain moderate fertility, avoiding excess nitrogen. Gazanias are very tolerant of heat, drought, salt spray, and wind and thrive in coastal conditions. Propagate by seed or by division in spring or fall. Nursery plants are sold in flats or individual containers; space 12 in. apart for complete cover. Plants are most often used as a fast-growing ground cover or filler, but gazanias also do well in containers.

■ *ringens* p. 214
Treasure flower, gazania. A showy perennial with daisylike
flowers 2–3 in. wide on stalks 12 in. tall. Can also be grown
as an annual in cold-winter climates. There are many cultivars
and hybrids, with single or double flowers in shades of red,
purple, pink, orange, yellow, white, and bicolors. Blooms winter to late spring in Mediterranean climates; continues all summer if plants receive moisture. Forms basal rosettes of slender
leaves that are dark green above, white below. Zone 9.

■ *ringens* var. *leucolaena*
Trailing gazania. A trailing plant with bright orange-yellow
blossoms on stalks that reach up to 12 in. tall, above a low,
dense patch of small, slender, gray leaves. Usually grown as
a groundcover. Zone 9.

Gelsemium
Jel-see´mee-um
Loganiaceae. Buddleia family

Description
Woody evergreen vines with fragrant, yellow, funnel-shaped
flowers. All parts of the plant are poisonous. Only 2 or 3
species, one or two from eastern North America, the other
from eastern Asia.

How to Grow
Full or part sun. Ordinary soil and watering. Tolerates hot
sun, wind, and salt spray. Climbs by twining around a trellis, tree trunk, or other support. Prune after flowering to encourage branching and to keep it tidy.

■ *sempervirens* p. 194
Carolina jasmine, yellow jasmine. An evergreen vine that can
climb to 20 ft. or taller but is easily kept shorter and bushier
by pruning. Clusters of fragrant yellow blossoms, about 1 in.
long, start opening in very early spring and continue for several weeks. The slender leaves are dark green in summer, purplish in winter. 'Pride of Augusta' has double flowers. Native
from Virginia to Texas. Zone 8.

Gleditsia
Gle-dit´see-a. Honey locust
Leguminosae. Legume family

Description
Deciduous trees with pinnately compound leaves, stout branched thorns, small greenish flowers, and large flattened woody pods. About 14 species, native to the Old and New World.

How to Grow
Full or part sun. Native to rich bottomlands throughout the eastern United States but isn't fussy in cultivation. Tolerates poor soil, salt spray, wind, and drought. Casts a light shade and has deep roots, so it can be underplanted with turfgrass, ground covers, perennials, or shrubs. Fast-growing and needs little care or pruning.

■ *triacanthos* p. 91
Honey locust. A large deciduous tree, 40–60 ft. tall, with a spreading crown. The lacy, fernlike, compound leaves are dark green in summer, turning gold in fall. Flowers are inconspicuous. Wild or seedling trees have startling thorns and shed profuse crops of long, curving pods. Selected cultivars such as 'Imperial', 'Moraine', 'Shademaster', and 'Skyline' are thornless and bear few pods, and they have better-than-average vigor and shape. Zone 4.

Gypsophila
Jip-sof′fil-la. Baby's breath
Caryophyllaceae. Pink family

Description
Annuals or perennials with opposite small leaves that disappear under a cloud of bloom. Flowers are small but very numerous, borne in profusely branched panicles. About 125 species, native to the Old World.

How to Grow
Full sun. Needs well-drained soil with plenty of lime. The double cultivars are often grafted; if so, plant with the graft below the soil surface. Large plants may need staking. Shear back after flowering to promote repeat bloom.

■ *paniculata* p. 215
Baby's breath. A popular perennial for flower beds and arrangements, bearing hundreds of small, single or double, white or pink flowers. Stems branch repeatedly and make a clump about 3 ft. tall and wide. The gray-green leaves are narrow and sparse. There are also dwarf forms, under 2 ft. tall. Creeping baby's breath, *G. repens,* has similar flowers

but forms a low mat of woolly gray foliage, good for rock gardens. Zone 4.

Hakea

Hay'kee-a. Pincushion tree
Proteaceae. Protea family

Description
Drought-tolerant evergreen shrubs with unusual stiff foliage. About 125 species, native to Australia.

How to Grow
Full sun. Tolerates poor, infertile soil but needs good drainage and will not tolerate excess water. Very tolerant of coastal conditions, heat, and drought once established. Can be used as a barrier, windbreak, background, or screen. Propagated by seed.

■ *suaveolens* p. 158
Sweet hakea. An evergreen shrub, usually 10–12 ft. tall. Forms a broad mound with upright sweeping branches. Resembles a pine, partly because its leaves are divided into prickly, needlelike segments. Fluffy round heads of fragrant white flowers appear mostly in fall and winter. Woody, nutlike fruits are prized for use in dried arrangements. Zone 9.

Hardenbergia

Har-den-ber'gee-a
Leguminosae. Legume family

Description
Small shrubs or vines with evergreen foliage and showy flowers. Only 3 species, native to Australia.

How to Grow
Full sun. Any well-drained soil; can't take extra water. Will climb a support or trail over a bank. Prune after flowering to encourage branching and to control size and shape.

■ *violacea* p. 195
Lilac vine. A shrubby vine that sprawls or climbs by twining, reaching 8–10 ft. tall. Evergreen leaves are slender, oblong, 2–4 in. long. Drooping clusters of small pealike pink-purple or white flowers are showy for several weeks in early spring. Zone 9.

Hebe

He´be
Scrophulariaceae. Foxglove family

Description
Evergreen shrubs or trees with opposite leaves and spikes of small flowers. Closely related to *Veronica*. About 75 species, most from Australia and New Zealand.

How to Grow
Full sun. Does best in light, sandy soil amended with organic matter. Water regularly during dry periods. Subject to fungal root rot in heavy clay soil or if overwatered. Grows quickly. Prune as needed to shape the plant and to remove old flower heads. Thrives near the seashore but doesn't live long in hot inland situations.

■ *speciosa* *p. 158*
Showy hebe. A dense, spreading evergreen shrub, 2–5 ft. tall, depending on growing conditions. Opposite leaves are glossy, deep green, about 4 in. long. Bottlebrush-like spikes of small reddish purple flowers cover the bush from midsummer to early fall. Zone 7.

Helenium

Hell-lee´nee-um. Sneezeweed
Compositae. Daisy family

Description
Annuals or perennials with clusters of composite flowers, usually in shades of yellow, maroon, reddish brown, or purple. About 40 species, native to North America.

How to Grow
Full sun. Prefers fertile, organic soil and regular watering. Tolerates damp sites. Easy to grow. Prune stems back by one-third in early summer to force branching and to reduce height. Propagate by division in spring or fall.

■ *autumnale* *p. 215*
Helen's flower, sneezeweed. An adaptable perennial that spreads to make a patch of leafy stems 4–5 ft. tall. Bears daisylike blossoms 2–3 in. wide over a long season from midsummer to fall. Good for informal borders or meadow gardens, in combination with other wildflowers and grasses. There are several cultivars and hybrids with yellow, red, orange, or bronze flowers. All make good cut flowers. Zone 3.

Hemerocallis

Hem-mer-o-kal'lis. Daylily
Liliaceae. Lily family

Description

Perennials with funnel- or bell-shaped flowers held on a branched stalk above a clump of narrow arching leaves. About 15 species, most native to China or Japan, and many hybrids. There are thousands of named cultivars.

How to Grow

Full sun or light afternoon shade where summers are hot. For best results, prepare the soil well by digging about 12 in. deep and working in plenty of organic matter. Space plants 18–24 in. apart and mulch well. Water regularly from spring to fall. Rarely touched by insects or diseases, daylilies require very little maintenance. Some multiply fast enough to be divided every few years; others can grow undisturbed for decades. Divide crowded plants in spring or fall and replant in freshly prepared soil.

■ **hybrids** *p. 216*
Hybrid daylilies. Popular, carefree perennials that form dense clumps of patches of slender grassy foliage and bear showy flowers on stalks 1–6 ft. tall. Each flower lasts only a day, but new buds open over a period of weeks. Flowers range from 2 in. to 7 in. wide, in shades of cream, yellow, orange, pink, and red. Most cultivars bloom for just a month or so, but by planting several different kinds, you can have a nonstop show from May or June through late September. 'Stella d'Oro', one of the most popular daylilies, blooms almost continually, with gold flowers 3 in. wide on stalks only 1 ft. tall. Zone 4.

Heuchera

Hew'ker-a. Alumroot
Saxifragaceae. Saxifrage family

Description

Perennials with thick rhizomes, a tuft of rounded or lobed basal leaves, and many tiny cup-shaped flowers on slender stalks. About 55 species, native to North America.

How to Grow

Full sun or part shade. Well-drained soil with frequent watering during dry spells. Makes a good edging or ground cover. Space about 18 in. apart, positioning the crown level with the soil surface. Divide every few years in early spring. Remove stalks of faded flowers to prolong bloom.

■ **hybrids** *p. 217*
Coralbells. An old-fashioned perennial that makes a low mound of thick, leathery, almost evergreen leaves, which may be round or kidney-shaped, toothed or lobed, crimped or ruffled. Wiry stalks 12–24 in. tall hold tiny flowers well above the foliage, forming an airy cloud of bloom. Blooms for weeks in early summer. There are many cultivars, with dark or bright red, pale or rosy pink, or pure white flowers. 'Palace Purple' has insignificant flowers but lovely purple-bronze leaves. Zone 4.

Hibiscus

Hy-bis′kus. Mallow
Malvaceae. Mallow family

Description
A diverse group of annuals, perennials, shrubs, and trees, most with showy bell-shaped flowers. About 200 species, occurring worldwide.

How to Grow
Full sun. The species below are native to damp sites and prefer moist, fertile soil but grow well with ordinary soil and watering. Cut down old stalks in fall or early spring. Be patient; new shoots don't emerge until quite late in spring. Clumps don't spread much and fill the same space year after year. Propagate by seed. It's difficult to move or divide established plants.

■ *moscheutos* *p. 217*
Rose mallow. A big, bold perennial that makes a clump of leafy stalks 4–6 ft. tall. Giant hollyhock-like flowers are white, pink, rose, or red, often with darker-colored centers. The 'Dixie Belle' and 'Southern Belle' strains have especially large flowers (up to 12 in. wide) on compact (2–4 ft. tall) plants. Too big and bold for most perennial borders but good for summer color in a hedge of spring-blooming shrubs. Try massing several over a bed of daffodils or other spring bulbs; the mallows emerge late, then fill in quickly and cover the yellowing bulb leaves. Native along the East Coast from Connecticut to Florida. Zone 5.

Hippophae

Hi-pof'ay-ee
Elaeagnaceae. Buckthorn family

Description

Deciduous shrubs or small trees, covered with silvery scales.
Only 3 species, native to Eurasia.

How to Grow

Full sun. Tolerates poor, dry, sandy soil; wind; salt spray; and
other coastal conditions. Not common at nurseries but easy
to grow if you can get it, and it makes an unusual and showy
specimen. Needs little pruning but can be trimmed to control
size and shape.

■ *rhamnoides* *p. 134*

Sea buckthorn. Usually a rugged-looking shrub 6–10 ft. tall
but can grow as a tree up to 30 ft. Deciduous leaves are slender and willowlike and have a silvery surface. Small male and
female flowers are borne on separate plants; if pollinated, females bear abundant crops of bright orange berries in fall.
The berries are edible, but most people leave them for the
birds. Zone 3.

Hydrangea

Hy-dran'jee-a
Saxifragaceae. Saxifrage family

Description

Deciduous or evergreen shrubs with opposite rounded leaves
and bushy clusters of white, pink, or blue flowers. More than
20 species, native to North and South America and eastern
Asia.

How to Grow

Full or part sun. The following hydrangeas prefer rich, fertile
soil amended with plenty of organic matter and need regular
watering throughout the growing season, but they tolerate
coastal conditions well. Once established, they are carefree
and long-lived.

■ *anomala* ssp. *petiolaris* *p. 195*

Climbing hydrangea. An excellent vine, slow at first but eventually climbing to 50 ft. or more up a tree, chimney, or wall.
(It clings by rootlets that don't harm masonry.) Leafy flowering branches extend 3 ft. from the anchored stems, bearing

flat lacy clusters of slightly fragrant white flowers for several
weeks in summer. The rounded leaves are glossy dark green.
The trunk and twigs have beautiful, peeling, cinnamon-col-
ored bark. Zone 5.

■ *macrophylla* *p. 134*
Garden hydrangea. A deciduous shrub with stout, erect, un-
branched stems 3–6 ft. tall, topped with rounded clusters of
white, pink, rose, or blue flowers in summer and fall. Broad
opposite leaves have a thick texture and shiny green color.
There are hundreds of cultivars, in two groups. 'Pia', 'Nikko
Blue', and other "hortensia" types have domed clusters of
flowers that are all sterile, with conspicuous, papery, petallike
sepals. 'Mariesii' and other "lacecap" types have flatter clusters with small fertile flowers in the middle and a lacy ring of
sterile flowers around the edge. Flower color varies with soil
pH: acidic conditions improve blue coloring; neutral to alkaline conditions favor the pink and red colors. Severe winter
cold can destroy hydrangea flower buds, which form on the
previous year's growth, but hydrangeas bloom reliably where
winters are mild. The plants are hardy to Zone 6.

Iberis
Eye-beer´is. Candytuft
Cruciferae. Mustard family

Description
Annuals or evergreen perennials, mostly small and low, with
clusters of white, pink, or purplish flowers. About 30 species,
native to Europe and the Mediterranean region.

How to Grow
Full or part sun. Needs well-drained, neutral or limy soil.
Water occasionally during long dry spells. Makes a good edging for raised beds or stone terraces and combines well with
early spring bulbs. Shear hard after blooming to keep plants
neat and compact. Propagate by seed or by division in spring
or fall.

■ *sempervirens* *p. 218*
Evergreen candytuft. A shrubby perennial, 6–12 in. tall, that
makes a spreading mat of trailing stems densely packed with
blunt, oblong, evergreen leaves. Small, 4-petaled, bright white
flowers form clusters up and down the stems in spring, continuing for weeks if the weather stays cool. Sometimes re-
blooms in fall. Zone 3.

Ilex

Eye'lecks. Holly
Aquifoliaceae. Holly family

Description

A diverse genus of trees and shrubs. Most are evergreen and have glossy leaves, often with spines around the edge. Some are deciduous, with smooth spineless leaves. Clusters of small flowers are borne in spring on separate male and female plants. Females produce round red, gold, white, or black berries, which can last from late summer until spring. About 400 species, native worldwide, and many hybrids and cultivars.

How to Grow

Full sun, part sun, or shade. Average garden soil. The following hollies are well adapted to coastal conditions. Once established, they need little care. Prune in winter, if desired, to control shape and size. Use dormant oil spray in winter to control various insect pests, particularly scale.

For good berry production, you need both sexes. Usually one male will suffice to pollinate 10–20 females. They don't need to be planted side by side, as bees will carry the pollen several hundred yards. If there's already a suitable male holly in your neighborhood, you don't need to plant another.

■ *aquifolium* p. 106

English holly. An evergreen tree that makes a neat, pyramidal specimen up to 30 ft. tall. Leaves are spiny and very glossy. The small white flowers open for about 2 weeks in May or June and have a sweet fragrance. Abundant crops of red berries are showy all winter. Although best adapted to the Pacific Northwest, it can also be grown in parts of the Mid-Atlantic states and Southeast where summers are not too hot and humid. Where it thrives, it makes a wonderful specimen, screen, or hedge. There are hundreds of cultivars, differing in leaf color (many are variegated with white or yellow), leaf size, spininess, sex, and hardiness. 'Argentea-marginata' is a female with white-edged leaves. 'Balkans' (both male and female) is the hardiest English holly. 'Sparkler' bears heavy crops of shiny berries, even as a young plant. Zone 6.

■ *cornuta* p. 159

Chinese holly. A tough evergreen shrub, usually under 10 ft. tall, that thrives in hot weather. There are several cultivars; most make irregular mounded shrubs, useful in foundation plantings and for hedges and specimens. The evergreen leaves feel like plastic and have a shiny rich green color. Berries are very big, bright red, and long-lasting, but plants need a long hot summer for berries to develop.

The typical Chinese holly has nearly rectangular leaves, 2–3 in. long, with sharp spines at the corners and tip. It makes a large upright shrub. 'Burfordii' is a vigorous grower that gets 15–20 ft. tall, has almost spineless leaves that cup downward, and bears a heavy crop of berries. It makes a good hedge or can be pruned into tree form. 'Dwarf Burford' has smaller leaves and berries and stays under 10 ft. 'Carissa' has spineless leaves, does not produce berries, and stays under 4 ft. tall. 'Rotunda' has stout spines on the leaves and no berries; it grows to 4 ft. tall and makes a formidable burglar-proof barrier planting under windows. Zone 7.

■ *glabra* p. 159

Inkberry. A hardy evergreen shrub, up to 8 ft. tall, with narrow spineless leaves about 2 in. long and small blue-black berries. Native to wet sites along the East Coast, but it also tolerates dry soil. Tends to grow upright and leggy, but shearing or pruning forces more branching near the base. 'Compacta' is a dense-growing female, 4–6 ft. tall, good for hedging. Zone 5.

■ × *meserveae* p. 160

Meserve hybrid hollies. These hybrid hollies are evergreen shrubs, 8–12 ft. tall, with beautiful foliage, large bright red berries, and good cold-hardiness. 'Blue Girl', 'Blue Boy', and the other "Blue" cultivars all have very dark blue-green foliage. Most grow into shrubby upright pyramids. A related group of hybrids, the 'China Boy', 'China Girl', and other "China" hollies are handsome mounded plants with rich dark green leaves; they tolerate hot weather better than the "Blue" hollies do. All do best if shaded from direct sun in winter; avoid planting on the south side of a building. Zone 5.

■ 'Nellie R. Stevens' p. 160

'Nellie R. Stevens' holly. A tough, durable hybrid holly that makes a handsome pyramidal tree 15–25 ft. tall or can be pruned into a dense hedge (space 5–10 ft. apart). Fast-growing and trouble-free. The dark green evergreen leaves are waxy-textured, 1–2 in. long, with just a few spines. If pollinated by a male Chinese holly (*I. cornuta*), it bears a heavy crop of bright red berries. Zone 7.

■ *opaca* p. 107 *Pictured on next page*

American holly. An evergreen tree native to the eastern United States, where its cultivars are common and popular. Grows upright with a rounded or pyramidal crown. Can reach 50

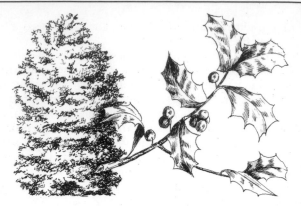

ft., but 20–30 ft. is more common. The leathery leaves have spiny edges and may be dark green or a yellowish olive green. Berries are dull red. Selected cultivars such as 'Christmas Carol', 'Merry Christmas', and 'Greenleaf' have much prettier leaves and berries than most wild plants do. Prefers moist soil and needs a site protected from winter sun and wind. Zone 5.

■ *vomitoria* p. 161

Yaupon holly. An evergreen shrub or tree native to the southeastern United States, with small, narrow, dark green leaves and huge crops of small, juicy-looking, red berries. Easily trained as a small multitrunked tree, 15–20 ft. tall, with picturesque crooked trunks and limbs. Dwarf cultivars make compact mounds of foliage and can be sheared into any desired shape. Adapts to almost any soil. Grows quickly and makes a good hedge or screen; also popular for foundation plantings. Zone 7.

Juniperus

Jew-nip'er-us. Juniper
Cupressaceae. Cypress family

Description

Evergreen conifers, including low, spreading shrubs and upright trees. Leaves are needlelike or scalelike. Female cones are berrylike. Wood, foliage, and fruits are often very fragrant. About 50 species, native to the Old and New World.

How to Grow

The following junipers all need full sun and well-drained soil. They are easy to transplant and need little care. Once established, they tolerate drought. Prune in late winter if desired.

Subject to bagworms and spider mites inland but generally trouble-free in coastal sites.

■ *chinensis* cultivars *p. 161*
Junipers. This useful group of evergreen shrubs and trees includes several cultivars that thrive by the sea and make excellent ground covers, screens, or specimens. Most have needlelike juvenile foliage and scalelike adult foliage, sometimes mixed on the same plant; the foliage has a pleasant sweet fragrance when crushed. Fruits are pea-sized blue balls.

The following cultivars are especially tolerant of coastal sun, wind, and salt. They are sometimes listed under the species *J. × media*. 'Armstrongii' has scaly olive green leaves and grows about 3 ft. tall and wide. Zone 6. 'Hetzii' is a fast grower that gets 10 ft. tall and 12 ft. or wider, with many trunks that reach out in all directions at a 45° angle. Its foliage is blue-green, often discoloring in winter. Zone 4. 'Maney' is bushy and upright, about 6 ft. tall and wide, with blue-green foliage. Zone 4. Var. *sargentii* has short bright green needles and grows only 2 ft. tall but spreads up to 10 ft. wide. Zone 4. 'Torulosa' or 'Kaizuka', commonly called Hollywood juniper, grows upright to 20 ft. or more, with irregular branching that makes an interesting asymmetric profile. It has dense, scalelike, bright green foliage. The various Pfitzer cultivars, also in this species, are more sensitive to salt and don't do as well by the sea. Zone 5.

■ *conferta* *p. 182*
Shore juniper. A low, spreading evergreen that makes an excellent ground cover for seashore gardens. Stays only 1-2 ft. tall and spreads 8–10 ft. wide. The needles are thin and about $\frac{1}{2}$ in. long and have a fairly soft texture. 'Blue Pacific', with bright blue-gray foliage, and 'Emerald Sea', with green foliage, are especially prostrate, fast-growing, and attractive. These junipers can be used to cover rocky hillsides, trail over walls, or stabilize sandy coastal dunes. Zone 6.

■ *horizontalis* cultivars
Creeping junipers. These low, spreading shrubs, usually under 2 ft. tall and spreading to 6 ft. or wider, are excellent ground covers. There are hundreds of cultivars, varying in foliage texture, color, and habit. Some of the best for seashore gardens, with excellent salt tolerance, are 'Bar Harbor', which has flat matted foliage, blue-gray in summer and blue-purple in winter; 'Blue Chip', mounding higher, with a good silver-blue color most of the year; and 'Wiltonii' or 'Blue Rug', which is flat and trailing and has silvery blue foliage. 'Plumosa' or 'An-

dorra', with fluffy shoots that arch like a low fountain, is popular inland but sensitive to salt and needs protection from sea winds. Zone 2.

■ *procumbens* 'Nana' *p. 183*
Dwarf Japanese garden juniper. A compact, slow-growing shrub, excellent for foundation plantings and small gardens because it grows only 1 ft. tall and 3 ft. wide, with an irregular mounded shape. The needlelike leaves are bright green. Zone 5.

■ *virginiana* *p. 107*
Eastern red cedar. An evergreen tree up to 30 ft. tall, common throughout the eastern United States. Tough and adaptable, it makes a fast screen and provides shelter and berries for birds. Young shoots are prickly; older branches have flat fans of scalelike foliage. Selected cultivars have distinct shapes and more attractive foliage than wild or seedling trees. 'Canaert' is upright with spreading branches and stays rich green all year. 'Gray Owl' is a spreading form, under 3–4 ft. tall, with silvery blue foliage. Zone 2.

Kniphofia
Nip-ho´fee-a. Red-hot-poker, torch lily
Liliaceae. Lily family

Description
Perennials with thick roots, tough grassy leaves, and showy spikes of bright red or yellow flowers. About 65 species, native to Africa, and dozens of hybrid cultivars.

How to Grow
Full or part sun. Ordinary or dry soil. Remove old flower stalks after bloom, and trim foliage to the ground in late fall. Increase by division, taking care not to break too many of the thonglike roots. Trouble-free.

■ hybrids *p. 218*
Torch lilies. Showy perennials with glowing scarlet, orange-red, golden, or yellow flowers on dramatic spikes up to 6 ft. tall. Plants bloom in spring or summer. The 2-in.-long tubular flowers are very attractive to hummingbirds, and the spikes are spectacular and long-lasting in cut arrangements. The basal foliage is a tangled mound of coarse, strongly keeled, gray-green leaves, 1 in. wide and up to 3 ft. long. Cultivars differ in flower color, bloom period, and height. Zone 5.

Koelreuteria

Kel-roo-teer'ee-a. Golden-rain tree
Sapindaceae. Soapberry family

Description

Deciduous trees with pinnate leaves and big clusters of yellow flowers, followed by papery inflated pods. Only 3 species, native to China and Taiwan.

How to Grow

Full sun. Not fussy about soil. Needs watering when young but tolerates drought once established. Must be pruned to shape; branching tends to be haphazard. Sometimes self-seeds. No serious pests.

■ *paniculata* p. 92
Golden-rain tree. A tough, adaptable, and showy deciduous tree, 30–35 ft. tall. Develops a spreading crown, good for shading lawns and patios. The large leaves are compound, with many jagged leaflets. Profuse clusters of bright yellow flowers cover the crown in midsummer. The puffy, pinkish beige seedpods that follow are almost as showy as the flowers and hang on into winter. Zone 5.

Kosteletzkya

Kos-tel-etz'kee-a
Malvaceae. Mallow family

Description

Perennials or small shrubs with tough stems, simple alternate leaves, and hibiscus-like flowers. About 30 species, mostly tropical.

How to Grow

Full sun. Average or constantly moist soil. Purchase container-grown plants or start your own from seed. Once established, they're difficult to move or divide. Cut stalks to the ground after frost.

■ *virginica* p. 219
Seashore mallow. A big, bushy perennial that makes a vase-shaped clump of stiff branching stems, 4–6 ft. tall. Widely spaced, irregularly lobed foliage gives an open, not dense, effect. Bears hundreds of soft pink flowers, 2–3 in. wide with 5 rounded petals, over a long season in late summer and early fall. Native to salt marshes along the East Coast. Zone 5.

Lantana

Lan-ta′na
Verbenaceae. Verbena family

Description
Perennials or shrubs, often with prickly stems and rough leaves, that bear rounded clusters of small bright flowers and black berries. About 150 species, most native to tropical America. Many of the newest cultivars are hybrids between the 2 species listed below.

How to Grow
Full sun. Not fussy about soil. Lantanas tolerate heat, wind, drought, and salt. They freeze back in cold winters but recover from the base; remove damaged wood in spring. Prune to shape as desired.

■ *camara* p. 162
Lantana. A semievergreen shrub that forms a low mound, 2–4 ft. high and 2–6 ft. wide. Hardy in mild climates and often grown as a bedding plant where winters are cold. It also grows well in containers — anything from patio half-barrels to hanging baskets. It blooms from late spring to frost, with rounded clusters of small flowers in shades of creamy white, yellow, gold, pink, orange, red, and bicolor. The simple, opposite, dark green leaves feel scratchy and smell pungent; they drop off when temperatures fall below freezing. Zone 9.

■ *montevidensis* p. 183 *Pictured above*
Trailing lantana. A sprawling shrub that spreads 2–4 ft. wide, with dark green foliage and lavender blossoms. It trails from planter boxes or makes a good ground cover, and it's somewhat more cold-hardy than common lantana. Zone 8.

Laurus

Law′rus. Laurel, bay
Lauraceae. Laurel family

Description
Evergreen trees with aromatic leaves, long used as a flavoring. Only 2 species, native to the Mediterranean region and adjacent Atlantic islands.

How to Grow
Full sun or afternoon shade. Ordinary soil and watering; tolerates dry spells once established. Space 3–4 ft. apart for a hedge. Shape with pruning shears, not hedge shears, to avoid mutilating the foliage. Can be trained into lollipop standards or formal cones, balls, or pyramids. Use horticultural oil spray to control scale and psyllids.

■ *nobilis* *p. 108*
Sweet bay, bay laurel. A dense evergreen shrub or tree, 10–40 ft. tall, that can be an impenetrable screen or a carefully shaped specimen. The pointed oval leaves are stiff, leathery, dark green, and pleasantly fragrant when crushed. Tight clusters of small greenish yellow flowers are inconspicuous in early spring, but shiny black fruits are sometimes evident in fall. Zone 8.

Lavandula
La-van´dew-la. Lavender
Labiatae. Mint family

Description
Perennials or shrubs, mostly evergreen in mild climates, with very fragrant foliage and flowers. About 20 species, native to the Mediterranean region and surrounding areas.

How to Grow
Full sun. Needs well-drained neutral or alkaline, not acidic, soil. Tolerates drought once established. Where the soil is heavy, plant "high" by positioning the crown above the surrounding grade so that water will run away from the plant. In cold areas, prune back frozen shoots in late spring and remove old stalks as flowers fade. Don't prune after midsummer, or soft new shoots will be killed in winter. In mild regions, prune as desired. Can be cut back hard to renew leggy, untidy plants. Pest-free.

■ *angustifolia* *p. 219*
English lavender, common lavender. A low shrub or perennial that makes a bushy mound of foliage 1–3 ft. tall and wide. The closely spaced leaves are stiff and slender, 1–2 in. long,

with a fuzzy gray surface. Makes a soft low hedge or edging, or can be massed with other drought-tolerant shrubs to fill a dry sunny slope. Evergreen only in mild climates; it discolors and then freezes back where winters are cold. Wonderfully fragrant flowers form crowded spikes on slender stalks above the foliage and bloom for several weeks in summer. Herb nurseries offer dozens of cultivars. 'Hidcote' has dark purple flowers, 'Jean Davis' has pale pink, and 'Munstead' has lavender-blue. *L.* × *intermedia,* lavandin, is a hardy, vigorous, hybrid lavender that has even sweeter, more intensely scented flowers. Zone 5.

Leptospermum

Lep-to-sper´mum. Tea tree
Myrtaceae. Myrtle family

Description
Evergreen shrubs or small trees, most with slender aromatic leaves and small flowers, usually white. About 30 species, most native to Australia.

How to Grow
Full sun. Needs well-drained soil. Tolerates sandy or rocky sites but succumbs to root rot in clay. Thrives in ocean wind. Pinch tips of young plants to encourage dense growth. Shear mature plants to shape. Don't prune back to bare wood. Pest-free.

■ *scoparium p. 163*
New Zealand tea tree. A fine-textured evergreen shrub, 6–10 ft. tall, with small, tough, needlelike leaves. Small, single or double, white, pink, or red flowers are crowded along the branches over a long season in spring and summer. Combines well with other drought-tolerant plants in a mixed border, or can be trained as a single-stemmed standard in the ground or in a container. There are several good cultivars. *L. laevigatum,* the Australian tea tree, grows larger and has oval gray-green leaves, white flowers, and a picturesque angular profile. Both species are hardy to Zone 9.

Leucothoe

Loo-ko´tho-ee. Fetterbush
Ericaceae. Heath family

Description

Evergreen (and a few deciduous) shrubs with simple alternate leaves and clusters of small, pink or white, bell-shaped flowers. More than 40 species, native to North and South America and eastern Asia.

How to Grow

Part sun or shade. Needs fertile, acidic, organic soil and constant moisture. Prune after flowering. The species below is less common at nurseries than *L. fontanesiana*, drooping leucothoe, but it is more compact, tolerates heat better, and has healthier foliage.

■ *axillaris* p. 163

Coast leucothoe. A very hardy and graceful evergreen shrub, 2–4 ft. tall. Branches arch into a spreading mound and tend to zigzag. Glossy leathery leaves, 1–3 in. long, are dark green in summer and reddish purple or purplish bronze in winter. Clusters of small fragrant white flowers bloom in spring. A good plant for small gardens or foundation plantings. Native from Virginia to Florida. Zone 5.

Ligustrum

Li-gus'trum. Privet
Oleaceae. Olive family

Description

Deciduous or evergreen shrubs or trees with opposite leaves; clusters of small, white, fragrant flowers; and black berries. About 50 species, native to the Old World.

How to Grow

Full or part sun. Privets grow in any well-drained soil and tolerate heat, wind, drought, and salt spray. They are easy to transplant. Space 5–10 ft. apart for hedges and screens. Renew old plantings by pruning back hard in early spring. Most privets have dense, shallow root systems; cover them with mulch and put other plants at least 2–3 ft. away.

■ *japonicum* p. 164

Japanese ligustrum, wax-leaf ligustrum. A fast-growing evergreen shrub or tree, 10–15 ft. tall, commonly used for hedges and foundation plantings, where it tolerates — and often needs — frequent pruning. Its smooth, glossy leaves are dark green, 2–4 in. long. Clusters of small white flowers form at the tips of new shoots in May or June, followed by blue-black

berries that weigh down the branches. Good for formal specimens at the corners of a building. Zone 8.

■ *lucidum*   *p. 108*
Glossy privet. An evergreen tree or large shrub, often reaching 30 ft. or more. Similar to wax-leaf ligustrum but larger,
with a looser, more open habit and glossy dark green leaves
4–6 in. long. The flower clusters are also larger and looser.
Responds well to pruning and can be used for medium-height
or tall hedges; also makes a fine single- or multitrunked tree.
Zone 8.

Limonium

Lee-mo′nee-um
Plumbaginaceae. Plumbago family

Description
Perennials or subshrubs with sprays of small flowers that
have colorful, papery, persistent calyxes. About 150 species,
native worldwide.

How to Grow
Full sun. Needs well-drained soil and tolerates considerable
drought in seashore conditions; subject to root rot in heavy
or wet soil. Needs only routine deadheading and grooming.
Plants are hard to divide but grow readily from seed.

■ *perezii*   *p. 220*
Sea statice, sea lavender. A fast-growing perennial that produces generous bouquets of flowers for fresh and dried
arrangements. Forms a basal mound of large, thick, evergreen
leaves. Airy, much-branched sprays of rich purple-blue
flowers with white centers are held on leafless stalks up to 2
ft. tall. Blooms mostly from spring to early fall, but nearly
year-round where winters are mild. Zone 9.

Liquidambar

Li-quid-am′bar. Sweet gum
Hamamelidaceae. Witch hazel family

Description
Deciduous trees that produce a sticky fragrant resin used in
medicines and perfumes. The leaves turn bright colors in fall.
Only 4 species, native to North America and Asia.

How to Grow

Full sun. Ordinary soil and watering. Tolerates heat, dryness, and wind. Surface roots can heave sidewalks or interfere with lawns; occasional deep soaking helps promote deeper roots. Prune only to remove lower limbs as needed. Pest-free and easy to grow.

■ *styraciflua* *p. 92* *Pictured above*
Sweet gum. A deciduous tree, up to 60 ft. tall. Forms a narrow pyramid when young, spreading wider with age. The star-shaped leaves, 6 in. wide, turn bright orange, red, or purplish in fall. The twigs have unique corky wings, and the trunk has ridged bark. The prickly seed balls, 1 in. wide, look interesting on the bare limbs but make rough litter on a lawn or sidewalk. 'Palo Alto' has bright orange or red fall foliage; 'Burgundy' turns purplish red and holds its leaves into winter. 'Rotundiloba' has leaves with rounded rather than pointed lobes and doesn't set fruit. Native to the eastern United States. Zone 6.

Liriope

Li-rie'oh-pee. Lilyturf
Liliaceae. Lily family

Description

Evergreen perennials forming tufts or spreading mats of grassy foliage. Only 5 species, native to southeastern Asia.

How to Grow

Part sun or shade. Grows best in well-drained soil with regular watering but tolerates short dry spells. Space sprigs 4–6 in. apart; plants from quart or gallon pots can go 12–18 in. apart. Foliage is evergreen where winters are mild but freezes back in colder zones. Renew by shearing in spring with grass shears or a lawn mower. No serious pests or problems.

■ *spicata* p. 184
Liriope, creeping lilyturf. A spreading perennial that makes a
grassy mat of soft dark green leaves about 12–18 in. long.
Short spikes of pale violet flowers form in midsummer. Makes
a good ground cover under trees or shrubs or in shady areas
where grass won't grow. Not good for edging, as it invades
adjacent beds. *L. muscari* forms clumps instead of creeping
and has wider leaves that may be striped with white or gold.
Zone 6.

Lonicera

Lon-iss´er-a. Honeysuckle
Caprifoliaceae. Honeysuckle family

Description
Shrubs or woody vines, deciduous or evergreen, with simple
opposite leaves. Small or large flowers, often sweetly fragrant,
are borne in pairs or whorls, followed by soft berries. About
180 species, native to the Northern Hemisphere.

How to Grow
Full or part sun. Honeysuckles tolerate shade but may not
flower there. They grow in any well-drained soil and tolerate
dry spells once established. Prune as needed to control size
and to remove old wood. Overgrown plants can be cut to the
ground for renewal. Subject to aphids and various other pests
and diseases, but the damage is usually cosmetic, not serious.

■ × *heckrottii* p. 196
Gold-flame honeysuckle. A woody vine that climbs 10–20 ft.
high. Smooth, rounded, blue-green leaves are evergreen where
winters are mild and hang on late even in cold climates. Clusters of slender flowers are borne at the tips of each stem,
blooming most heavily in late spring but continuing sporadically until fall. The flowers are carmine outside, yellow inside, with a sweet fragrance that's especially noticeable in the
evening. Plant it on a trellis or arbor upwind of a patio or
open window, let it spill over a retaining wall, or use it as a
ground cover. Doesn't set berries, so it doesn't spread like
Japanese honeysuckle. Zone 5.

■ *sempervirens* p. 196
Trumpet honeysuckle. A woody vine that usually doesn't
climb higher than 10–15 ft. and tends to be shrubby and restrained, not aggressive. The glossy, oval, blue-green leaves
are semievergreen. Clusters of 2-in. tubular flowers, usually

coral-red but sometimes yellow, are scentless but attract hummingbirds. Blooms heavily for a month or so in early summer, then intermittently through fall. Makes red berries but rarely self-sows. An excellent, carefree vine for covering fences, mailbox or lamp posts, or trellises. Native to the eastern United States. Zone 4.

Lycianthes
Lie-see-an'theez
Solanaceae. Nightshade family

Description
Shrubs and vines with simple alternate leaves, 5-petaled flowers, and fleshy fruits. This genus was previously combined with *Solanum*. About 200 species, from tropical climates.

How to Grow
Full sun or part shade. Ordinary soil with regular watering during dry spells. Grows rapidly, providing quick fill. Good for informal settings or as a background or ground cover, but needs frequent heavy pruning to keep it in bounds. Watch for aphids and whiteflies.

■ *rantonnetii* p. 164
Blue potato bush. A woody plant that can be shaped into a loose, open shrub 6–8 ft. tall; encouraged to sprawl like a ground cover; or, if fastened to a support, will climb like a vine up to 12 ft. tall. Oval, slightly hairy leaves are usually evergreen but may drop after a sudden cold snap. Blooms continually from spring to early fall, providing a spectacular show. The rich blue-violet flowers are shaped like small petunias. Zone 9.

Lyonothamnus
Lie-oh-no-tham'nus
Rosaceae. Rose family

Description
An evergreen tree with attractive foliage and flowers. Only 1 species, native to the Channel Islands off southern California.

How to Grow
Full sun. Does best in deep, well-drained soil with moderate fertility; the foliage turns pale green in heavy, poorly drained

soils. Once established it is drought-tolerant, but it looks better with occasional watering. Grows well only in coastal locations. Prune off faded flowers to keep the plant looking tidy, and thin lightly to expose the handsome trunk and bark. Grows quickly but is very susceptible to deer feeding.

■ *floribundus* ssp. *asplenifolius*   *p. 109*
Fernleaf Catalina ironwood. A graceful, slender, evergreen tree 30–50 ft. tall. Interesting fernlike leaves, 5 in. long, are divided into many notched segments, glossy dark green above and gray below. Impressive large trusses of creamy white flowers are borne in late spring. Lovely when planted in small groups or groves. Zone 9.

Magnolia
Mag-no′lee-a
Magnoliaceae. Magnolia family

Description
Deciduous or evergreen shrubs or trees with large simple leaves, showy flowers in spring or summer, and conelike fruits in fall. About 125 species, most native to eastern Asia or eastern North America. There are also many hybrids and cultivars.

How to Grow
Full or part sun. Well-drained acidic or neutral soil amended with organic matter. Plant in spring, after new growth starts. Be careful not to break or bruise the thick, fleshy roots. Apply a thick layer of organic mulch to shade the soil and to retain moisture. Water deeply and regularly during droughts. Prune only to remove dead or damaged shoots. Magnolias have few pests or diseases.

■ *grandiflora*   *p. 109*
Southern magnolia. A medium to large evergreen tree, 30–60 ft. tall, with an erect trunk and horizontal limbs. The large oblong leaves are thick and glossy, dark green above, covered below with a dense coating of short woolly hairs. Creamy white flowers, 6–10 in. wide, have a rich lemony or fruity fragrance. Bloom peaks in early summer and continues sporadically through fall. Decorative brown fruits release shiny red seeds in fall. There are compact and hardier-than-average cultivars. Native along the coast from North Carolina to Texas. Zone 7.

Mahonia
Ma-ho´ni-a
Berberidaceae. Barberry family

Description
Evergreen shrubs with glossy leaves, yellow flowers, and blue-black berries. About 70 species, native to Asia and North America.

How to Grow
Can take full sun in summer but needs shelter from winter sun and dry winds in cold regions, or the leaves will turn brown and die. (The plant survives but recovers slowly.) Well-drained soil and ordinary watering. Spreads, but not too fast, by underground runners. You can dig and transplant well-rooted suckers. Cut off old, tattered, or too-tall stems at ground level in early spring.

■ *aquifolium* p. 165
Oregon grape. An evergreen shrub that makes a clump or grove of erect stems 6–8 ft. tall. Compound leaves have 5–9 spiny leaflets that are glossy green in summer, purplish in winter. Clusters of bright yellow flowers are showy for a few weeks in early spring. Small silvery blue berries attract birds in fall. Large clumps or mass plantings make a good screen or background. Other *Mahonia* species, hybrids, and cultivars are also good plants for seashore gardens. Native to the Pacific Northwest. Zone 6.

Melaleuca
Mel-a-loo´ka
Myrtaceae. Myrtle family

Description
Evergreen shrubs and small trees with bottlebrush-like flower heads. Many have bark with an unusual corky or papery texture. About 150 species, most native to Australia.

How to Grow
Full sun. The following species do best in slightly fertile, well-drained soil and tolerate moderate drought once established. Tip-prune when young to encourage branching. Prune shrub forms lightly after flowering to keep plants compact. Thin tree stems to show off the attractive bark. Resistant to deer feeding.

■ *nesophila* p. 165
Pink melaleuca. An upright open shrub or small tree, up to 20 ft. tall or lower if pruned, that develops a gnarled, windswept profile and has attractive peeling light-colored bark. Clusters of lavender to rose-pink flowers open in summer. The evergreen leaves are stiff, glossy, gray-green ovals about 1 in. long. Drooping melaleuca, *M. armillaris,* is a similar-size shrub with graceful drooping branches, flexible needlelike leaves, and creamy white flowers. Both are hardy to Zone 9.

■ *quinquenervia* p. 110
Cajeput tree. A slender upright tree, 30–35 ft. tall, often with multiple trunks. Evergreen leaves are pale green, 4 in. long, with 5 pronounced parallel veins. Creamy white or purplish flowers form 3-in. spikes in summer and fall. Makes a good lawn or street tree. Also known as *M. leucadendra* or *M. viridiflora* var. *rubriflora.* Zone 9.

Miscanthus
Mis-kan´thus
Gramineae. Grass family

Description
Large perennial grasses with feathery flower heads and long slender leaves with distinct midribs and rough margins. Most form erect clumps. More than 15 species, native to the Old World.

How to Grow
Full or part sun. Ordinary or unamended soil. Adapts to acidic or alkaline conditions. Looks best with regular watering, but established plants tolerate mild droughts. Cut to the ground in early spring, before new growth begins to show. Older plants can be divided at that time. Dig the entire clump and use a butcher knife, machete, or ax to chop it into smaller sections for replanting. Has no serious pests or diseases.

■ *sinensis* p. 233 *Pictured opposite*
Eulalia grass, Japanese silvergrass, maiden grass. A perennial grass that makes a large, fountainlike clump of long, slender, arching leaves and has showy flower heads and seed heads on stiff stalks 5–8 ft. tall. Different cultivars have leaves that are plain green or striped or banded with white or yellow. Flower heads form in late summer or fall. They open white, pink, or

reddish purple, then ripen into feathery buff or silver seed heads that remain attractive throughout the winter. These grasses make fine specimens for mixed borders and contrast dramatically with large-leaved perennials. Combine them with evergreens and berrying shrubs for winter interest. Space clumps side by side as a substitute for shrubs to make a screen, hedge, or background. There are several cultivars to choose from, and they are widely available and inexpensive. Zone 5.

Myoporum

My-o-por′um
Myoporaceae. Myoporum family

Description
Evergreen trees or shrubs with small bell-shaped flowers, bright-colored juicy berries, and dark leaves with small clear dots. More than 30 species, most native to Australia.

How to Grow
Full sun. Any well-drained soil. Tolerates drought once established. Plant 3–5 ft. apart for a ground cover that will fill in the first year. Prune to remove dead or damaged stems. Stems root where they touch loose, moist soil. May require edging to control its spread.

■ *parvifolium* *p. 184*
Prostrate myoporum. A low, wide-spreading evergreen shrub, used mostly as a ground cover. Stays under 3–6 in. tall but spreads to 6 ft. or wider. Bright green leaves, about 1 in. long, are crowded along the stems. Small, white or pink, bell-shaped flowers bloom in summer and early fall. Zone 9.

Myrica

Mir´i-ka, mir-i´ka
Myricaceae. Bayberry family

Description
Deciduous or evergreen shrubs or trees, most with fragrant leaves and small, round, waxy, fragrant fruits. Some are nitrogen-fixing. About 50 species, distributed worldwide.

How to Grow
Full sun or part shade. The species below are well adapted to infertile, dry, sandy soil and salt spray. They thrive in average garden soil. Space 6–10 ft. apart for informal hedges or screens. Little if any pruning is required.

■ *californica* p. 166
Pacific wax myrtle. An evergreen shrub with numerous upright trunks, or a small slender tree, reaching 20–25 ft. tall. Lustrous, dark green, oblong leaves are aromatic when crushed. Small purplish berries, covered with a white wax, are borne along the stems in autumn and attract birds. Native along the Pacific coast from Canada south. Southern wax myrtle, *M. cerifera,* is similar, but the leaves are lighter green and more slender and the berries are gray. Native along the Atlantic coast from Maryland south. Both are hardy to Zone 7.

■ *pensylvanica* p. 135
Bayberry. A deciduous shrub with an irregular mounded habit and dense twiggy growth. Slowly reaches 8–10 ft. tall and spreads equally wide or wider. The wavy-edged leaves are glossy bright green in summer, turning purple before dropping in late fall. Clusters of waxy silver-gray berries on female plants are conspicuous after the leaves drop in fall. A good shrub for foundation planting or for massing on dry banks. Native along the Atlantic coast from Maryland north. Zone 4.

Nephrolepis

Nef´-ro-lee´pis. Sword fern
Polypodiaceae. Fern family

Description
Tender ferns with creeping rhizomes that bear tufts of slender featherlike fronds. About 30 species, native to warm and tropical climates.

How to Grow

Usually grown in part to full shade but can take full sun in cool, coastal locations. Looks best in good garden soil with regular watering but tolerates poor soil, heat, and irregular watering better than most ferns do. Plant 2 ft. or farther apart. Grows vigorously and fills in quickly; may need confining. Prune out dead and discolored fronds, cutting them to the ground. Propagate by division.

■ *cordifolia* p. 220

Sword fern. An evergreen fern with slender upright fronds 30–36 in. tall. Spreads by underground runners and makes a dense ground cover under trees or tall shrubs. Fronds are bright green, divided into numerous paired segments. *N. exaltata* is similar but larger, with fronds 3–5 ft. long. Zone 9.

Nerium

Neer'i-um. Oleander
Apocynaceae. Dogbane family

Description

Evergreen shrubs with leafy stems and big clusters of showy 5-lobed flowers. All parts are extremely poisonous. Only 2 species, native from the Mediterranean region to Japan.

How to Grow

Full sun. Grows in almost any soil and tolerates poor drainage, drought, salt, heat, and wind. Used extensively for screening along beaches and highways wherever it is hardy. Damaged by severe frost but usually recovers. Prune in winter, cutting some of the stems to the ground. Flowers form on new growth. Use dormant oil spray to control scale insects.

■ *oleander* p. 166

Oleander. An evergreen shrub, usually 6–12 ft. tall and wide, that forms a big mound of slender leafy stems, erect or sometimes arching under the weight of the flowers. Blooms throughout the heat of summer, with clusters of single or double flowers in white, creamy yellow, pink, salmon, rose, or red. The long narrow leaves are smooth and leathery, dark green above, pale below. There are many cultivars, differing in size, flower color, and hardiness. Most are hardy to Zone 9; a few to Zone 8.

Nyssa

Nis′sa. Tupelo, sour gum
Nyssaceae. Tupelo family

Description
Deciduous trees with outstanding fall color. Only 5 species, native to North America and eastern Asia.

How to Grow
Full or part sun. Not fussy about soil. Tolerates poor drainage or occasional droughts. Foliage is not damaged by salt spray. Start with a container-grown plant. Slow-growing but adaptable and pest-free. Prune to shape as desired.

■ *sylvatica* *p. 93 Pictured above*
Sour gum, black gum. A deciduous tree with a narrow pyramidal crown, 30–60 ft. tall. Native to the eastern United States but grown in other regions too for its outstanding fall color. Glossy oval leaves, 2–5 in. long, turn from dark green to bright red. Color begins early and lasts until late fall. Flowers are insignificant, but birds like the small, dark blue fruits that ripen in late summer. Zone 3.

Olea

O′lee-a. Olive
Oleaceae. Olive family

Description
Evergreen trees or shrubs with leathery leaves, small flowers, and fruits with one large seed. Some species provide good timber. About 20 species, native to warm climates in the Old World.

How to Grow

Full sun. Ordinary or unamended soil. Thrives in heat and tolerates dry soil once established. Even large trees can be transplanted easily with a high chance of success. Grows quickly. Subject to scale infestation and verticillium wilt.

■ *europaea* p. 110

Olive. An evergreen tree, 25–30 ft. tall and wide. Makes a fine lawn or street tree with a rugged trunk and spreading limbs. Can also be sheared into formal shapes or used as a hedge. The slender leaves have a silvery color and leathery texture. The tiny flowers are inconspicuous, but many people are allergic to the pollen, and the dropping fruit can be a nuisance. Look for 'Swan Hill' or other cultivars that produce little pollen and no fruit. Zone 8.

Opuntia

Oh-pun'shee-a
Cactaceae. Cactus family

Description

Shrubby or treelike succulents with plump, green, flat or round stems divided into a series of joints or pads. Flowers are often large and bright with many waxy petals. Seedy fruits may be juicy or dry.

How to Grow

Full sun. Needs good drainage. Tolerates poor or dry soil. Useful on rough rocky hillsides, on sandy beaches, or in planter beds surrounded by hot pavement where little else will grow. Combines well with spreading conifers and clumping grasses for low-maintenance mass plantings. Avoid sites with blowing litter, as cleanup is difficult. Use a thick layer of gravel mulch to discourage weeds.

■ *humifusa* p. 185

Prickly pear cactus, hardy prickly pear. A shrubby evergreen succulent, under 1 ft. tall but spreading up to 5 ft. wide. The spiny stems are flattened into round or oval "joints" or sections about 6 in. long. The waxy yellow flowers, 3-in. wide, are as pretty as roses in early summer. Small, soft purplish fruits ripen in late summer. The stems turn reddish purple and wrinkle up like raisins in the winter; they get plump and green again come spring. Native from Massachusetts to Georgia. Zone 4.

Osmanthus

Oz-man'thus
Oleaceae. Olive family

Description

Evergreen shrubs or trees with tough leathery leaves, sometimes spiny-toothed, and small but very fragrant flowers.
About 15 species, most native to eastern Asia.

How to Grow

Full or part sun. Ordinary soil and watering. Allow plenty of
room for this large shrub. Use as a single specimen or for a
tall screen. Can be kept small in a container. Prune only to
shape, if desired. Pest-free.

■ *fragrans* p. 167

Sweet olive. A large evergreen shrub — dense, erect, and
eventually treelike, up to 30 ft. tall and 25 ft. wide. Clusters
of tiny white flowers are fragrant enough to perfume the entire garden in spring and summer and sporadically through
the year. Pointed oval leaves, to 4 in. long, are thick and
leathery. Zone 9.

In colder regions, choose O. × *fortunei,* a slow-growing
evergreen shrub with spiny-edged, hollylike leaves and fragrant flowers in autumn. It grows to 6 ft. or taller and is
hardy to Zone 7. Devilwood, O. *americanus,* is not common
at nurseries but grows wild from North Carolina to Mississippi and can be planted farther north. It has smooth-edged
leaves and fragrant white flowers in spring. Zone 6.

Osteospermum

Os-tee-oh-sper'mum
Compositae. Daisy family

Description

Shrubs or perennials with alternate leaves, often toothed or
lobed, and daisylike flower heads held above the foliage on
long stalks. About 70 species, most native to Africa.

How to Grow

Full sun. Any well-drained soil. Grows best with occasional
watering but tolerates drought once established. Prune out
older shoots to encourage new growth and abundant bloom.
Stems root as they spread, making it a good ground cover.
Pest-free.

■ *fruticosum* p. 185

Trailing African daisy. A trailing perennial, under 1 ft. tall and spreading 3–4 ft. wide. Makes a cheerful display of bright lilac and white flowers that open on sunny days but close at night or in cloudy weather. Blooms mostly in winter and early spring but continues intermittently all year. Foliage is dense and evergreen. Also available with pure white or purple flowers. Zone 9.

Seed catalogs list several strains of hybrid African daisies under the genus *Osteospermum* or the closely related genus *Dimorphotheca*. These are easy-to-grow annuals that bloom all summer in flower beds or containers, with large daisylike flowers in shades of white, pink, lilac, salmon, and orange.

Paeonia

Pee-oh´nee-a. Peony
Paeoniaceae. Peony family

Description

Perennials or low shrubs with compound leaves and rounded flowers, often large and showy. More than 30 species, most native to Europe or Asia. Most common garden peonies are hybrids.

How to Grow

Full sun or light afternoon shade. Well-drained, acidic or neutral soil amended with plenty of organic matter. Peonies thrive where winters are cold and don't do well where temperatures rarely dip below freezing. Bud formation requires winter chilling. Carefully choose and prepare the site before planting; peonies can continue in one place for decades. Plant in fall, positioning the pink buds or "eyes" 1–2 in. below soil level. After bloom, remove developing seedpods and fertilize lightly. Cut stems to the ground in early winter. A row of peonies makes an attractive low hedge along a walkway or fence.

■ **hybrids** *p. 221*

Herbaceous peonies. Peonies are long-lived perennials that form mounded clumps about 3 ft. tall and wide. Long-stemmed flowers 4–8 in. wide are excellent for cutting. They can be single or double, in shades of white, pink, rose, and red. Some of the double kinds are very fragrant. Compound leaves are a handsome glossy green all summer, turning purplish or gold in fall. There are hundreds of cultivars, varying in flower color, doubleness, fragrance, plant height, and season of bloom (ranging between late spring and early summer). Zone 3.

Panicum

Pan´i-kum. Panic grass
Gramineae. Grass family

Description
A diverse genus of annual and perennial grasses. About 600 species, native worldwide.

How to Grow
Full or part sun. Ordinary or unimproved soil and ordinary watering. Cut down to the ground in early spring. May spread but isn't invasive. Older clumps can be divided. Mass plantings provide shelter for birds. Makes a good low screen, effective from early summer through late winter.

■ *virgatum*   *p. 234*
Switch grass. A native perennial grass that forms sturdy, narrow, upright clumps 3–6 ft. tall. The slender leaves, 1–2 ft. long, are medium green in summer, turning bright yellow, gold, or orange in fall. Flower panicles form an airy mass 12–16 in. above the foliage and look good from July into fall. They open dark reddish purple and fade to beige. 'Heavy Metal' grows 4–5 ft. tall and has stiff, metallic blue leaves. 'Rostrahlbusch' grows 3–4 ft. tall and has red fall color. Zone 4.

Papaver

Pa-pay´ver. Poppy
Papaveraceae. Poppy family

Description
Annuals or perennials with showy flowers borne singly on long stalks, lobed or dissected basal leaves, and milky sap. About 50 species, native to Old and New World.

How to Grow
Full sun. Ordinary soil and watering. Plant when dormant in late summer or early fall. Place roots 3 in. below the surface. Divide every 5 years or so, when dormant. Poppies are long-lived and trouble-free in cold climates but don't live long where winters are mild.

■ *orientale p. 221*
Oriental poppy. An old-fashioned perennial with vivid flowers in late spring or early summer, on stalks up to 3 ft. tall. Flowers are 4–6 in. wide, with crinkled or ruffled petals in brilliant shades of scarlet, orange, red, pink, or white. The pinnately lobed foliage, pale green with bristly hairs, develops early but dies down in midsummer when the plants go dormant. Plant blanket flowers, Russian sage, seaside goldenrod, or other late-blooming perennials nearby to fill the gap for late summer and fall. Zone 2.

Annual poppies such as *P. nudicaule,* Iceland poppy, and *P. rhoeas,* corn poppy or Shirley poppy, also do very well in seashore gardens. They bloom abundantly for several weeks and often self-sow.

Parthenocissus
Par-then-o-cis´sus. Woodbine
Vitaceae. Grape family

Description
Deciduous woody vines with compound or lobed leaves. They climb by branching tendrils, often with sticky disks at the tips. About 10 species, native to North America and Asia.

How to Grow
Full sun, part sun, or shade. Grows in almost any soil with normal rainfall or ordinary watering. Space container-grown plants 1–2 ft. apart for a ground cover, or use one or more plants to decorate a tree trunk, hide an old stump, or cover a shed or fence. Think twice before planting it next to a house. Adhesive disks at the ends of the tendrils cling to any surface, including wood siding, shingles, and masonry; although you can pull down the actual vines if they reach too far, it's hard to remove the little disks.

■ *quinquefolia p. 197 Pictured above*
Virginia creeper. A deciduous woody vine valued for its carefree growth and bright fall foliage. Can climb to 25 ft. or

sprawl on the ground. Palmately compound leaves with 5 leaflets 3–6 in. long are glossy dark green in summer, turning bright red in early fall, before most trees start to color. Birds eat the dark purple berries as soon as they ripen in fall. Native throughout the eastern United States. Zone 2.

Passiflora

Pas-si-flo´ra. Passionflower
Passifloraceae. Passionflower family

Description
Mostly evergreen vines that climb by tendrils. Large round flowers are fascinating and complex and sometimes very fragrant. Some kinds are valued for their sweet fruits. About 350 species, most native to tropical America.

How to Grow
Full or part sun. Ordinary soil and watering. Grows quickly and needs annual pruning to thin the tangle of stems. Freezes back during severe cold snaps; usually recovers in spring but may not bloom well that year. Various caterpillars eat the leaves but do no serious harm.

■ *caerulea* p. 197
Blue passionflower. A vine that climbs by tendrils, often reaching 20–30 ft. Smooth evergreen leaves are divided into 5 lobes. Blooms in late spring and summer, with very fragrant white and blue-purple flowers up to 4 in. wide. Egg-sized yellow fruits are edible but seedy. Other species and hybrid passionflowers also do well in seashore conditions. Zone 8.

Pennisetum

Pen-ni-see´tum
Gramineae. Grass family

Description
Annual or perennial grasses with flat leaves and dense flower heads. About 70 species, most native to tropical or warm climates.

How to Grow
Full sun. Average soil with occasional deep watering during long dry spells. Cut back old foliage in February or March, especially if interplanted with bulbs. Can be (but doesn't need

to be) divided every 5–6 years. The center of the clump may die out, but that gap is noticeable only in early spring and doesn't matter later.

■ *alopecuroides* *p. 234*
Fountain grass. A clump-forming perennial grass that makes a vibrant, flowing fountain of 3-ft. leaves, dark green in summer and warm apricot, almond, or orange in fall. Flowers freely from July to October, with many fluffy spikes 6–8 in. long, shading from reddish purple to coppery tan. Combines well with spring bulbs, or use it as a ground cover or transition between natural and formal areas. Zone 5.

■ *setaceum* 'Burgundy Giant' *p. 235*
Crimson fountain grass. A clumping grass with fine-textured, purple-bronze foliage. Makes a mound about 2–3 ft. tall and wide. Fluffy nodding spikes of deep purple flowers are held well above the foliage from June through fall. 'Purpureum' and 'Rubrum' also have dark-colored foliage; the species itself has plain green leaves. Perennial to Zone 8; grown as an annual in colder zones.

Perovskia
Pe-rof´skee-a
Labiatae. Mint family

Description
Woody-based perennials with opposite leaves, square stems, and small 2-lipped flowers. Only 7 species, native from Iran to India.

How to Grow
Full sun. Ordinary soil and watering. Needs good drainage, especially in winter. Remove old stems, leaving short stubs, in late fall or early spring. Use pine boughs as a winter mulch in Zones 6 and 5, and don't remove them too early in spring. Established clumps endure for years. Problem-free.

■ *atriplicifolia* *p. 222*
Russian sage. A shrubby perennial that grows 3–5 ft. tall and makes an open, airy specimen. The stiff, twiglike stems and slender toothed leaves are silver-gray and aromatic. Tiered whorls of small lavender flowers top each stem in late summer. Graceful and easy to grow, it combines well with other perennials in a sunny bed or border. Zone 5.

Phalaris

Fa-lay´ris
Gramineae. Grass family

Description

Annual or perennial grasses, most with spreading rhizomes. Seeds of some species are used for bird feed. About 15 species, from around the north temperate zone.

How to Grow

Full or part sun. Not fussy about soil — tolerates sand or clay, acidic or alkaline conditions, wet or dry sites, and some salt. In most areas, the foliage is pretty in spring and early summer but looks worn by August. Cut it back to 6 in. and it will sprout fresh new growth for fall. Easily propagated by division.

■ *arundinacea* 'Picta' *p. 235*

Ribbon grass. A perennial grass, 2–3 ft. tall, that forms a spreading patch, not separate clumps. Upright stems hold leaves 4–10 in. long, bright green with lengthwise white stripes. Flowers in midsummer are small and inconspicuous. One clump can lighten a dark corner or provide a foil for clashing colors in a perennial border. Invasiveness is the main concern. Control spread by planting in a bottomless container. Planted in mass, it makes a tough ground cover and the rhizomes are an effective soil stabilizer. Zone 4.

Phlomis

Flo´mis. Jerusalem sage
Labiatae. Mint family

Description

Perennials or shrubs with square stems and opposite leaves, often quite woolly, and tubular 2-lipped flowers. About 100 species, most native to dry stony habitats in Europe and Asia.

How to Grow

Full sun. Does best in average soil with regular watering during dry spells but tolerates infertile soil, drought, and salt spray. Prune lightly soon after flowering to encourage re-bloom. Cut stems back halfway in late fall or early spring to shape the plant. Watch for mealybugs.

■ *fruticosa* p. 222
Jerusalem sage. A rounded, bushy perennial, up to 4 ft. tall
and 6 ft. wide, with many stems that are woody at the base
and soft on top. Thick, wrinkly leaves, 2–4 in. long, are gray-
green above, white and woolly below. Stems are topped with
a series of ball-shaped whorls of fuzzy buds and tubular
1-in. yellow flowers. Blooms off and on from spring to fall.
Zone 7.

Phlox
Flox
Polemoniaceae. Phlox family

Description
Annuals, perennials, or small shrubs with simple leaves and
round 5-petaled flowers. More than 60 species, all but one
native to North America.

How to Grow
Full sun or part shade. See descriptions below for specific requirements.

■ *paniculata* p. 223
Garden phlox. A popular perennial for late-summer bloom.
Makes erect clumps of leafy stems 2–4 ft. tall, topped with
domed clusters of fragrant flowers ³/₄ in. wide. It spreads over
time to form large patches. There are dozens of cultivars with
white, pink, salmon, red, purple, or bicolor flowers. Carolina
phlox, *P. carolina,* and spotted phlox, *P. maculata,* are similar but bear purple, pink, or white flowers in early summer
and have thicker, healthier foliage. All need fertile, well-
drained soil and regular watering. Space 2 ft. apart. Increase
by division in spring or fall. Zone 4.

■ *subulata* p. 186
Moss phlox, moss pink. A low, creeping perennial, only 6 in.
tall but spreading up to several feet wide. It makes wonderful swaths of color in spring and is trouble-free and easy to
grow. Forms dense mats of somewhat woody stems with stiff,
needlelike leaves ¹/₂ in. long. Foliage is evergreen in mild climates, semievergreen in the North. Covers itself with white,
lilac, pink, or magenta flowers. Needs well-drained or sandy
soil. Space 1 ft. apart for a ground cover. Shear back after
flowering (use a lawn mower for big areas). Increase by division in early fall. Zone 2.

Phoenix

Fee′nix
Palmae. Palm family

Description
Palm trees with long, pinnately divided leaves on short or tall trunks. The fruits are used for food; the leaves, for thatched roofs and basketry. About 17 species, native to Africa and Asia.

How to Grow
Full sun. Ordinary or dry soil. Very tolerant of heat and drought. Remove old leaf bases to expose the patterned trunk. Recovers slowly from severe frosts, which kill the leaves.

■ *canariensis* p. 167
Canary Island date palm. A palm up to 50 ft. tall, with a thick erect trunk topped with an umbrella of arching fronds 15–20 ft. long. Featherlike fronds have coarse dark green leaflets. Slow-growing when young but eventually gets quite large. Zone 9.

Phormium

For′mee-um
Agavaceae. Agave family

Description
Large clumping plants with spearlike leaves. Fibers from the leaves are woven into nets and fabrics. Only 2 species, native to New Zealand.

How to Grow
Full or part sun. Ordinary, well-drained soil and regular watering. Plant from containers and allow plenty of space — these plants soon get quite large. Needs no care beyond the removal of dead or damaged leaves and old flower stalks. May freeze back in cold winters but recovers in one season. Can be divided, but you'll need several helpers to tackle a large specimen.

■ *tenax* p. 168
New Zealand flax. A bold, dramatic perennial that forms clumps of sword-shaped leaves up to 9 ft. long and 5 in. wide. New cultivars offer a variety of foliage colors — bronzy, purplish, reddish, and striped with cream or yellow. Dull reddish brown flowers are trumpet-shaped, 2 in. long,

borne in branched clusters atop tall naked stalks in summer. Compact cultivars are available for smaller gardens. Zone 8.

Phyla

Fil'la
Verbenaceae. Verbena family

Description

Low, creeping perennials or subshrubs with opposite leaves and spikes of small flowers. About 15 species, from Central and South America.

How to Grow

Full sun to light shade. Grows in almost any soil but does best in amended fertile soils. Established plantings are fairly drought-tolerant but look better with regular watering. Space 12–15 in. apart for a quick, dense cover. Stems root where they contact moist soil. Fertilize in early spring to renew foliage color. Mow off flowers if you object to bees.

■ *nodiflora* p. 186
Lippia. An evergreen ground cover that forms a flat, tight, creeping mat of running stems, only 2–3 in. tall in full sun, up to 6 in. tall in light shade. The small leaves are gray-green and have toothed edges. Marble-sized heads of pale lilac flowers appear from spring to fall and attract bees. Makes a good lawn substitute and tolerates moderate foot traffic and mowing. Often listed as *Lippia repens*. Zone 9.

Phyllostachys

Fil-lo-stak'is
Gramineae. Grass family

Description

A large and useful group of hardy bamboos. Some grow quite tall, and all spread to make thickets or groves. The young shoots are eaten as a vegetable, and mature culms are used for fishing rods, plant stakes, fences, and timber. About 60 species, native to China.

How to Grow

Full sun or part sun. Ordinary soil and watering. Plant divisions in spring, container-grown plants anytime. These bamboos spread by underground rhizomes and can send up new shoots 20–30 ft. into your neighbor's yard. Mowing the shoots with a lawn mower won't keep the plant from spreading; you need to dig a trench and install a concrete, metal, fiberglass, or heavy plastic curb 2 ft. deep. Do this when you first plant the bamboo. It's a hard job, but easier than trying to eradicate an established grove that's gotten out of bounds. Maintenance is simple. Remove the oldest, tattered culms at ground level. Thin culms to create a grove. Shear hedges as desired.

■ *aurea* p. 168
Golden bamboo, fishpole bamboo. A hardy bamboo that forms a grove of culms 15–25 ft. tall and 1–2 in. thick, colored gold or yellow-brown. Slender, papery, light green leaves are 2–6 in. long. Yellow-groove bamboo, *P. aureosulcata,* is similar but has green culms with yellow grooves that run from node to node. Both can be used as a screen or hedge if you curb the rhizomes. Leaves and culms may freeze back in severe winters, but the rhizomes are quite hardy. Zone 6.

■ *nigra* p. 169
Black bamboo. A graceful bamboo with slender culms 15–25 ft. tall that mature to a rich black color. Narrow dark green leaves are 1–4 in. long. A confined grove makes a lovely specimen. Zone 7.

Picea
Py-see′a. Spruce
Pinaceae. Pine family

Description
Evergreen coniferous trees with drooping cones and stiff needles that make a distinct pattern of bumps where they attach to the twigs. About 34 species, native to cool regions of the Northern Hemisphere.

How to Grow
Full sun. Prefers well-drained acidic or neutral soil and needs regular watering. Protect the root zone with a layer of mulch; the roots are too shallow for underplanting. Container-grown or balled-and-burlapped plants are easy to transplant. Trees shape themselves naturally and don't need pruning. Native across Canada, this spruce withstands heat, wind, and dryness but needs cold winters.

■ *glauca* p. 111
White spruce. A Christmas-tree-shaped conifer that grows

60–70 ft. tall and 25 ft. wide, useful as a specimen, wind-break, or screen. More common than the species is 'Conica', a dwarf form with short, pale green needles densely crowded on the twigs. It takes decades to reach 10 ft. tall. 'Densata', often called Black Hills spruce, is another compact form that grows about 6 in. a year. It has dense, dark blue-green needles. Zone 3.

Pinus
Py′nus. Pine
Pinaceae. Pine family

Description
Evergreen coniferous trees with needlelike leaves, almost always borne in clusters of 2–5. The main trunk is strongly upright. Each year's growth makes a new whorl of branches on the main trunk and the side limbs. Woody cones may be small or large; a few kinds have edible seeds. The timber is very important for carpentry and woodworking, and the trees also provide turpentine, rosin, and fragrant oils. More than 90 species, native to both temperate and tropical climates in the Old and New World.

How to Grow
Full sun. The pines listed here adapt to any well-drained soil, even sandy or rocky sites, and are fairly drought-tolerant once established. Plant in early spring, before bud break, or in fall. The roots are vulnerable to drying out — even a few minutes' exposure to wind and sun can hinder subsequent growth, so be sure to keep the roots covered or protected while digging the planting hole. Water new trees regularly for the first year.

Various borers, beetles, rusts, and blights can cause problems, but in general pines are tough, adaptable trees. Pruning is not required, but if you want to improve the shape or reduce the size of a tree, you can thin or shorten the expanding buds, called candles, in spring. Snapping off the ends of the candles produces more compact growth.

■ *canariensis p. 111*
Canary Island pine. A graceful pine that reaches 60–75 ft. tall but remains narrow enough to fit into all but the smallest gardens. Grows quickly. Soft, drooping, dark green needles up to 10 in. long are carried in large billowy tufts, mostly near the ends of the stems. Cones are oval, 6–9 in. long. Zone 9.

■ *densiflorus 'Umbraculifera'*   *p. 112*
Japanese umbrella pine, tanyosho pine. An unusual pine that slowly grows 10–25 ft. tall and makes a distinct, umbrella-shaped crown with many close-set branches. Handsome at all ages, it makes a fine specimen for any garden. Multiple trunks have attractive flaking red-orange bark. Needles are soft, twisted, 3-5 in. long. Cones are 2 in. long, borne even on young trees. This cultivar is more widely grown than the species, which is a round-headed tree, to 60 ft. or more, with interesting irregular branching. Zone 5.

■ *halepensis*   *p. 112   Pictured above*
Aleppo pine. A large, fast-growing pine that reaches 50-60 ft. tall, often with two or three main trunks. Has interesting irregular branching even when young, and older trees develop a round crown with branches that look windswept. Needles are pale green, 2–3 in. long. Oblong cones are 3 in. long. Very tolerant of sea wind, salt spray, heat, and drought. Zone 8.

■ *mugo*   *p. 113*
Mugo pine. More like a shrub than a tree, this slow-growing pine is broad and bushy. It can reach 15 ft. tall and wide, good for screens or boundary plantings. Nurseries sell several dwarf strains, often labeled as *P. mugo* var. *mugo;* some are more compact than others. All have dense, dark green foliage that is undamaged by salt spray. Needles are stiff, 2 in. long. Oval cones are 1–2 in. long. Zone 3.

■ *nigra*   *p. 113*
Austrian pine. A large pine, 40–60 ft. tall and 20–30 ft. wide, with a stout trunk and spreading limbs. Conical when young, it becomes broad and flat-topped with age. The foliage is rich dark green, even in winter, and makes a good background for other plantings. Stiff needles are 4–6 in. long. Oval cones are 3 in. long. Tolerates wind and salt and makes a good windbreak or screen. Recently subject to a fatal blight inland but not (yet) along the shore. Zone 4.

■ *pinea*   *p. 114*
Swiss stone pine, Italian stone pine. A slow-growing pine, conical when young but maturing into a large tree, 70–80 ft.

tall, with an umbrella-shaped or flat-topped crown and multiple trunks with attractive orange or yellow-brown bark. The needles are glossy green, twisted, 5–7 in. long. Broad oval cones up to 6 in. long contain edible seeds called pine nuts. Well adapted to coastal conditions. Zone 8.

■ *sylvestris* p. 114
Scotch pine. An adaptable, fast-growing pine that reaches 70 ft. or taller and spreads 30–40 ft. Young plants quickly develop a conical shape and are widely planted for Christmas trees. Older trees become quite picturesque, with open branching and an irregular rounded crown. The twigs and branches have orange bark that peels off in papery layers. Stiff, twisted needles with sharp points are 1–4 in. long, in groups of 2. Rounded cones are 2–3 in. long. There are dwarf, fastigiate, and blue-needled cultivars. Zone 3.

■ *taeda* p. 115
Loblolly pine. A fast-growing pine, reaching 80 ft. or taller, with an erect trunk and round crown. Young trees are full and conical; older trees get straggly but still provide some shade. The needles are 6–9 in. long, light green in summer but often yellowish in winter. Clusters of oblong, spiny cones, 2–6 in. long, hang on the branches for years. Native to the Southeast and very tolerant of heat and humidity. Adapts to wet or dry soil. Zone 7.

■ *thunbergiana* p. 115
Japanese black pine. A fast-growing and adaptable pine, widely planted along the Atlantic and Pacific coasts because it is very tolerant of salt spray, wind, and poor, sandy soil. Usually grows 20–40 ft. tall but can get taller. Young trees are more or less conical and can be pruned or sheared for dense rounded growth. Older trees develop a crooked trunk and an irregular, spreading crown. Needles are stiff, dark green, about 3 in. long. Cones are 2–3 in. long. Also known as *P. thunbergii*. Zone 6; sometimes listed as Zone 5 but subject to freeze damage there.

Pittosporum

Pit-o-spo′rum
Pittosporaceae. Pittosporum family

Description
Evergreen shrubs or trees with shiny, leathery leaves and attractive, often fragrant flowers. About 200 species, native to warm and tropical climates in the Old World.

How to Grow
Full or part sun. Ordinary soil with regular watering during dry spells. Prune or shear hedges to promote dense growth. Stake and train trees during the formative years. Watch for aphids, scale, and mealybugs. Foliage tolerates sea winds and salt spray.

■ *crassifolium* p. 169
Karo. An evergreen shrub that can reach 10 ft. tall and wide but is usually kept smaller by annual pruning. The gray-green leaves are thick and leathery, 1–2 in. long, and have rounded tips. Clusters of small purple flowers in late spring are less conspicuous than the blue-purple fruits that follow. 'Compactum' is a dwarf form. Zone 8.

■ *tobira* p. 170
Mock orange. A tough and durable shrub that can reach 10–15 ft. or taller but is usually kept shorter by pruning. It makes an irregular but dense mound of glossy evergreen foliage. Large, thick, dark green leaves with rounded tips are clustered at the tips of the branches. 'Variegata' has gray-green leaves mottled with white and grows about 6 ft. tall. 'Wheeler's Dwarf' has small dark green leaves and grows only 3–4 ft. tall; it does well in planters or containers. All bear clusters of small, creamy white, very fragrant flowers in early summer. Tough and adaptable, mock orange is good for foundation plantings, hedges, or mixed borders. Zone 8.

■ *undulatum* p. 116
Victorian box. A round-headed evergreen tree, 35–40 ft. tall, or large shrub with spread nearly equal to its height. The shiny, dark green leaves are 6 in. long and have a wavy (undulating) margin. Creamy white flowers are intensely fragrant in late spring. Clusters of showy orange fruits open to reveal dark, sticky seeds but are messy if they land on a patio or sidewalk. Grows quickly and makes a good lawn tree or a broad informal screen. Zone 9.

Platanus

Plat´a-nus. Sycamore, plane tree
Platanaceae. Plane tree family

Description
Large deciduous trees with thick trunks, spreading limbs, flaking bark, lobed leaves, and round flower heads and fruits. Only 6 or 7 species, several native to North America.

How to Grow
Full sun. Average or fertile soil with regular watering. Grows quickly and soon needs plenty of space. Subject to various insect pests.

■ *occidentalis* p. 93
American sycamore, buttonwood, buttonball tree. A large deciduous tree, up to 100 ft. tall and wide, best known for its distinctive bark — smooth and white on the new limbs, flaking in irregular patches of cream, gray, olive green, and tan on the trunk and main branches. It has a stout trunk and twisting, wide-reaching limbs. Large toothed leaves have a soft texture and are medium green in summer, tan in fall. Dry, brown, golf-ball-sized fruits are borne singly. Native throughout the eastern United States. Zone 5.

London plane tree, *P. × acerifolia,* has similar bark and leaves, but the fruits are borne in pairs. Zone 5. California sycamore, *P. racemosa,* has strings of 3–7 fruits and more deeply lobed leaves. Native to California. Zone 9.

Plumbago
Plum-bay'go. Leadwort
Plumbaginaceae. Plumbago family

Description
Perennials or shrubs with simple leaves and flowers with long tubes that flare into 5 lobes. About 10 species, native to tropical climates.

How to Grow
Full sun. Ordinary soil and watering, tolerates heat and dry soil once established. Slow to start but trouble-free once established. Makes a good ground cover along driveways or on banks. Can be trained on a fence or trellis, or used as a screen or boundary planting. Remove frost-damaged shoots in spring. Thin out the oldest stems periodically.

■ *auriculata* p. 170
Cape plumbago. A spreading, mounding, or climbing evergreen shrub that reaches 6–8 ft. tall or wide. Blooms from early summer to fall, with clusters of white, pale blue, or sky blue flowers. Buy plants in bloom to get the color you want. The pale green leaves are smooth and thin. Previously known as *P. capensis.* Zone 9.

Podocarpus

Po-do-kar'pus
Podocarpaceae. Podocarpus family

Description
Coniferous trees or shrubs with flat, narrow, evergreen leaves. Many are harvested for timber. More than 90 species, most native to the Southern Hemisphere.

How to Grow
Full sun or part shade. Needs well-drained soil and tolerates drought once established. Easy and adaptable, with no serious pests or diseases. Prune to shape as desired.

■ *macrophyllus* *p. 116*
Yew pine. An evergreen shrub or tree that can reach 30 ft. tall but is usually kept much smaller. Glossy, leathery, needle-like leaves are 3–4 in. long and ¼ in. wide. Creamy clusters of male flowers are conspicuous in early summer. Edible reddish purple fruits show up in fall. Responds well to pruning; makes a dense hedge or screen, or can be espaliered or used for topiary. Can also be trained as a columnar or rounded specimen tree. Var. *maki* is a narrow, compact form that slowly reaches 10 ft. or more. Popular for foundation plantings, it also does very well in containers. Zone 8.

Polygonum

Po-lig'o-num. Knotweed
Polygonaceae. Buckwheat family

Description
Annuals, perennials, or vines, some aquatic. The stems usually have swollen nodes. Leaves are alternate. Flowers are small but sometimes showy. Some species are very weedy, spreading by seed or rhizome. About 150 species, native worldwide.

How to Grow
Full or part sun. Ordinary or unimproved soil. Tolerates drought once established. Plant in spring for flowers the first year. Freezes back to the ground each winter in the North. Where winters are mild, cut it back hard in spring to limit its spread. Propagate by division. May be attacked by Japanese beetles.

■ *aubertii* p. 198
Silver fleece vine. A fast-growing deciduous vine that climbs up to 15 ft. the first year and 25–35 ft. in later years. Has a very soft, relaxed appearance when scrambling over a wall or fence or climbing into shrubs or trees. Soft leaves up to 4 in. long are reddish at first, bright green later. Blooms in midsummer on new growth, literally covering itself with slender drooping clusters of mildly fragrant, white or pinkish flowers. Zone 5.

Populus

Pop'you-lus. Cottonwood, poplar, aspen
Salicaceae. Willow family

Description
Deciduous trees that are very fast-growing but usually short-lived. They have soft, light wood; simple leaves; and dangling catkins in early spring. Closely related to willows (*Salix*). About 35 species, native to the north temperate zone, and several hybrids.

How to Grow
Full sun. Average or infertile soil. Grows well in sandy soil with regular watering during dry spells. Not damaged by salt spray. Makes a good tree for windbreaks, or can be cut back hard each spring and used as a hedge. Avoid planting near driveways or patios, as the roots can lift pavement; or near drains or sewers, as the roots can penetrate and clog pipes.

■ *alba* p. 94
White poplar. An adaptable, fast-growing, deciduous tree, 50–60 ft. tall, with an erect trunk and a broad crown. The attractive bark is white or gray-green with horizontal rows of black dots. The lobed leaves, dark green above and bright white below, make an eye-catching display when tossed by the wind. 'Bolleana' has a narrow, columnar shape. Zone 3.

Potentilla

Po-ten-til′la. Cinquefoil
Rosaceae. Rose family

Description
Annuals, perennials, or shrubs with stiff or wiry stems, compound leaves, and 5-petaled flowers. About 500 species, native to the north temperate zone.

How to Grow
Full sun. Ordinary soil and watering are best, but it tolerates dry sandy soil. Space 2–3 ft. apart for hedges or mass plantings. Blooms on first-year wood, so it can be cut to the ground and still flower. This should be done at least every other year in early spring to keep the plant dense and compact.

■ *fruticosa* *p. 135*
Bush cinquefoil. A deciduous shrub, 2–3 ft. tall and 3–4 ft. wide, that makes a plump round specimen or a low hedge. Blooms all summer, with round flowers about 1 in. wide. Palmately compound leaves with 3–7 slender leaflets are covered with silky hairs. Hard to beat for ease of care and reliable bloom. 'Katherine Dykes' has pale yellow flowers. Other cultivars have white, dark yellow, yellow-orange, or pinkish flowers. Zone 2.

Prunus
Proo'nus
Rosaceae. Rose family

Description
A valuable group of deciduous and evergreen trees and shrubs. All have alternate simple leaves, pink or white flowers, and fleshy fruits with one hard seed or pit. This genus includes cherries, prunes, plums, peaches, and apricots. Many species are grown as ornamentals, and some are used for timber. About 400 species, most native to the Northern Hemisphere.

How to Grow
Full or part sun. See individual entries for soil requirements. Most species are subject to various insects and diseases that may disfigure the leaves but rarely do serious damage.

■ *caroliniana* *p. 117*
Carolina cherry laurel. A fast-growing tree, up to 30 ft. tall, with an upright oval crown and glossy, dark, evergreen leaves. When crushed, the leaves and twigs have a strong maraschino cherry odor. Small starry flowers in clusters at each leaf axil release a heavy sweet aroma for a few weeks in early spring. Birds flock to eat the small black cherries when they ripen and distribute the seeds throughout the neighborhood. Often used for hedges or screens, but it needs frequent severe pruning to control the size and shape. 'Bright 'N Tight'

is a more compact plant with smaller leaves. Grows very fast in rich, moist soil; adapts well to average soil and watering. Can't take extreme heat or drought. Native along the coast from North Carolina to Texas. Zone 7.

■ *laurocerasus* p. 117 *Pictured above*
Cherry laurel. A small evergreen tree, 10–25 ft. tall, with a broad, dense, rounded crown of thick glossy leaves, 4–6 in. long and 2 in. wide. Upright clusters of very sweet-scented small white flowers stand out like exclamation points against the foliage in midspring. Can be used as a tall screen, but avoid shearing, as it chops the leaves. 'Otto Luyken', 'Schipkaensis', and 'Zabeliana' are shrublike cultivars that grow only 3–6 ft. tall but spread 6–10 ft. wide. Cherry laurel grows in sun or shade and prefers average soil and watering but tolerates dry, infertile soil. Zone 7.

■ *maritima* p. 136
Beach plum. A low-growing deciduous shrub, usually under 6 ft. tall, that grows wild in sandy, acidic soil along the Atlantic coast from Maine to Virginia. White flowers are showy in spring. Red or yellow plums about 1 in. long ripen in summer and make excellent jam. Leaves sometimes develop good fall color. Very salt-tolerant and hardy. Propagated by seed; sow in place or buy container-grown plants. Zone 3.

■ *serotina* p. 94
Black cherry. A deciduous tree, 60–75 ft. tall, with attractive, reddish, birchlike bark; dangling clusters of white flowers in spring; and dark green leaves that turn gold or orange in fall. The black cherries are edible but small and tart. Birds love them. Needs full or part sun, average soil, and regular watering. A good lawn or shade tree for seashore gardens. Native throughout the eastern United States. Zone 3.

Punica

Pew'ni-ka. Pomegranate
Punicaceae. Pomegranate family

Description
Deciduous shrubs or small trees with showy flowers and large fruits with juicy pulp. Only 2 species, native to Eurasia.

How to Grow
Full sun. Well-drained average or fertile soil with occasional deep watering during long droughts. Prune in spring, removing tangled inner branches and cutting back long shoots. Flowers on new wood. No serious pests or diseases.

■ *granatum* p. 136
Pomegranate. A deciduous shrub or small tree, 15–20 ft. tall, that can be used as a specimen or hedge, trained as a single- or multitrunked tree with a spreading crown, or espaliered. It blooms for months in hot weather. Single or double flowers, 1–2 in. wide, are usually bright orange-red, but new cultivars have salmon-pink, yellow, white, or two-tone flowers. Round fruits, 3–5 in. thick, have a leathery red rind and are stuffed with sweet juicy seeds. Narrow pointed leaves are glossy bright green in summer, yellow in fall. 'Wonderful' has the most delicious fruits. 'Nana' is a dwarf form, under 3 ft. tall, that can live in the same pot for years. It has near-evergreen foliage, single orange-red flowers, and small dry fruits. Zone 8.

Pyracantha

Py-ra-kan'tha. Firethorn
Rosaceae. Rose family

Description
Vigorous thorny shrubs with simple leaves, round clusters of small white flowers, and red or orange berries. The berries are very showy from fall to spring, and birds don't eat them until other food sources are depleted. Only 6 species, native to southeastern Europe and Asia, and many hybrids.

How to Grow
Pyracanthas need full sun for maximum fruit production but grow fine in part shade. Well-drained soil with regular watering at first; established plants endure drought. Depending on cultivar, they can be used in foundation plantings or hedges, trained into small multitrunked trees, or espaliered.

Prune in early spring, removing frost-damaged shoots and shaping as desired. Subject to fire blight, which makes the shoots die back from the tips; scab, which makes hard dark spots on the berries and leaves; and various insect pests.

■ **hybrid cultivars** *p. 171*
Pyracanthas. Most cultivated pyracanthas are hybrids derived from *P. coccinea, P. koidzumii,* and other species. All are semievergreen shrubs with glossy foliage, clusters of white flowers in spring, and bright berries. They differ in size, habit, vigor, hardiness, and fruit color. 'Gnome' is compact and dense, usually under 6 ft. tall, with orange berries. Susceptible to scab. Zone 5. 'Lalandii' is vigorous and fast-growing, 10–15 ft. tall, with orange-red berries. Zone 6. 'Mohave' grows narrowly upright to about 10 ft., with huge crops of bright orange berries that color early. Disease-resistant. Zone 7 or 6. 'Navaho' makes a broad mound, 6 ft. tall, with orange-red fruits. Disease-resistant. Zone 7. 'Teton' grows upright, to 10 ft. or more, with yellow-orange fruits. It is one of the hardiest cultivars. Zone 5. 'Watereri' is a vigorous rounded shrub with dark red berries. Zone 7.

Quercus
Kwer'kus. Oak
Fagaceae. Beech family

Description
A great and complex genus of evergreen and deciduous trees, some shrubby and some immense. All have alternate leaves, usually lobed or toothed; dangling catkins of male flowers; and woody acorns. Many are harvested for the hard, durable, attractive timber. About 600 species, nearly all from the Northern Hemisphere.

How to Grow
Full sun. Soil and moisture requirements vary; see individual entries. Most oaks do best if transplanted when young. They need little pruning; just remove damaged, crossing, or spindly shoots. In general, the following oaks are trouble-free.

■ *agrifolia* *p. 118 Pictured on next page*
Coast live oak, California live oak. An evergreen tree native to coastal California, growing up to 75 ft. tall, with a wide-spreading canopy of graceful limbs. The leaves are glossy dark green above, paler below, 1–2 in. long, with a few spiny points around the edge. Does best in fertile, well-drained soil.

Young trees can grow 2 ft. a year under ideal conditions. Existing native trees are notably intolerant of summer watering and should not be underplanted with a lawn; surround them only with low-water-use plants. Young, nursery-grown plants usually adapt to moderate lawn watering. Zone 9.

■ *coccinea* p. 95
Scarlet oak. A deciduous tree, 50 ft. or taller, with an upright oval crown. Leaves are 4–6 in. long with deep, bristle-tipped lobes, rich green in summer and bright red in fall. Does well as a shade tree in lawns; the deep roots don't compete with grass. Prefers light, sandy soil. Native all along the East Coast. Zone 5.

■ *ilex* p. 118
Holly oak, holm oak. A rugged, fairly fast-growing, evergreen oak for West Coast gardens. It can make a spreading, irregular tree up to 50 ft. tall, but it's often used as a hedge or screen and can be pruned as desired. The leathery leaves are 1–3 in. long, toothed or smooth-edged. New growth in spring is covered with white down and gives the effect of a flowering tree. Very tolerant of wind, dry soil, and salt. Zone 7.

■ *stellata* p. 95
Post oak. A rugged deciduous tree, usually 30–50 ft. tall, that grows slowly but tolerates poor sandy soil, wet or dry, and salt spray. Often develops a gnarled profile, with a crooked trunk and thick, spreading limbs. Dark green leaves have deep, rounded lobes. Native along the East Coast from Massachusetts to Texas. Zone 6.

■ *virginiana* p. 119
Live oak. A majestic evergreen tree that thrives in hot, humid climates. Old trees reach 60 ft. tall and 100 ft. wide and have short thick trunks and strong twisted limbs that spread like outstretched arms. Young trees are more erect, with dense,

rounded crowns. Smooth-edged leaves, 2–5 in. long, are dark green above, fuzzy white below. Grows wild along the Atlantic and Gulf coasts from Virginia to Texas, where Spanish moss often drapes the limbs. Prefers acidic or neutral soil. Tolerates dry spells but grows better with regular watering and does well in irrigated lawns. Zone 7.

Rhaphiolepis
Ra-fee-ol′e-pis, ra-fee-o-lcep′is
Rosaceae. Rose family

Description
Evergreen shrubs with thick leathery leaves and small but showy flowers. About 14 species, native to eastern Asia.

How to Grow
Needs full sun for maximum flowering. Ordinary soil and watering. Tolerates short dry spells but not prolonged drought. Prune after flowering to shape as desired. Often used in foundation plantings. Also makes a good low hedge or mass planting.

■ *indica* *p. 171*
Indian hawthorn. A mounded evergreen shrub, 2–5 ft. tall and 4–6 ft. wide, with thick, glossy, dark green leaves and abundant clusters of pink or white flowers for several weeks in spring. Individual flowers are only $1/2$ in. wide, but clusters can be 4–6 in. wide. Small blue berries ripen in late summer. Oval leaves with pointed tips are clustered at the ends of the branches. There are many cultivars, differing in habit and flower color 'Jack Evans' is an upright cultivar with pink flowers. *R. umbellata* is a similar species with rounded leaves and fragrant white flowers $3/4$ in. wide; some cultivars are hybrids between these two species. Zone 8.

Rhus
Roos. Sumac
Anacardiaceae. Sumac family

Description
Deciduous or evergreen trees, shrubs, or vines with simple or compound leaves, milky or resinous sap, and terminal clusters of small flowers and berries. This genus includes poison ivy, poison oak, and a few other species that cause skin

rashes, but the species listed below are harmless. About 200 species, native worldwide.

How to Grow
Full or part sun. These species adapt to any well-drained soil and are drought-tolerant once established, but they look better if watered during dry spells. They tolerate coastal wind and salt spray. Prune to shape in late winter.

■ *copallina* p. 137 *Pictured above*
Shining sumac. A deciduous shrub up to 12 ft. tall. Given room, it spreads underground to make a dome-shaped colony of upright stems. It is, however, easily controlled by mowing or pulling the outer suckers. It makes a good background screen or single specimen. The large compound leaves have 9–15 small toothed leaflets and are shiny bright green in summer and crimson in fall. Greenish yellow flower clusters develop in summer and mature into red fruits that last through the winter. Native to the eastern United States. Smooth sumac, *R. glabra,* and staghorn sumac, *R. typhina,* are similar but larger shrubs that form thickets of erect, sparsely branched stems with bright fall foliage and conspicuous red fruit clusters. All are hardy to Zone 4.

■ *integrifolia* p. 172
Lemonade berry. An evergreen shrub 10–12 ft. tall or a small tree up to 25 ft. tall, native to coastal southern California. Can be used for a hedge or bank cover or trained into an espalier or specimen tree. The slate green leaves are leathery, oval, 2 in. long. Small clusters of white or pink flowers in late winter are followed by sticky, orange-red fruits that have an acid flavor and make a lemonade-like beverage. Zone 9.

Robinia
Row-bin'ee-a. Locust
Leguminosae. Pea family

Description
Deciduous trees or shrubs with compound leaves, thorny stems, and showy white or pink flowers. Only a few species, native to North America.

How to Grow
Full sun. Grows best in rich, moist soil but adapts to very poor soil and tolerates drought once established. Tolerates fog and salt spray, but hurricanes or severe coastal storms can break limbs off older trees.

■ *pseudoacacia*   *p. 96*
Black locust. A fast-growing deciduous tree, 40–50 ft. tall. A healthy, well-cared-for specimen is very attractive, with large clusters of very fragrant white flowers in late spring, lacy compound leaves that cast a light filtered shade all summer and turn clear yellow in fall, and rugged bark with deep ridges and furrows. Unfortunately, it can be weedy, spreading by suckers and volunteer seedlings; it also suffers from several insect pests, and the young shoots are studded with pairs of very sharp thorns. 'Frisia' is a unique selection with golden yellow foliage that stays bright all summer. Native to the eastern United States. Zone 4.

Romneya
Rom´nee-a. Matilija poppy
Papaveraceae. Poppy family

Description
A large perennial with white flowers. Only 1 species, native to California and Baja California.

How to Grow
Full sun. Needs well drained, sandy soil where water will not collect around the crown. Keep growth in check by avoiding fertile soil and withholding summer water once established. Buy a container-grown plant from a nursery; don't try to transplant wild plants. Plant in fall. In following years, cut back in late summer. New growth comes with the fall rains. Good for naturalizing in out-of-the-way places, but use with care near other plants because it is invasive. In colder parts of Zone 8 and protected areas of Zone 7, it doesn't get as big and is less invasive.

■ *coulteri*   *p. 223*
Matilija poppy. A perennial California wildflower that forms

a big vigorous patch, reaching up to 8 ft. tall and spreading 8–10 ft. wide. The poppylike flowers, up to 5 in. wide, have 6 snow-white, frilled petals and a big central tuft of golden stamens. Each flower lasts only a few days, but flowering continues from late spring to midsummer. The large, blue-green leaves are divided or deeply lobed. Zone 8.

Rosa

Ro´za. Rose
Rosaceae. Rose family

Description
Deciduous or evergreen shrubs with thorny stems, pinnately compound leaves, and an upright, climbing, or trailing habit. Wild rose flowers have 5 petals and many stamens. Garden roses often have many petals. Rose fruits, called hips, have a fleshy hull with several hairy seeds inside. There are about 100 species, native worldwide, and about 20,000 cultivars, mostly hybrids.

How to Grow
Full sun. The roses listed here need well-drained, average soil with regular deep watering during summer dry spells. They are healthy, vigorous plants that tolerate coastal conditions, and once established they are relatively carefree. Prune in early spring to remove damaged shoots and older canes, to control size and shape, and to promote maximum flowering.

■ 'Betty Prior' *p. 137*
'Betty Prior' rose. A vigorous, bushy floribunda rose that grows 2–3 ft. tall and wide. Starts blooming in early summer and continues through late fall, with generous clusters of rich pink, spicy-scented, single flowers 3 in. wide. Zone 4.

■ 'Chevy Chase' *p. 138*
'Chevy Chase' rose. A rambler rose that can climb 15 ft. if supported. Blooms for a month in midsummer, with no fall repeat. Bright crimson flowers are fully double, 1½–2 in. wide. Foliage has good disease resistance. Zone 6.

■ 'Duet' *p. 138*
'Duet' rose. A hybrid tea rose. Grows upright, 3–4 ft. tall, with large, dark, healthy leaves. Two-tone flowers are light pink with a deep pink reverse, double, 4 in. wide, and have mild fragrance. Blooms abundantly, and buds and flowers are long-lasting. Zone 5.

■ **'Fruhlingsgold'** *p. 139*

'Fruhlingsgold' or 'Spring Gold' rose. An upright bush, about 5 ft. tall, with vigorous, arching canes and delicate-looking but healthy foliage. Blooms in spring, with single, pale yellow flowers 3 in. wide. 'Fruhlingsmorgen' or 'Spring Morning' is similar but has pink and yellow flowers. Both bear heavy crops of small red hips in fall. Zone 4.

■ **'Petite Pink Scotch'** *p. 139*

'Petite Pink Scotch' rose (sometimes called 'Petite Scotch Pink' rose). A low shrub, under 3 ft. tall, with cascading stems and tiny, very glossy green leaves. It tolerates poor soil and can be used to stabilize and cover sandy banks or as a low hedge. Double pink flowers about 1 in. wide are borne up and down the stems in early summer, with no repeat. This is an heirloom rose, introduced by Scotch immigrants and grown since colonial days along the East Coast. Despite its name, it bears no relationship to the Scotch rose, *R. spinosissima*. Zone 5.

■ *rugosa* *p. 140*

Rugosa rose, salt-spray rose. A hardy rose that's especially tolerant of cold, wind, sandy soil, and salt spray. Makes a patch of upright, bristly stems, 2–5 ft. tall, with glossy green, richly textured foliage. The flowers are very fragrant, single, about 3 in. wide, purple-pink or white. The shiny red-orange hips are the size of cherry tomatoes and are very showy from fall into winter. Some people gather them for tea or preserves. Many hybrid cultivars have been developed from this species. 'Alba' has white flowers. Zone 4.

■ *virginiana* *p. 141*

Virginia rose. A wild rose that spreads to make a thicket of erect canes 3–6 ft. tall. Blooms in summer, with fragrant, medium pink, single flowers about 2 in. wide. The foliage turns bright colors in fall, and the red hips and red-barked canes are attractive all winter. Native along the Atlantic coast. Several other wild roses, such as the prairie rose, *R. setigera*, also tolerate seashore conditions. Zone 4.

■ *wichuraiana* *p. 141*

Memorial rose. A trailing shrub that makes a fast, carefree ground cover. Stems grow 6–10 ft. or more in a season, rooting where they touch moist soil. Glossy, healthy, dark green foliage is semievergreen in mild regions. Fragrant, single, white or pink flowers, 2 in. wide, are borne in clusters in midsummer, followed by red hips in fall. This is a parent of many hybrid climbing roses. Zone 5.

Rosmarinus

Ros-ma-ry´nus. Rosemary
Labiatae. Mint family

Description
Evergreen shrubs with slender opposite leaves and small 2-lipped flowers. The fragrant leaves are a favorite culinary herb. Only 2 species, native to the Mediterranean region.

How to Grow
Full sun. Well-drained, ordinary or unimproved soil. Tolerates heat, drought, coastal fog, wind, and salt spray. Plant 2 ft. apart for ground cover (prostrate types) or hedge (upright growers). Pinch growing tips to promote full, bushy growth. Watch for spider mites in hot, dry summers.

■ *officinalis* *p. 172*
Rosemary. An evergreen shrub with very aromatic, gray-green, needlelike leaves about 1 in. long. Small light blue, lilac, or white flowers form on old wood and last for weeks in winter and spring. Usually grows bushy and upright, reaching about 4 ft. tall and wide, and can be trained and pruned into formal shapes or hedges. There are also creeping or prostrate forms that stay under 1 ft. tall and spread as a ground cover or trail over a wall or bank. Herb nurseries offer several cultivars that differ in habit, leaf size and color, flower color, and hardiness. Zone 8.

Rudbeckia

Rood-bek´ee-a. Coneflower
Compositae. Daisy family

Description
Annuals or perennials with showy daisylike blossoms, usually with gold, reddish, or rusty brown rays. About 15 species, native to North America.

How to Grow
Full sun. Ordinary soil. Water it often during hot weather, or the leaves will droop. Deadhead to prolong bloom. Very easy to grow and trouble-free. Divide every few years in early spring or fall.

■ *fulgida* 'Goldsturm' *p. 224* *Pictured opposite*
Black-eyed Susan. A popular perennial that forms a low mound of large, oval, dark green leaves early in the season, then sends up stiff branching flower stalks 18–30 in. tall in midsummer. Blooms for several weeks and combines well with daylilies, asters, and grasses. Cut the flowers for fresh or dried arrangements. Native to the southeastern United States. Zone 3.

Sabal

Say′bal. Palmetto
Palmae. Palm family

Description
Palms with fanlike fronds, often used in basketry or for thatched roofs. About 14 species, native from the southeastern United States to South America.

How to Grow
Full sun, part sun, or full shade. Palmettos are tough, adaptable plants that tolerate poor soil, standing water or seasonal drought, and any amount of salt. They grow slowly but need virtually no care; simply remove old foliage and bloom stalks. Buy container-grown plants from a nursery. Wild plants are difficult to move.

■ *minor* *p. 173*
Dwarf palmetto. A shrubby palm, 4–10 ft. tall. Large rounded fronds on long stiff stalks stick up and out in all directions. The blades are split into many thin segments that flutter in the wind. The trunk is very short, often remaining underground. Bears white flowers in spring and black berries in fall. Tolerates shade and grows well along the edge of a woods or under a grove of trees. Native from North Carolina to Texas. Zone 8.

■ *palmetto* *p. 119*
Cabbage palmetto. A native palm tree with a slender, erect trunk 20–60 ft. tall, topped by a dense, rounded crown. Shiny, dark green fronds, 5 ft. or more in diameter, are divided fanlike into dozens of slender segments. Large drooping clusters of creamy white flowers in spring are followed by dark blue-black fruits in fall. The state tree of South Carolina and Florida, it thrives along the southern Atlantic and Gulf coasts. Zone 9.

Salix

Say'licks. Willow
Salicaceae. Willow family

Description
Deciduous trees or shrubs with simple leaves and separate catkins of small male and female flowers. Most willows are fast-growing but relatively short-lived. About 300 species, nearly all native to cold or temperate climates in the Northern Hemisphere.

How to Grow
Full sun. These willows grow in any average soil and tolerate, but do not require, constant moisture. Willows grow fast and tolerate seashore conditions well, but they get brittle with age and are subject to storm damage. Don't plant them near water or sewer lines, as the roots are invasive.

■ *alba* 'Tristis' *p. 96*
Weeping willow. A deciduous tree that grows up to 50 ft. tall and wide, with a short trunk, spreading limbs, and graceful drooping branchlets. Makes a fine specimen on a large lawn. The twigs have bright yellow bark, conspicuous in winter. Slender leaves, 2–4 in. long, are light green on top and silky white below. They unfold in very early spring, along with the yellow catkins, and turn clear yellow before dropping in late fall. Young trees must be staked to develop a strong, straight trunk. This tree is sometimes listed under several other names. Zone 2.

■ *discolor* *p. 142*
Pussy willow. A deciduous shrub or small tree up to 20 ft. tall, with thick, erect twigs. The fuzzy gray catkins open in very early spring; male catkins get larger than female and are covered with gold pollen. Slender leaves are 2–5 in. long, bright green in summer, turning yellow in late fall. Prune hard right after it flowers, cutting it back almost to the ground, to promote vigorous and strong new growth. Native throughout the northeastern United States. Zone 3.

Santolina

San-to-ly'na
Compositae. Daisy family

Description
Perennials or shrubs with pungent foliage and round flower heads. About 18 species, native to the Mediterranean region.

How to Grow

Full sun. Santolinas need good drainage and thrive in sandy or gravelly soils. They tolerate repeated pruning and can be used for clipped edgings along walkways or around formal beds. Older plants get woody at the base and split open in the middle. Cut back hard in spring to renew, or, better yet, replace them with fresh plants.

■ *chamaecyparissus* p. 224

Lavender cotton, gray santolina. A low, shrubby perennial, about 2 ft. tall and 3 ft. wide. Grows naturally into a low, spreading mound that combines well with rosemary, lavender, sages, rock roses, and wild buckwheats. The silvery gray, aromatic foliage has a rough, curly texture, like terry cloth. Buttonlike yellow flower heads, $3/4$ in. wide, perch on 6-in. stalks in summer. Zone 6.

■ *virens* p. 225

Green santolina. A low, shrubby perennial, about 2 ft. tall and 3 ft. wide, with pungent, dark green foliage. The slender leaves, 1–2 in. long, look like twisted pine needles. Blooms in summer, with pale yellow, round flower heads $1/2$ in. wide on stalks 6 in. tall. Often combined with gray santolina and other gray-leaved plants and used as a clipped edging or a mass planting on dry banks. Sometimes listed as *S. rosmarinifolia*. Zone 6.

Satureja

Sat-you-ree'ya. Savory
Labiatae. Mint family

Description

Annuals or perennials with square stems and opposite leaves, used medicinally and for flavoring. About 30 species, native to the Old and New World.

How to Grow

Full sun or part shade. Grows best in rich, well-drained, light-textured, moist soil, where it spreads quickly and strikes roots wherever the stems touch the ground. Space 15–18 in. apart for a ground cover or underplanting. Easily propagated by replanting rooted stems.

■ *douglasii* p. 187

Yerba buena (meaning "good herb"). A low, creeping perennial, 3–4 in. tall in sunny sites, up to 10 in. tall in part shade.

Trailing stems spread up to 3 ft. wide. Leaves are light green, round or oval with a wavy edge, about 1 in. long, with a pleasant minty aroma. Tiny white or pale pink flowers bloom from spring to fall. Combines well with ferns, columbines, coast redwood, and Pacific wax myrtle. Native along the Pacific coast. Sometimes listed as *Micromeria chamissonis*. Zone 8.

Schinus

Sky´nus
Anacardiaceae. Sumac family

Description
Evergreen trees with simple or compound leaves and showy clusters of small flowers and round fruits. About 27 species, native to tropical America. Fruits of the species below are sold for seasoning as "pink peppercorns"; some people are allergic to them, so use with caution.

How to Grow
Full sun. Ordinary or unamended soil with regular watering at first; tolerates drought once established. Roots are aggressive and can invade water pipes or sewers or lift sidewalks. Train trees to establish one or more trunks, and remove suckers and low branches that get in the way. Can also be planted 2–3 ft. apart and pruned as a hedge. Subject to aphids, scale, and psyllids.

■ *molle* p. 120
California pepper tree. An evergreen tree, up to 40 ft. tall and wide. Old specimens have a lot of character, with heavy, gnarled trunks and limbs and graceful weeping branches. The fine-textured compound leaves are shiny bright green. Drooping clusters of small rose-pink berries last for months in fall and winter. Brazilian pepper tree or Florida holly, *S. terebinthifolius*, has a single straight trunk; a rounded crown of dark green, leathery foliage; and clusters of bright red berries. It's a showy tree, but it shouldn't be planted in Florida, where bird-sown seedlings have become a major weed problem. So far, it hasn't spread invasively in California. Both species are hardy to Zone 9.

Sedum

See´dum. Stonecrop
Crassulaceae. Orpine family

Description
Small perennials, sometimes shrubby, with succulent leaves and stems. There are 300 or more species, most from the north temperate zone, and several hybrids and cultivars. Authorities disagree on the taxonomy of this group, so some plants are listed under various Latin names, but the cultivar names go along unchanged.

How to Grow
Full or part sun. Well-drained or average soil. Sedums need little care. Just cut down the stalks after the flowers fade and divide crowded plants every few years.

■ *acre*   *p. 187*
Goldmoss sedum. A low, creeping perennial, only 4–6 in. tall, that spreads indefinitely and makes a good ground cover. Small succulent leaves are bright green all summer, darker in cold weather. Bright yellow flowers cover the foliage for a few weeks in late spring. Zone 4.

■ 'Autumn Joy'   *p. 225   Pictured above*
'Autumn Joy' sedum. An attractive and easy-to-grow perennial that flowers for many weeks in late summer and fall. Forms a spreading clump of thick unbranched stems, 2–3 ft. tall, surrounded with plump, succulent, blunt-toothed leaves. Tiny starry flowers form clusters like broccoli, 4–6 in. wide, starting out pink, then deepening to dark salmon and finally rusty red. Zone 3.

Sempervivum
Sem-per-vy´vum
Crassulaceae. Orpine family

Description
Low-growing perennials that make a dense rosette of succulent leaves and multiply by offsets. About 40 species, native mostly to Europe.

How to Grow
Full or part sun. Needs well-drained soil and regular water-ing. Very easy and trouble-free. Plant it against a stone, in the crevices of a wall or steps, along a path, or in a shallow con-tainer. Let the colony spread, or detach "chicks" to plant else-where or to give away.

■ *tectorum* p. 226
Hen-and-chickens. An endearing perennial that thrives with virtually no care. It forms dense clusters of tight rosettes, usu-ally only 1–4 in. tall, and spreads gradually to 1 ft. or wider. Each "hen" rosette is closely surrounded by many smaller "chicks." Flat clusters of starry reddish flowers top thick stems that stick up 6–12 in. tall in midsummer. There are dozens of selections in different sizes and colors. Zone 4.

Senecio
Se-nee´see-oh
Compositae. Daisy family

Description
A huge and diverse group of annuals, perennials, vines, and shrubs, including some succulents. Although many species have been reassigned to other groups in recent years, this is still one of the largest plant genera, with more than 1,500 species worldwide.

How to Grow
Full sun. Ordinary or unimproved soil. Does best with regu-lar watering but tolerates dry spells. Easily propagated by seed or cuttings. Subject to fungal infections in wet soil or humid weather but otherwise trouble-free.

■ *cineraria* p. 226
Dusty miller. A shrubby perennial, often grown as an annual, valued for its beautiful silvery gray or white leaves. It com-bines well with almost any plant and makes a good foil for bright-colored flowers. Useful for bedding and edgings and in containers. Forms a woody crown and a spreading rosette of lobed leaves. Leaf size and shape vary among cultivars — some are very deeply cut and lacy, but others are broad and bold. The leaves are evergreen in mild climates. Overwintered plants have small yellow flowers on 2-ft. stalks the second and following years, but they are insignificant compared with the foliage. Hardy to Zone 8; grown as an annual in all zones.

Sequoia

See-kwoy'a. Redwood
Taxodiaceae. Bald cypress family.

Description

A majestic conifer that grows taller than any other tree. Only 1 species, native along the Pacific coast from Oregon to central California.

How to Grow

Full sun or part shade. Tolerates nearly any soil but does best in a sheltered, cool, humid location with regular watering. If new needles turn yellowish in summer, try adding iron to the soil in the form of iron chelate or iron sulfate. Young plants should be staked to encourage a straight trunk. Used as a lawn tree or planted in groves. Sometimes grown as a hedge, with plants spaced 7–10 ft. apart and their tops sheared as needed.

■ *sempervirens p. 120*

Redwood, coast redwood. A fast-growing evergreen conifer that can reach 70–80 ft. in 25 years in good garden conditions. Has one or a few strong vertical trunks covered with reddish brown bark. Slightly pendulous branches are lined with narrow, flat, 1-in. needles that spread left and right into a flat spray and give a light, airy appearance. Needle color ranges from deep green to blue-gray. Cultivars propagated from cuttings offer a selection of foliage colors and plant forms. Zone 8.

Solandra

So-lan'dra
Solanaceae. Nightshade family

Description

Woody vines with leathery foliage and large fragrant flowers. Only 8 species, native to tropical America.

How to Grow

Full or part sun. Rich, well-drained soil with regular watering during the early part of the season, but water should be withheld beginning in late summer to ripen newly formed flowering wood. Very tolerant of salt spray and ocean wind. Grows rapidly once established. Provide a substantial support. Prune back to strong stubs to control growth and to maximize flower production.

■ *maxima* p. 198
Cup-of-gold vine. A rampant evergreen vine that climbs
12–15 ft. tall and spreads 35–40 ft. wide, depending on the
support. Has an exotic, tropical appearance. The trumpet-
shaped flowers open 6 in. wide and are deep golden yellow
with brownish purple stripes. Blooms in fall and spring, intermittently through the winter in warm, sheltered locations.
The broad oval leaves are glossy bright green. Makes a billowy bank cover without support and can be trained along
fences or eaves. Zone 9.

Solidago
Sol-i-day´go. Goldenrod
Compositae. Daisy family

Description
Perennials with leafy erect stalks and clusters of gold flowers
in late summer or fall. About 100 species, most native to
North America.

How to Grow
Full sun. Adapts to most soils, including sandy, salty, or
marshy sites along the coast. Plants bloom in the second year
when grown from seed. Easily propagated by dividing the rhizomes in spring.

■ *sempervirens* p. 227
Seaside goldenrod. A showy wildflower that forms a clump
of sturdy stems 2–6 ft. tall, topped with one-sided clusters of
bright yellow flowers for several weeks in fall. The leaves are
narrow with smooth edges and have a glossy, almost fleshy
appearance and feeling. Combines well with grasses, asters,
and bayberry. Native along the Atlantic coast. Zone 5.

Sollya
Sol´ya
Pittosporaceae. Pittosporum family

Description
Evergreen shrubs or vines with small leaves and flowers. Only
3 species, native to Australia.

How to Grow
Full sun or part shade. Any well-drained soil. Withstands
moderate drought but looks much better with regular water-

ing during dry periods. Prune back long, wayward stems to keep it dense and compact. Watch for scale insects.

■ *heterophylla* p. 188
Australian bluebells. A billowy, mounding shrub, 24–30 in. tall, with dense evergreen foliage and clusters of rich blue, bell-shaped flowers from summer to midfall. Can also be trained as a vine up to 6 ft. tall in ideal growing conditions. The glossy leaves are narrow, about 1½ in. long. Has a delicate appearance and looks good spilling over a low wall, in containers, or as a ground cover. Zone 9.

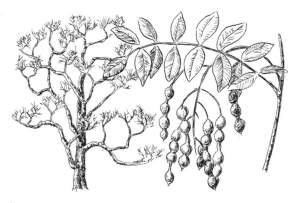

Sophora
So-for′ra
Leguminosae. Pea family

Description
Deciduous or evergreen trees with alternate compound leaves and showy pealike flowers. Woody pods are constricted between the beanlike seeds. More than 50 species, native to the Old and New World.

How to Grow
Full sun. Ordinary soil and watering. Tolerates dry spells once established. Young trees are sensitive to cold. Wrap with burlap for the first year or two and hope for mild winters. Subject to powdery mildew and leafhoppers but generally trouble-free.

■ *japonica* p. 97 *Pictured above*
Pagoda tree, scholar tree. A deciduous tree, 50–60 ft. tall, with glossy green compound leaves. Young trees don't bloom, but older trees bear very showy clusters of creamy white, mildly fragrant flowers for a few weeks in midsummer and

bright yellow-green, beanlike pods in fall. The flowers and fruits are messy on pavement, but it makes a wonderful lawn specimen. The cultivar 'Regent' grows faster, has better foliage, and blooms at a younger age. Zone 5.

Spiraea

Spy-ree´a. Spirea
Rosaceae. Rose family

Description
Deciduous shrubs with simple alternate leaves and clusters of small white or pink flowers. About 70 species, native to the north temperate zone.

How to Grow
Full or part sun. Well-drained soil. Spireas tolerate short dry spells once established but do better with regular watering. Plant from containers in spring or fall. Remove spent blooms to prolong flowering. Prune to shape in early spring. Easy to grow. No serious pests or diseases.

■ × *bumalda cultivars* p. 142
Spireas. These deciduous shrubs form low, twiggy, fine-textured mounds 2–3 ft. tall and 2–4 ft. wide. Leaves are small, usually under 1 in. long. Round flat clusters of dainty little flowers last for several weeks in summer. The following cultivars are most popular. 'Anthony Waterer' has rosy pink flowers and green foliage; 'Coccinea' is similar but has deeper, reddish pink flowers. 'Crispa' has light pink flowers and crinkled, toothed leaves that darken from pinkish to red to green as they mature. 'Goldflame' has crimson flowers and leaves that are pure gold in summer, touched with red and copper in both spring and fall. 'Lime Mound' has light pink flowers and leaves that change from yellow to lime green to orange-red as the season progresses. Others species and hybrids of spireas are also good seashore plants. Zone 3.

Stachys

Stay´kis
Labiatae. Mint family

Description
Perennials or shrubs with square stems and opposite leaves. Some kinds are used in medicine or cooking. About 300 species, native to temperate climates.

How to Grow
Full or part sun. Well-drained, average soil. Water during long dry spells. Space 12–18 in. apart for edging or small-scale ground cover. Trim back in spring and groom frequently to remove old leaves. Divide in early spring or fall. Subject to fungal diseases in hot, humid weather.

■ *byzantina* p. 227 *Pictured above*
Lamb's ears. A low, spreading perennial that forms semievergreen mats about 6–8 in. high and 18–24 in. wide. White, ear-shaped leaves, 3–6 in. long, are covered with soft, thick "wool." Scattered pink or purple flowers develop in late spring or early summer on fat square stalks 12–18 in. tall. Many gardeners remove them or choose 'Silver Carpet', a nonflowering cultivar. 'Helen Van Stein' is a new cultivar that does flower but has unusually attractive, larger-than-average leaves. Sometimes listed as *S. lanata*. Zone 5.

Syagrus
Sigh-ag'rus
Palmae. Palm family.

Description
Short or tall palms with pinnate fronds. About 32 species, native to South America.

How to Grow
Full sun. Tolerates unamended soil but needs regular watering. Transplant when small. Remove old dead fronds to expose the handsome trunk.

■ *romanzoffianus* p. 121
Queen palm. A fast-growing palm tree, 30–60 ft. tall, with an exceptionally straight trunk, topped with a cluster of glossy

green, featherlike fronds up to 15 ft. tall. Often used as a street tree in the mild regions of Florida, Texas, and California. Formerly called *Arecastrum romanzoffianum*. Zone 9.

Symphoricarpos
Sim-for-i-kar′pos
Caprifoliaceae. Honeysuckle family

Description
Hardy deciduous shrubs with thin stems, opposite leaves, small flowers, and showy fruits borne in pairs or small clusters. About 17 species, all native to the United States, except for one Chinese species.

How to Grow
Sun or shade. Tolerates any well-drained soil. Very easy to transplant. Prune in early spring so that flowers and subsequent fruits aren't cut off. Remove old stems and unwanted suckers to the ground, and cut the most vigorous shoots back partway to induce branching. Spreads by suckers and stabilizes loose soil or steep banks. Subject to aphids and powdery mildew.

■ *orbiculatus* *p. 188*
Coralberry. A deciduous shrub, 2–3 ft. tall, with many slender stems that bow under the weight of the abundant orange-red or red-purple berries that form in fall and last into winter. Has small pinkish flowers in early summer and dainty blue-green leaves. Other species and hybrids are equally adaptable and have pink or white berries. Native from New Jersey to Texas. Zone 3.

Syringa
Sir-ring′a. Lilac
Oleaceae. Olive family

Description
Deciduous shrubs or small trees with opposite leaves and clusters of small flowers, often very fragrant. About 25 species, most native to Asia.

How to Grow
Full or part sun. Average garden soil with regular watering during dry spells. Add lime to acidic soil. Prune after flower-

ing, removing spent blooms. Can be rejuvenated by cutting to the ground in early spring.

■ *reticulata* *p. 97*

Japanese tree lilac. A deciduous tree up to 30 ft. tall, with one or more trunks and an upright oval crown. Large fluffy clusters of creamy white flowers last for about 2 weeks in June. The flowers are quite fragrant, but they smell like privet, not like common lilacs. The leaves are oval, about 5 in. long, and fairly resistant to mildew. The cherrylike bark adds winter interest; it is smooth, glossy, and reddish brown, with small white horizontal marks. Zone 3.

■ *vulgaris* *p. 143* *Pictured above*

Common lilac. A deciduous shrub with many erect stems 5–15 ft. tall. Large cone-shaped clusters of very fragrant flowers top each stem for 2–3 weeks in spring. The heart-shaped leaves are dark green, 2–5 in. long. There are many cultivars, with single or double flowers in shades of lilac, purple, pink, or white, blooming in sequence from mid- to late spring. Most lilacs need cold winters to induce blooming, but the "Descanso hybrids" bloom even in southern California where winters are mild. Zone 4.

Tamarix

Tam´a-ricks
Tamaricaceae. Tamarisk family

Description

Shrubs or trees with slender twigs, scalelike leaves, and clusters of tiny flowers. About 55 species, native to Eurasia.

How to Grow
Full sun. Well-drained soil. Tamarisks are very tolerant of sand and salt. They have deep, extensive root systems; avoid planting near water pipes or sewers. Prune in early spring, since flowers form on new wood. Renew old or shabby specimens by cutting them to the ground. Makes a fast-growing, tough, and attractive screen or windbreak.

■ *ramosissima* *p. 143*
Tamarisk, salt cedar. A deciduous shrub, 6–10 ft. tall, with many arching stems. Looks almost fluffy, with very fine-textured, blue-green or blue-gray foliage and masses of pale or bright pink flowers in midsummer. This species is often listed as *T. pentandra.* Zone 4. Spring tamarisk, *T. parviflora,* is similar but grows 10–15 ft. tall and blooms in spring on the previous year's wood, so prune after flowering. Zone 6.

Taxus
Tax´us. Yew
Taxaceae. Yew family

Description
Conifers with dense, fine-grained timber; flat needlelike leaves; and fleshy red or brown fruits with one hard seed inside. The foliage and seeds contain poisonous compounds. Only 7 species, native to the Old and New World.

How to Grow
Full sun, part sun, or shade. Well-drained, average soil. Plant in spring or fall and water regularly for the first year or two. Yews tolerate and respond well to repeated pruning, but you can minimize the need for pruning by choosing cultivars of appropriate size, habit, and rate of growth. If you do want a formal, neatly sheared effect, clip new growth after it has lengthened, but before it has hardened.

■ *cuspidata* cultivars *p. 173*
Japanese yews. Slow-growing evergreen shrubs with an upright or spreading habit and dense, dark green foliage. The needles are flat and narrow, under 1 in. long, and have pointed tips. Females have bright red berries in fall. 'Capitata' forms a broad pyramid up to 25 ft. tall and has foliage that turns bronze in winter. 'Columnaris' is narrowly upright, good for hedging, and stays green all year. There are several slow-growing, spreading forms, good for foundation plant-

ings 'Greenwave' forms a low mound with arching branches. 'Nana' is very dense and spreads about twice as wide as it is tall. Both have good green winter color. Cultivars of *T. × media,* hybrid yew, are also good seaside plants. Most yews are hardy to Zone 5.

Tecomaria
Te-ko-may´ree-a
Bignoniaceae. Trumpet creeper family

Description
An evergreen shrub or vine with very showy flowers. Only 1 species, native to South Africa.

How to Grow
Full sun or part shade. Looks best in loose amended garden soil but grows in nearly any well-drained soil. Needs regular watering during summer dry spells to produce spectacular flower displays. Tolerates hard pruning as a shrub or to renew old specimens, but don't prune after mid-August. Watch for aphids.

■ *capensis p. 174*
Cape honeysuckle. A mounding, sprawling, evergreen shrub, 8–10 ft. tall, with long arching stems. If supported, it can climb as a vine 10–12 ft. tall. Useful as a barrier, windbreak, or screen, or to cover a bank or hide a fence. Blooms in late fall through winter, with clusters of fiery orange-scarlet, tubular flowers at the stem ends. The glossy bright green leaves are compound with several leaflets. 'Aurea' has bright yellow flowers but is smaller and less vigorous. May freeze back in cold parts of Zone 9, but established plants quickly recover. Zone 9.

Thuja
Thew´ya. Arborvitae
Cupressaceae. Cypress family

Description
Tall evergreen conifers, usually with scalelike foliage arranged in flat fans or sprays. There are only 5 species, native to eastern Asia and North America, but there are hundreds of selected cultivars.

How to Grow
Full sun or part shade. Ordinary soil and watering. Tolerates heavy clay soil and alkaline conditions. Can't take extreme heat or dryness. Easy to transplant but may pause a year or two before it regains speed. Needs no pruning and is generally trouble-free.

■ *plicata*   p. 121
Western red cedar. An evergreen tree that can reach 200 ft. tall in its native habitat along the Pacific Northwest coast and that often reaches 50–70 ft. in gardens. Young trees grow fast and make a narrow cone or pyramid. Older trees slow down and spread wider. Flat fans of fragrant, ferny-looking foliage spread from the graceful, drooping branches. Foliage is glossy bright green in summer, turning golden brown in cold winters. Holds its branches and foliage all the way to the ground unless you remove them. Makes a lovely specimen or tall hedge. Zone 5.

Trachelospermum
Tra-kel-o-sper′mum
Apocynaceae. Dogbane family

Description
Woody vines with twining stems, evergreen leaves, milky sap, and fragrant 5-petaled flowers. About 20 species, all but one native to southeastern Asia.

How to Grow
Sun or shade. Not fussy about soil. Tolerates some dryness but needs watering during droughts. For a ground cover, space 1-gal. plants 2 ft. apart. Use one plant against a tree or trellis, and start training it right away. Fasten the stems to the support until they catch on. Prune out old woody stems as needed to renew growth. Trouble-free.

■ *jasminoides* p. 199 *Pictured opposite*
Star jasmine, Confederate jasmine. An evergreen vine that can
climb to 20 ft. or sprawl as a ground cover. The dark green
leaves are shiny, stiff ovals about 1 in. long. Blooms heavily
for several weeks in late spring and early summer, with clusters of pinwheel-shaped flowers $1/2$ in. wide, opening white
and fading to creamy yellow. They are very fragrant, especially in the evening. Zone 8.

Trachycarpus

Tra-kee-kar′pus
Palmae. Palm family

Description
Small to medium-size fan palms that provide fibers and
fronds for cordage and basketry. Only 4 species, native to the
Himalaya region.

How to Grow
Full or part sun. Grows best in well-drained soil with regular watering. Tolerates salt spray and some dryness but not
constantly wet soil. Needs only occasional grooming. Trouble-
free.

■ *fortunei* p. 122
Windmill palm. A small palm, under 20 ft. tall, that's slow
but easy to grow. Forms a single trunk covered with coarse
black fibers, topped with an umbrella-shaped or rounded
crown. Long-stalked fronds, about 3 ft. in diameter, are
palmately divided into dozens of long slender segments that
droop at the tips. Flowers and fruits are not showy. Use as a
specimen, in the ground or a container. Zone 8.

Tristania

Tris-tay′ni-a
Myrtaceae. Myrtle family

Description
Evergreen trees and shrubs with simple alternate leaves and
small white or yellow flowers. About 20 species, most native
to Australia.

How to Grow
Full or part sun. Ordinary soil and watering. Tolerates dry

soil once established. Needs only routine training and pruning. Trouble-free.

■ *conferta* p. 122
Brisbane box. An evergreen tree, 40–60 ft. tall, with an erect trunk, a rounded crown, and leathery bright green leaves 4–6 in. long. Small white flowers that look like snowflakes bloom in summer. Dark red-brown outer bark peels off to expose smooth tan inner bark. Grown as a shade tree, mostly in California. Sometimes listed as *Lophostemon confertus*. Zone 9.

Umbellularia
Um-bel-you-lay′ree-a
Lauraceae. Laurel family

Description
An evergreen tree with aromatic foliage. Only 1 species, native to California and Oregon.

How to Grow
Full sun. Average well-drained soil. Established plants tolerate dry spells. Young plants need shelter from cold and dry winter winds. Watch for scale insects.

■ *californica* p. 123
California bay, Oregon myrtle. A dense, round-headed evergreen tree 60–75 ft. tall, sometimes with multiple trunks. Alternate leaves are smooth and leathery, 2–5 in. long, shiny green on top and dull below, with a strong aroma. Clusters of greenish yellow flowers in spring are followed by dark purple fruits in fall. Zone 7.

Vaccinium
Vak-sin′i-um. Blueberry, cranberry
Ericaceae. Heath family

Description
Deciduous or evergreen shrubs and a few small trees or vines. Many have edible fruits. About 450 species, native worldwide.

How to Grow
Full sun or part shade. (The more shade, the fewer berries.) Needs fertile, acidic soil with plenty of moisture. Use a thick

layer of mulch to protect the shallow roots and keep them cool and damp. Prune after harvest to remove old or weak stems.

■ *corymbosum* *p. 144* *Pictured above*
Highbush blueberry. A deciduous shrub, 6 ft. or taller, with many erect, branching stems. Makes an informal rounded hedge, both attractive and productive. It has small pinkish white flowers for weeks in spring, tasty berries in summer, fine-textured foliage with good fall color, and bright twiggy stems in winter. Native to the eastern United States. Lowbush blueberry, *V. angustifolium,* is another eastern native. A low shrub, it spreads to make extensive patches and is a good ground cover for acidic soil, with outstanding fall color and small but very tasty berries. Both are hardy to Zone 3.

Evergreen huckleberry, *V. ovatum,* is a Northwest native, found in coastal forests. It grows to 6 ft. or taller and has beautiful glossy evergreen foliage, pinkish white flowers, and small tasty berries. Zone 7.

Verbena

Ver-bee´na
Verbenaceae. Verbena family

Description
Annuals, perennials, or shrubs with toothed or dissected foliage and spikes or clusters of small flowers. About 250 species, nearly all native to the New World.

How to Grow
Full sun. Well-drained soil with occasional watering during long dry spells. Space 1 ft. apart for a ground cover. Shear back after flowering or if plants get straggly.

■ *tenuisecta* p. 189
Moss verbena. A low perennial that forms a mat of sprawling stems, only a few inches tall but spreading about 3 ft.
wide. It's useful as a ground cover for sunny banks and sandy
soil. The leaves are divided into threadlike segments. Blooms
all summer with short spikes of small mauve, lavender, or
white flowers. Can be grown as an annual where winters are
cold. Zone 9.

Viburnum

Vy-bur´num
Caprifoliaceae. Honeysuckle family

Description
Deciduous or evergreen shrubs or small trees with simple opposite leaves and showy clusters of 5-petaled flowers, usually
white or pink and sometimes very fragrant. About 150
species, native to the Old and New World, and several hybrids.

How to Grow
Full or part sun. Average well-drained garden soil and regular watering. Apply a thick organic mulch to keep the roots
cool and moist. You can prune after flowering to improve
shape and to make plants denser and more compact, but
pruning removes the fruits. Renew established plants by cutting old and weak stems to the ground in early spring. Watch
for aphids.

■ *carlesii* p. 144
Korean spice viburnum. A deciduous shrub, 4–5 ft. tall and
wide, valued for its extremely fragrant flowers, which open
in midspring, just as the leaves expand. Pink buds open into
small white flowers in dome-shaped clusters 2–3 in. wide.
Broad oval leaves are covered with soft hairs and are dull
green in summer, sometimes turning reddish in fall. 'Compactum' has similar flowers and foliage but makes a neat
sphere only 3 ft. tall and wide. 'Cayuga' is a hybrid with especially healthy and attractive foliage and generous clusters
of pink buds and white flowers. It grows about 5 ft. tall and
wide. *V.* × *burkwoodii* and *V.* × *juddii* are related hybrids
with equally fragrant flowers. Zone 5.

■ *prunifolium* p. 145
Black haw. A deciduous shrub or small tree, up to 15 ft. tall,

with just a few upright trunks and an upright oval crown. The oval leaves are healthy, smooth, and lustrous; 2–3 in. long; deep green in summer and reddish purple in fall. Clusters of small white flowers are showy in spring. Dark blue-black berries attract birds in fall. Native to the eastern United States. Zone 4.

■ *tinus* p. 174 *Pictured above*
Laurustinus. An erect, narrow, evergreen shrub, 6–10 ft. tall. It responds well to pruning and makes a good hedge for smaller gardens. Dark green leaves are smooth, shiny ovals, 2–3 in. long. Dense clusters of pink buds and white flowers, slightly fragrant, last for weeks in late winter and early spring. Pretty blue berries ripen in summer. There are a few cultivars with larger, smaller, or variegated leaves. Zone 7.

Vinca
Ving´ka. Periwinkle
Apocynaceae. Dogbane family

Description
Trailing vinelike perennials with opposite leaves and 5-petaled flowers. Only 7 species, native to the Old World.

How to Grow
Sun or shade. Average soil with regular watering in full sun. Shaded plants can tolerate short dry spells but will grow slowly. Space rooted runners or purchased starts 6 in. apart for a ground cover. For the first year or two, shear or prune long runners to encourage branching and make a denser cover. Established plantings need minimal care. Pest-free.

■ *minor*   p. 189   *Pictured above*
Periwinkle. An evergreen perennial ground cover, about 6 in.
tall. It makes a dense, weed-proof mat of wiry stems, and its
tenacious roots can secure steep banks against erosion. The
paired leaves are small ovals, about 1 in. long. Soft-textured
and light green when they unfold in early spring, they turn
thick, leathery, and dark green by summer. Winter sun and
cold can color the foliage a dull purplish bronze. Short upright stems hold flat round flowers, about 1 in. wide, for several weeks in spring. The more sun, the more flowers; plants
in deep shade may not bloom at all. The flowers are usually
lavender-blue, but pale blue, darker purple, and white forms
are also available. Zone 4.

Vitex
Vy´tex
Verbenaceae. Verbena family

Description
Deciduous or evergreen shrubs or trees with opposite compound leaves and clusters of small flowers. Both foliage and
flowers can be aromatic. About 250 species, mostly tropical,
native to the Old and New World.

How to Grow
Full sun. Tolerates poor, dry soil but grows faster with ordinary garden soil and regular watering. May freeze back in
cold winters but recovers and blooms on new wood. Renew
straggly older plants with a hard pruning in spring. Trouble-
free.

■ *agnus-castus*   p. 145
Chaste tree, pepperbush. A deciduous shrub or small multitrunked tree, 10–20 ft. tall, with a loose, open, umbrella-
shaped crown. The palmately compound leaves are dark

green above and gray-green or silvery below. They release a spicy or peppery fragrance when crushed. Blooms from midsummer to fall, as long as the weather is hot, with arching clusters of small lilac or lavender flowers on the tips of each branch. Adaptable and easy to grow, it makes a fine lawn or border specimen. Selections with white or pink flowers are also available. Zone 7.

Washingtonia
Wash-ing-toe′nee-a
Palmae. Palm family

Description
Large palm trees with tall trunks and palmately divided leaves. Only 2 species, native to the arid Southwest.

How to Grow
Full sun. Adapts to any well-drained site. Grows fastest in well-drained, fertile soil with regular watering during dry spells but tolerates drought once established. Well suited to coastal conditions. Naturally retains its thatch or shag, made of dead fronds hanging on the trunk below the live fronds. Though it looks interesting, shag is a significant fire hazard and often serves as a breeding area for rodents; remove it if desired.

■ *robusta* *p. 123*
Mexican fan palm. A palm tree, 75–90 ft. tall, with a very slender, straight trunk and a compact, rounded head. Bright green fan-shaped fronds are 3–4 ft. wide. Tiny apricot-pink flowers on sprays up to 8 ft. long appear in spring but may be partially hidden by the foliage. Often planted along streets or in groups or groves. California fan palm, *W. filifera,* is similar but has a thicker trunk and grows only 50–60 ft. tall. Both are hardy to Zone 8.

Wisteria
Wis-tee′ree-a, wis-tair′ee-a
Leguminosae. Pea family

Description
Woody vines with twining stems; pinnately compound leaves; clusters of pealike blossoms, often very fragrant; and thick pods. All parts are poisonous. Only 6 species, native to North America and eastern Asia.

How to Grow
Tolerates part shade but needs full sun for maximum flowering. Ordinary soil and watering. Requires several years to reach flowering size and may be balky. Administer treatment in early summer to promote flowering the next spring — cut back vigorous shoots, prune the roots by cutting vertically with a sharp shovel, then fertilize with superphosphate. An established plant can be very aggressive and cover whole trees. Don't hesitate to prune it back severely. No serious pests.

■ *sinensis p. 199 Pictured above*
Chinese wisteria. A vigorous vine that climbs by twining and grows several feet a year, usually reaching 30 ft. or more. Dangling clusters of very fragrant violet, blue, or white flowers open in spring, followed by large velvety pods. Deciduous leaves are compound, with 7–13 leaflets. Japanese wisteria, *W. floribunda,* is similar but has longer flower clusters and 13–19 leaflets, and twines in the opposite direction. Both form thick woody trunks and need a strong support, or they can be trained into a small weeping standard. There are many cultivars, selected for flower color and length of the flower clusters. Grafted plants of named cultivars tend to flower earlier and more freely than unnamed seedling plants. Zone 5.

Yucca
Yuk′a
Agavaceae. Agave family

Description
Woody perennials with short or medium-height trunks; stiff, swordlike, fibrous leaves; erect branched stalks of large

flowers, usually white; and large woody or fleshy fruits. About 40 species, native to North America.

How to Grow

Full sun. Yuccas need good drainage and tolerate poor, dry soil but do better in fertile garden soil with regular watering during droughts. Transplant container-grown plants in spring, or propagate by removing offsets from the base of an older plant. Established plants persist for decades with no care beyond the removal of old flower stalks and dead leaves.

■ *elephantipes* p. 175

Giant yucca. An evergreen shrub, 20–25 ft. tall, with several vertical to gracefully curving stems, each usually swollen near the base, with foliage clusters near the top. Deep green, sword-shaped leaves are 3–4 ft. long, 3 in. wide. Immense spikes of very showy white flowers are held above the foliage in late spring or summer. Makes a striking specimen. Zone 9.

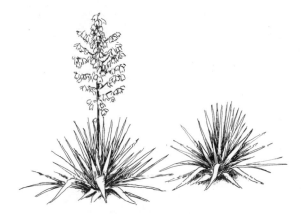

■ *filamentosa* p. 175 *Pictured above*

Bear grass, Adam's needle. A low evergreen shrub that spreads slowly to make a dense patch of crowded rosettes. The leaves are 2–3 ft. long, 1 in. wide, with sharp tips and curly fibers along the edges. There are variegated forms with gold or cream stripes on the leaves. Stiff, branched stalks 5–6 ft. tall hold giant clusters of large white flowers in June. Combines well with perennials, ground covers, and low shrubs in a mixed border or foundation planting. Native along the Atlantic coast. Zone 5.

Hardiness Zone Map

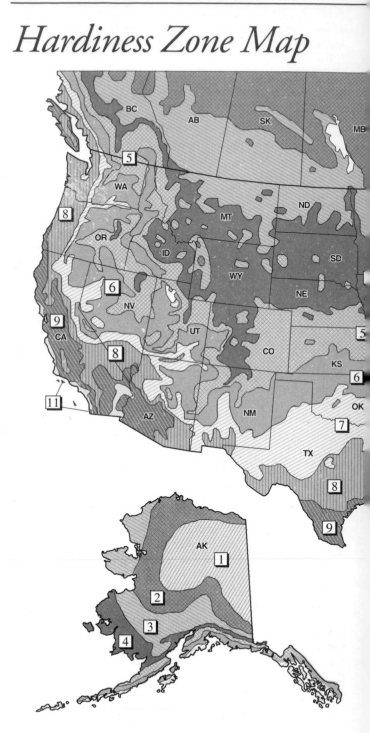

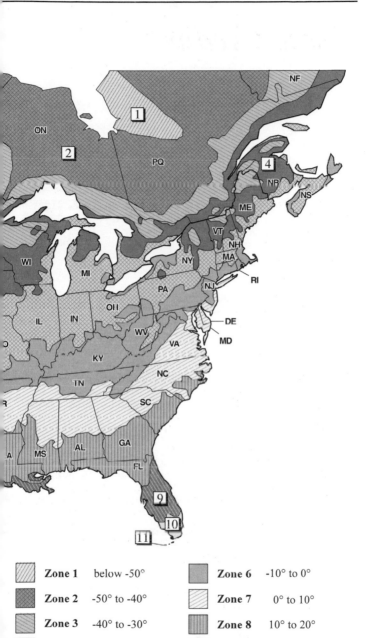

	Zone 1	below -50°		**Zone 6**	-10° to 0°
	Zone 2	-50° to -40°		**Zone 7**	0° to 10°
	Zone 3	-40° to -30°		**Zone 8**	10° to 20°
	Zone 4	-30° to -20°		**Zone 9**	20° to 30°
	Zone 5	-20° to -10°		**Zone 10**	30° to 40°
				Zone 11	above 40°

Photo Credits

Allan Armitage: 129A, 172B, 175B, 179B, 183B, 184A, 186A, 187B, 189A, 193B, 195A, 202A, B, 203A, B, 204A, B, 205B, 206B, 207A, 208A, B, 209A, B, 210A, 211B, 212A, B, 213B, 214A, 215A, B, 216A, B, 217B, 218A, B, 220A, 221A, B, 222A, B, 223A, 224A, B, 225A, B, 226B, 227B

Philip Beaurline/PhotoNats: 90B

Gay Bumgarner/PhotoNats: 94B

Chuck Crandall: 72–73, 100A, 104B, 106A

Tom Eltzroth: 76, 82, 96B, 100B, 103A, 104A, 109A, 111B, 112B, 114A, 117A, 118B, 121A, 123A, 141A, 149A, 150B, 151A, 152B, 153B, 154B, 155B, 158A, 164A, 165B, 166A, 168B, 169A, 173A, 176–177, 180A, B, 184B, 186B, 187A, 188A, 194A, 206A, 228–229, 231A, 234A, B

Derek Fell: 86–87, 88B, 89A, B, 92B, 95A, 97A, 98–99, 101A, 103B, 107B, 110A, 115A, 118A, 119A, B, 120A, 124–125, 132B, 135A, 137B, 138A, 139A, 140B, 142A, 143A, 145A, 146–147, 149B, 152A, 158B, 162B, 164B, 170B, 175A, 189B, 220B, 230A, 232A

Charles Marden Fitch: 90A, 96A, 97B, 102A, B, 105A, B, 107A, 108A, B, 109B, 110B, 112A, 113A, B, 114B, 115B, 116A, B, 117B, 120B, 122A, B, 123B, 126B, 128A, B, 129B, 130A, 131B, 132A, 133A, B, 134B, 135B, 136A, B, 140A, 142B, 144A, B, 145B, 148A, B, 150A, 151B, 153A, 154A, 155A, 156A, B, 159A, B, 160A, 163A, B, 165A, 166B, 167A, B, 168A, 169B, 170A, 171A, B, 172A, 174A, 178B, 179A, 181A, 182B, 183A, 185A, B, 190–191, 192A, 193A, 194B, 195B, 196A, 197A, B, 198A, B, 199A, B, 211A, 213A, 214B, 226A, 227A, 230B, 231B, 233A, B, 235A, B

Galen Gates/PhotoSynthesis: 95B, 106B, 126A, 137A, 162A

Sam Jones: 127B, 161A, 196B, 219A

Dency Kane: 207B

Ron Lutsko: 92A, 101B, 192B, 200–201, 210B, 217A, 219B, 223B

John A. Lynch/PhotoNats: 93B

Jerry Pavia: 91B, 93A, 111A, 121B, 127A, 130B, 131A, 138B, 157A, 160B, 161B, 173B, 205A, 232B

Joanne Pavia: 157B, 174B, 178A

Ann Reilly/PhotoNats: 141B

Steven Still: 88A, 91A, 134A, 181B, 182A, 188B

George Taloumis: 74–75, 77, 78–79, 80–81, 83, 84–85, 94A, 143B

Virginia Twinam-Smith/PhotoNats: 139B

Index

Titles available in the Taylor's Guide series:

Taylor's Guide to Annuals	$19.95
Taylor's Guide to Perennials	19.95
Taylor's Guide to Roses, Revised Edition	19.95
Taylor's Guide to Bulbs	19.95
Taylor's Guide to Ground Covers	19.95
Taylor's Guide to Houseplants	19.95
Taylor's Guide to Vegetables	19.95
Taylor's Guide to Shrubs	19.95
Taylor's Guide to Trees	19.95
Taylor's Guide to Garden Design	19.95
Taylor's Guide to Water-Saving Gardening	19.95
Taylor's Guide to Garden Techniques	19.95
Taylor's Guide to Gardening in the South	19.95
Taylor's Guide to Gardening in the Southwest	19.95
Taylor's Guide to Natural Gardening	19.95
Taylor's Guide to Specialty Nurseries	16.95
Taylor's Guide to Shade Gardening	19.95
Taylor's Guide to Herbs	19.95
Taylor's Guide to Container Gardening	19.95
Taylor's Guide to Heirloom Vegetables	19.95
Taylor's Guide to Fruits and Berries	19.95
Taylor's Guide to Orchids	19.95
Taylor's Guide to Seashore Gardening	19.95
Taylor's Master Guide to Gardening	60.00

At your bookstore or by calling 1-800-225-3362

Prices subject to change without notice